AF880828

FOR MOTHER

I Need a Website, What Do I Do Now?

A Simple Guide to Understanding Your Options

Candace Carson

Third-Party Materials: Material in this book may include information, products or services by third parties. The Third-Party materials consist of products and opinions expressed by their owners. The author does not assume responsibility or liability for any Third-Party material or opinions. The publication of such Third-Party materials does not constitute the author's guarantee of any information, instruction, opinion products or services contained with the Third-Party material. The use of recommended Third Party material does not guarantee any success and/or earnings related to you or your business. Publication of such Third-Party material is simply a recommendation and an expression of the author's own opinion of that material. All trademarks and registered trademarks appearing in this book are the property of their respective owners. Users of this book are advised to do their own due diligence when it comes to making business decisions and all information, products, and services that have been provided should independently be verified by your qualified professionals. By reading this book, you agree that the author is not responsible for the success or failure of your business decisions relating to any information presented in this book.

LIMIT OF LIABILITY/DISCLAIMER OF WARRANTY: THE AUTHOR MAKES NO REPRESENTATIONS OR WARRANTIES WITH RESPECT TO THEIR ACCURACY OR COMPLETENESS OF THE CONTENTS OF THIS WORK AND SPECIFICALLY DISCLAIMS ALL WARRANTIES, INCLUDING WITHOUT LIMITATION WARRANTIES OF FITNESS FOR A PARTICULAR PURPOSE. NO WARRANTY MAY BE CREATED OR EXTENDED BY SALES OR PROMOTIONAL MATERIALS. THE ADVICE AND STRATEGIES CONTAINED HEREIN MAY NOT BE SUITABLE FOR EVERY SITUATION. THIS BOOK IS SOLD WITH THE UNDERSTANDING THAT THE AUTHOR IS NOT ENGAGED IN RENDERING LEGAL ACCOUNTING OR OTHER PROFESSIONAL SERVICES. IF PROFESSIONAL ASSISTANCE IS REQUIRED, THE SERVICES OF A COMPETENT PROFESSIONAL PERSON SHOULD BE SOUGHT. THE AUTHOR SHALL NOT BE LIABLE FOR DAMAGES ARISING HEREFROM THE FACT THAT AN ORGANIZATION OR WEBSITE IS REFERRED TO IN THIS WORK AS A CITATION AND/OR A POTENTIAL SOURCE OF FURTHER INFORMATION DOES NOT MEAN THAT THE AUTHOR ENDORSES THE INFORMATION THE ORGANIZATION OR WEBSITE MAY PROVIDE OR RECOMMENDATIONS IT MAY MAKE. FURTHER, READERS SHOULD BE AWARE THAT INTERNET WEBSITES LISTED IN THIS BOOK MAY HAVE CHANGED OR DISAPPEARED BETWEEN WHEN THIS WORK WAS WRITTEN AND WHEN IT IS READ.

Cover Image Courtesy of College Degrees 360 via Flickr.com
https://www.flickr.com/photos/83633410@N07/7658284016/in/dateposted/
Changes to the cover image made by Candace Carson

Published by Sigi & LuLu Productions, Sarasota, Florida 34238
https://AmazingWebsites.org

Library of Congress Control Number: 2019918613
Paperback Edition: ISBN 978-1-937339-17-3
E-Book Edition: ISBN 978-1-937339-18-0

INTRODUCTION

"There comes a time when you've got to say, "Let's get off our asses and go ... I have always found that if I move with 75 percent or more of the facts, I usually never regret it. It's the guys who wait to have everything perfect that drive you crazy."
—**Lee Iacocca**

If you think you don't need a website in today's market, you are delusional. If you own a business, you need a website. End of story.

There are more than a billion websites in the world today, yet almost 46% of U.S. small businesses don't have a website, and only about 36% use their website to communicate news to customers and potential customers.

Wake up—times have changed.

89% of Americans are on the web looking for products and services. Those people are looking at company websites before making a purchase decision. A website shows that your business exists. It informs the public of your location and phone number, shows pictures of your products, and explains your services. It introduces you to the world.

It is short-sighted to be in the marketplace without the benefit of having a website. Why even bother? But you already know that. You are smart. You realize that a website is vital to your success.

This book is a *simple* guide to acquaint you with the choices you have in developing a website, the importance of branding, and the aspects of good design. We cover the integral components of a website, what works and what doesn't, design principles, SEO, Google Analytics, and maintenance requirements.

If you are a small business owner, this book is for you. I am here to assist you through the technological maze and help you focus on what's important in building your website. I have been in your shoes, and I know what you are going through. It's not rocket science, but it can be daunting. So, don't give up. READ MY BOOK!

FORWARD

"Wealth is not about having a lot of money; it's about having a lot of options."
—**Chris Rock**

When I was in art school, I observed a class of students standing in front of their easels practicing drawing a straight line. They spent the entire class hour doing this exercise. I related the experience to one of my teachers, Richard Lindblom, who said, "Why not use a ruler?".

Today we have so many tools at our fingertips– we should use them. If you love reading about the intricacies of developing a website—Go for it. Take a class or study online.

But if you are like most people who need a website for their business, you simply do not have the desire nor the time to devote to acquiring the knowledge and skills needed to build a website from scratch. You are running a business!

Good news--you have options. This book will guide you through the best of them.

CONTENTS

GET INTO THE GAME

Small businesses need a website—duh.

A website is a vital investment in the future of your business. It is your most important marketing tool. It will save you time and money, advertise your skills and products to a wider audience, build long-term relationships, increase productivity, generate sales, give you credibility, and make you competitive in today's market. Its value to your business is monumental.

- Everyone uses the internet to find products and research businesses. It is the best marketing tool you can have. By 2020 there will be 6.1 billion Smartphone users in the world, which is close to 70% of the world population (Ericsson). Each user can find your business, phone number, and address in seconds.

- No one uses phone books anymore. What do you do when a phone book is left at your door? You recycle it. It is no longer worth the paper on which it is printed. A website is the best way for someone to find your business.

- It gives your business legitimacy. Your customers expect it. If you do not have a website, you do not exist in the marketplace. Potential customers will not trust you. You will seem out-of-date. That is true today but just wait until the 2020s.

• You control the narrative. You create your own story. Take the initiative to show the public who you are and what you do. There may be negative comments about you online, but with a website, you get to tell your side of the story.

• It's cheap advertising. You reach thousands of potential customers for pennies. Think about how much flyers, brochures, and ads cost. You save a bundle– yet, many still worry that they cannot afford a website. "Penny-wise, pound-foolish."

• It showcases your business. Your services and products are available to everyone–all 6.1 billion!

• Data Collection - You can collect email addresses, which is an invaluable resource when establishing customer relationships. Companies pay for that kind of information, and you can collect it for free!

• Customer Service - You are available 24 hours a day providing your customers with contact information, location, hours of operation, products, services, company news, FAQ, and customer support.

• Customer contact - Engage customers by advertising sales, specials, events, and new products. Inform customers with blogs and newsletters.

• Update anytime - Add new images and text, how-to videos, newsletters, blogs, new products and services, and pictures of new employees.

• Mobile-Friendly - 89% of all searches are made on a mobile device. If you have a Smartphone, you look businesses up.

- Your competition has a website. Trust me, if not today, tomorrow. If you are not competitive with your competition, you are giving shoppers a reason to buy from someone else.

- It's open 24/7 every day of the year. What beats that?

A small business website is like yesterday's business card. It is a must-have, only a lot better. You can throw a business card away, but your website is online as long as you want it to be.

So, why are you waiting? Get into the game today!

MY APPROACH

Many websites overlook the personal aspect of small business. We are a community of people working together. Identify your distinctiveness and project that image to the public. It gives you a voice in the crowd.

Check out my website, https://amazingwebsites.org
It does not look like any other Website Design company. It may not be your cup-of-tea, but it is me; no one else. Summon up the courage to be yourself. It is where your success lies.

I look at small business websites every day and most use the same format, the same fonts, and the same stock photos. They are slick but empty. They have no identity.

You are different.
You should not look like everyone else. Find out why your business is unique and then show the world. Today, people want to relate. They want to get a sense of who you are and what you do before they meet you. They want to feel comfortable with you—even if they only visit you online.

Define who you are and what you do.
Use your website to highlight your personality and display your company's unique qualities. Being "real" is your competitive edge in the marketplace.

Every business owner should ask, "Why me?"
A website is a valuable tool not only to promote your business but also to define what makes you different from everyone else. How are you better than your competitors?

Your website has to be engaging and it's got to be current. It is an essential part of your business. It lives to advertise your products and services, share your business philosophy, and to make and maintain relationships with your customers.

You welcome web customers into your business, just as if they walked through the door. Invite, engage, and impress using your website. You are developing business relationships.

Be Real—and don't forget it.
It is easier than you think.
It's not that hard to spot a fake online.
Websites that use:

• Trite, Tired, Overused Phrases:

Out of the box	To be honest
Push the envelope	One-stop shop
It is what it is	On the same page
Move the needle	Proactive
Raise the bar	My door is open
Reach out	Low-hanging fruit
Paradigm shift	Value-added
Going forward	Game-changing
Win-win	With all due respect
Synergize	At the end of the day
Robust	Cutting Edge
Next-Generation	Mission-Critical

Use your own words to describe your business—not overused canned phrases.

• <u>Stock Photos</u>

People relate to real people, not actors pretending to be real people. Use pictures of you and your staff....and make sure you are smiling!

• **Boring Design**

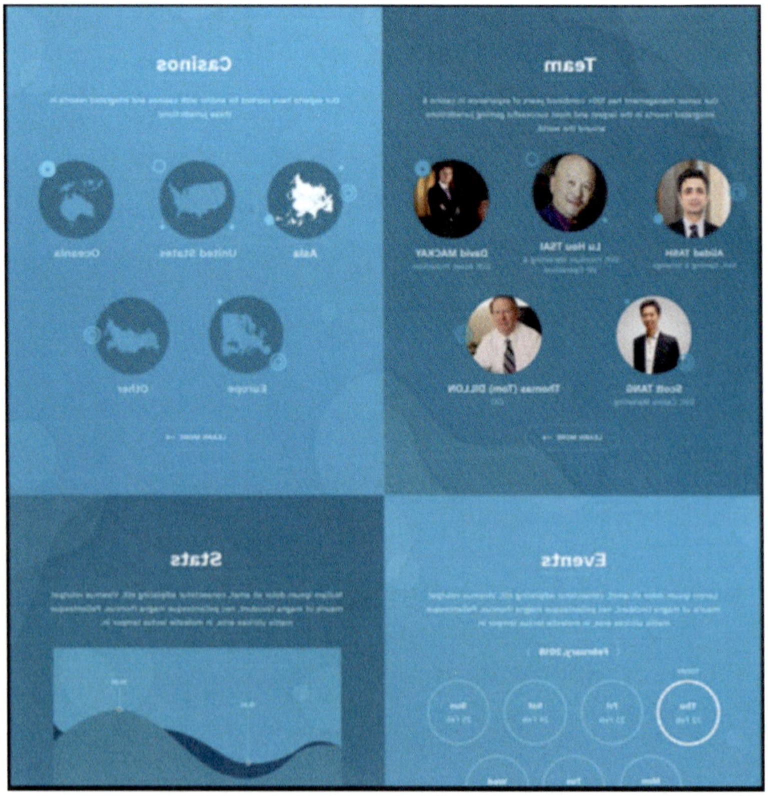

If you don’t take the time to personalize, not only do you look like everyone else, you look lazy. You didn’t invest the time. You are not genuine.

Don’t settle for cheap design. Take a chance. Convince them you are legitimate, and they will return.

"Knowing yourself is the beginning of all wisdom."
–Aristotle

CHAPTER ONE

FIRST THINGS FIRST – Introspection and Identification

Introspection and identification are the foundation of your website. Invest in the time to understand why you are in business and identify what you want to accomplish. Get this right, and the rest is easy.

WHO

Define your brand. Who are you, and how do you want to present your business? Branding will determine all the choices you make in the future.

Branding is the face of your company. It defines you, confirms your credibility, sets you apart from your competition, motivates the buyer to purchase your products, and generates referrals. Customers will connect with you and feel good when they buy your product.

Examples of successful branding:

Examples of good branding of other companies:

THE WIENERS CIRCLE
Vienna Beef

Sun microsystems

VIA Rail Canada

KÖLNER ZOO

goodwill

Firefox

Formula 1

NATIONAL GEOGRAPHIC

TOBLERONE

HONEYSUCKLE
H F
OYSTER FARM

LG

CISCO

DEATH WISH COFFEE Co.

TOSTITOS

TENTSILE

k._lled
PRODUCTIONS

WHY

Define your purpose. Define the reason for your website. Is your site informational? Will you be selling online? Do you want to connect with your customers using newsletters and blogs? How do you want to grow your business? Do you want to set up a customer database?

WHERE

Define your audience. Where is your target market? Where do you fit into their needs? Do you want to serve a local market, or are you interested in expanding your reach?

WHAT

What structure will you use? What kind of website do you want? What is your budget? Will the theme be conservative, modern, contemporary, or do you want to be a little crazy? Think about style. What colors do you want to use (try to stick with two or three)? What about fonts? Take a look - there are thousands. Which ones seem more like you? What pictures will you use? What content is important? How will you explain your business? Keep it brief—no one will read paragraphs. Don't get too technical (TMI); keep it light.

HOW

Decide on a navigation plan. How will you ensure that your viewer gets information easily and quickly?

WHEN

That's simple—you should have started YESTERDAY!

"The best time to plant a tree was 20 years ago. The second best time is now." Chinese Proverb

"The beginning is always today." —Mary Shelley

CHAPTER 2

So…let's begin.

RESEARCH

Spend time looking at websites. Visit the websites of similar businesses. What do you like/dislike about them? Look at the colors they use, the style, types of images, and the written text. How many pages do they have? Check out your competition -what do they lack? How would you do it better?

<u>DOMAIN NAME</u>

What's in a Name? —Actually, a lot.

It's your website address–how people find you, remember you, and share your company with others. It is the link between the real and virtual worlds. A good name can make a lasting impression; a bad name will be a detriment. Invest in the time to make it right.

- <u>Parts of a domain name:</u>

https://	URL (Uniform Resource Locator)
name	Name of your company
.com	Extension (letters after the dot)

Put the parts together and you have a domain name

https://amazingwebsites.org

Note: www. (World Wide Web) used to be included in the domain name after the URL. You can still add it, but it is not necessary anymore. Best to keep it short.

Tips: Short is best--no more than 30 characters
<u>Extensions:</u> .com is the best but if unavailable, use .org or .net.

Options to Consider for Your Domain Name:

FREE OR PAID

You can get a free domain name from website builders like Wix, Weebly, Squarespace, and WordPress. The problem: after your name, they add theirs before the extension.

Ex: *JohnsCarWash.wordpress.com or AnnDalyCuts.wix.com*

Don't do it. I know it is free, but it is not a good idea. You don't own the name; the website builder does. If you decide to switch to another provider, you cannot take the name with you. It reeks of unprofessionalism and makes you look cheap. People don't like cheap. If you look cheap, they assume you will not give them the best product.

YOUR DOMAIN NAME SHOULD:

- Be relevant.

  It should identify your business (*Amazing Websites!*). Make it easier to find by including a description in the name. If you are a plumber, put it in the name. It's all about customers being able to find you. Don't be generic; make it relatable.

  SamsPlumbing.com not *AmericanPlumbers.com*

- Be easy to spell.

  Unique spellings are a bad idea. If there is confusion about how to spell a name, potential customers give up and go elsewhere. Keep it simple; no hyphens, no numbers. Make it easy to pronounce, too. You want your customers to tell others about you.

  CindysCoffeeShop.com not *SyndiesKoffeeShop.com*

- Be easy to remember.

  Keep it short, under 25 characters is best. Remember, you will be printing it on your business cards and in all advertising. If it is too long, it will be difficult to remember, take up too much space, and will be hard to type correctly.

  CindysCornerStoreCoffeeandDonutShop.com
  Better: *Cindy'sCornerStore.com*

  SamsWholeHousePlumbingContractors.com
  Better: *SamsPlumbing.com*

• <u>Have a positive connotation.</u>
Your name should have a positive vibe. People will (consciously or unconsciously) associate your domain name with your brand. Keep it positive.

EdsReliableMovers.com not *EdsPushyMovers.com*

• <u>Use your name.</u>
If you are an artist (actor, artist, vocalist, etc.), you want people to find you by using your name, not by what you do.

Once you settle on a name, look it up on www.whois.com

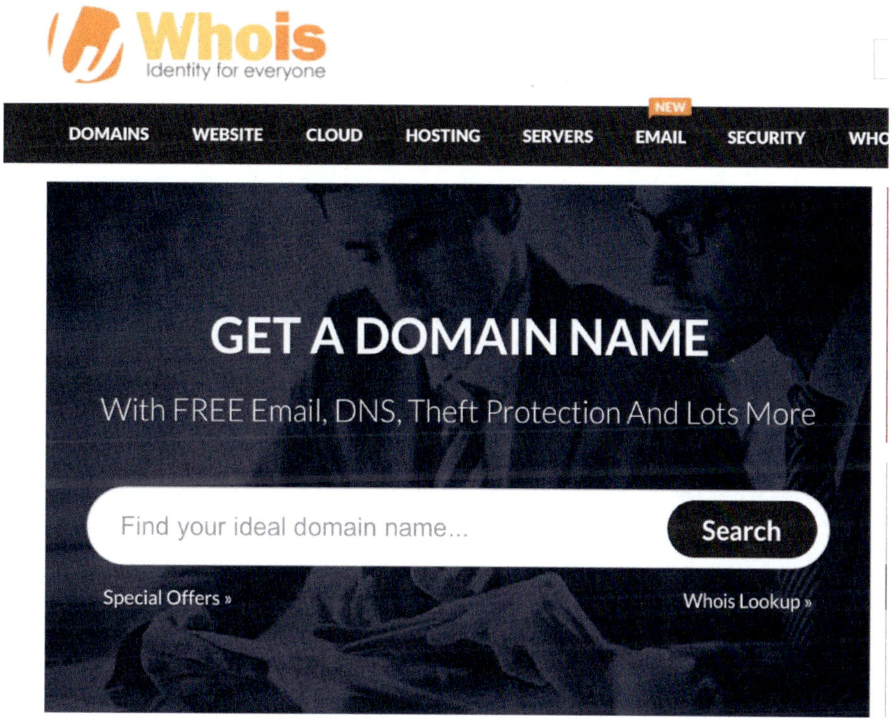

If someone has previously registered the name, you must buy it from them or choose another name. You can make alterations by changing the extension from .com to .net, .org, etc.

You can add "My" or "The" in the name or personalize by using your name. This is not the best solution. Do this only if you are steadfast with your name choice.

If *WineShop.com* is taken, use:
TheWineShop.com or *FranksWineShop.com*

Cybersquatters are people who buy up domains with the names of famous people or brands to extort money. Governor Chris Christie did not own his domain name and had to purchase it from a cybersquatter. Senator Rand Paul reportedly paid $100,000 to get the rights to his domain. *AmazingWebsites.com* domain was registered in 2001. The purchase price has been $49,999.00, but the price fluctuates. Recently, the price was $11,612.70. Needless to say, I can live without .com at the end!

A Note About Trademarks

Avoid legal issues and stay away from names that are trademarked. You don't want the hassle.

You don't need a lawyer if you wish to trademark your name. The basic cost is $225 and takes about nine months to complete the process. Renewals are due every five years for $125. Apply for a trademark at https://www.uspto.gov/trademark.

Amazing Websites!®

DOMAIN NAME REGISTRATION

Making it real. You are doing this!

Once you decide on a domain name, you have the option to register it in different places. Listed are some reputable companies:

bluehost HOSTINGER

DOMAIN.COM GoDaddy®

HostGator hover

Google Domains BETA namecheap

How to Choose?

Here are a few guidelines:

- Pricing: Registering, renewal, and extensions (some charge more for .com)
- Transfer: It should be free—some charge a fee.
- Support: What does the company offer?
- Privacy Protection: Fees vary

The rules change. Shop around and review each company.

Your domain registration expires every year. You must renew annually, or you will lose the name. You will receive an email before the expiration date, but it is best to schedule the date on your calendar to ensure you don't let your domain registration lapse.

It will cost you $15+ each year.

THREE CHOICES TO REGISTER YOUR DOMAIN NAME

1. Get it free from a website builder.
   After your name, website builders will add their name before the extension.
   Example: AmazingWebsites.wix.com

   It may be free but looks cheap and is not professional. It is better to use: *AmazingWebsites.org*

   Also, you do not own the name—they do. If you want to move your website to another company, you will have to find another domain name. This could be disastrous for your business.

2. Use a website builder.
   If you choose a premium plan and pay annually, most website builders will pay the domain registration fee for the first year. They make it easy to connect the domain name to your website, but it isn't rocket science. It's easy to do. Still, they make it convenient.

   If you purchase your domain name from a website builder and want to change to another, you can transfer it to any platform. The new website builder will talk you through it, but it is time-consuming and may take seven days to complete.

Make sure that the domain name is registered in your name—not theirs. If this is not done, you do not own the name. (See #1 above)

3. Register your name independently.
   You own the name separately from your host provider.

   Owning your name keeps your files in one place, apart from your website. You can transfer your website to another host with the help of your domain registrar.

   You have added security. If your website is hacked, your domain name is safe. "Don't put all your eggs in one basket."

MY ADVICE: Register your domain name with a domain registrar. You own it, you can easily transfer it, and it is more secure.

DOMAIN TRANSFER

Once you purchase the domain name, you own the right to use it and to transfer it anywhere, as long as you pay the annual fee.

If you purchase it from a domain registrar, it stays with the registrar. If you want to change to another website platform, you simply sever the connection with one platform and reconnect with the new platform.

PRIVACY PROTECTION

Domain privacy protection is an add-on service to protect your data and keep it hidden from the rest of the world.

Why You Need Domain Privacy Protection

- Your personal information is accessible to everyone.
- You might get bombarded with sales calls.
- You might get scammed.
- Your website might get hacked.
- Your data can be sold.
- You will get a ton of spam emails.
- Your competition will know a LOT about you.

Anyone can look up ownership and contact information of a domain by using Whois.com.

If you do not want the information public, you can privately register your domain name for about $15 a year.

MY ADVICE: Pay the $15 a year—it's well worth it.

"Invisible threads are the strongest ties."
—Friedrich Nietzsche

CHAPTER 3

WEB HOSTING

A Web Hosting company stores your website's content online. When anyone types in your domain name, the web retrieves it from your website host. The web host delivers content, keeps your site open to the public 24/7, and offers support.

You have four main options:

1. FREE HOSTING

Some companies offer free service with their hosting packages. This service puts several subscribers onto a single server, which is shared between them.

There are some problems:

- You cannot have a custom name. Most require you to have the hostname in your URL ex: *SamsFish.hostingcompany.com*

- You do not own your domain name–they do. There will be complications if you want to move to another platform.

- Search engines (like Google) won't take your name as seriously. This is important because search engines locate you on the web.

- You are not viewed as credible. You are telling the world that you are cheap. As stated earlier, you never, ever want to look cheap.

- It is not a great deal if you are competing in the marketplace because they offer very few features.
- Speed, storage capacity, and bandwidth are limited.

- Uptime (the amount of time your site is up–not down) can be an issue.

- File size is limited to 1 MB per file–which limits the use of images, graphics, and special features.

- Ads are on your site. They could be anywhere on your site: top, side, bottom. They change every few seconds. It is an annoying distraction for a viewer.

There is a restaurant near me that has free hosting with an ad about stomach worms–ugh.

Examples of ads displayed on free websites:

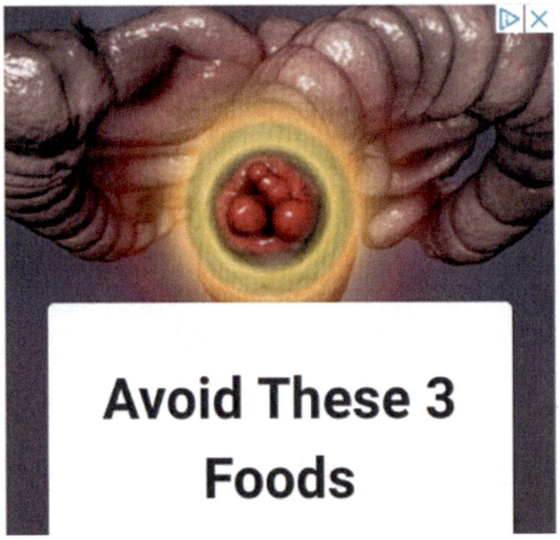

Advertisements

Advertisements

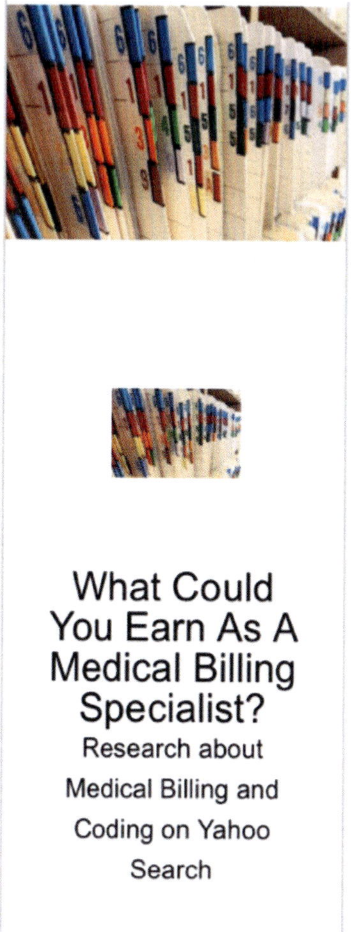

- You have no SSL (Secure Sockets Layer) certificate, which assures the viewer that your site is secure. SSL's establish an encrypted connection between the browser (Yahoo, Google, Chrome, Firefox, etc.) and the user's computer to protect sensitive data, such as credit card information.

"Not Secure" will appear in front of your website address. In today' s world everyone is afraid of being hacked--you don't want that!

Not Secure — sunnysidecafesrq.com/?utm_source=tripadvisor&utm_medium=referral

- Your site will have limited bandwidth. Once you are over your allotment, your site will go down.

- Customer support is limited, if at all.

If you still want to consider free hosting, these are the best:

- Hostinger.com is almost free because it charges $.80 a month. It is faster than other free hosting sites.

- 000WebHost.com is free, but off-line an hour a day. It once suffered a security hack, and 13 million user's information was leaked. Uptime is very slow.

- FreeHosting.com support is exceedingly slow.

2. SHARED HOSTING

Fee-based, shared packages provide subscribers with more features than free hosts. Shared hosting is inexpensive—under $10 a month for basic plans.

The advantage of Shared Hosting is that it is inexpensive. The disadvantage is that you share a server with lots of other websites, and performance can be impaired during peak times.

You can purchase shared hosting separately or with a website builder platform. PC Magazine consistently rates BlueHost as one of the best Shared Hosts to use. BlueHost charges $3 - $8 a month. It works with WordPress, a free website platform.

Shared Hosting is included with website builder platforms like Wix, Weebly, and GoDaddy. The monthly fee includes hosting. The first year is usually half-price. The $15 monthly payment in the first year will increase to $30 in the second year--still cheap, but not a bargain like the first year.

3. VIRTUAL PRIVATE HOSTING (VPS)

A Virtual Private Server is a hybrid between shared hosting and dedicated hosting. Fewer websites are housed on the same server than in shared hosting. Each website has individual resources when spikes in usage occur. Fees range from $40 to $60+ a month.

4. DEDICATED HOSTING

Dedicated Hosting is when a website has a private host. Big businesses who want the highest level of security, have lots of traffic, and hundreds of clients can lease private servers that can be accessed and used only by them. These are the most expensive packages, but they provide the most power, security, and flexibility. They are expensive --$150+ a month.

MY ADVICE: Choose fee-based Shared Hosting. You should not need the extensive services provided by Virtual and Dedicated Hosting.

Do not choose Free Hosting. Keep in mind the adage, "You get what you pay for."

Note: WordPress is free, and when used with BlueHost is the best choice economically, but there is a steep learning curve. They offer hundreds of templates and plug-ins to customize your website.

WordPress is difficult for those who have limited computer experience, design background, and time to invest. It is not easy to learn. Certainly, not for the faint-of-heart. Bluehost offers a program to assist in building a WordPress site for $99 month. If you choose the WordPress platform, consider hiring a freelancer to work with you.

The other "drag and drop" website builders are easier to use but cost more. The learning curve is not as steep. Limited support is available. Knowledge of basic computer skills is helpful. Popular platforms are Wix, Weebly, SquareSpace, and GoDaddy. Hiring a Freelancer is always an option.

"Look for your choices, pick the best one, then go with it."
—Pat Riley

CHAPTER 4

LET'S TALK PLATFORMS

You must decide what platform to use to build your website. Here are 4 options.

1. DO IT YOURSELF WEBSITE CREATION

Don't DIY unless you understand web code and design concepts. You can learn techniques by taking courses online. Two favorite sites are Udmeny.com and LinkedinLearning.com. They're not free and take a considerable amount of dedication.

If you can do this, you might be in the wrong business. Website creation might be your forte instead of whatever you are doing now.

Adobe Dreamweaver and RapidWeaver are website design programs popular with DIY users.

Basic Skills needed if you opt to go it alone:

- How to create your brand.
- Basic marketing concepts-selling your brand.
- Good writing skills.
- Good Photography skills-sharp images.
- Understanding Graphic Design Concepts.

Helpful to know:

Photoshop, Editing Skills, Code

2. <u>CONTENT MANAGEMENT SYSTEMS (CMS)</u>

CMS are platforms that handle most of the technical aspects of building a website allowing non-developers to manage the creation and modify the content of websites. Code writing is not a necessary skill.

There is little reason for a small business owner to learn to code a website. There are many free and paid themes available which allow you to set up most kinds of sites, including E-commerce sites, blogs, restaurants or cafe sites, and more.

<u>Two Types of CMS:</u>

1. <u>Customized Programs:</u> Three main platforms are **WordPress**, **Joomla!** and **Drupal.**

<u>WordPress</u> is both a customized program *and* a drag-and-drop program. It is more complicated than other drag-and-drop programs, but the easiest to use and the most popular customized program. 30% of all websites on the Internet are built with WordPress. It is free and often hosted by BlueHost.

<u>Examples of companies that use WordPress:</u>

Joomla! is second to WordPress in ease and popularity. The name means "all together" in Swahili. It powers about 3% of the websites on the internet.

Examples of companies that use Joomla!

Drupal ranks third with about 2% of the websites on the internet. It is popular with big websites and is the most technical. Knowledge of programming languages and code is required. It is the hardest to learn.

Examples of companies that use Drupal:

2. <u>Drag-and-Drop Programs</u>

Designed to help non-developers build a functional website utilizing a large number of customizable templates and drag-and-drop functions. They make website creation easier. Notice I did not say EASY. It will take some time, but drag-and-drop programs are the best option for novices. WordPress can be included in this type of platform.

Examples for business websites:

BOLDGRID SITEBUILDER.COM weebly

GoDaddy SQUARESPACE WiX.com

HostGator web.com WordPress

Examples for E-commerce websites:

shopify BIGCOMMERCE

<u>What are the differences?</u>

The Customized Programs require more skill and patience than the Drag-And-Drop Programs.

How good are you with computers? Are you confident in your computer skills? Can you invest time in building your site? Are interested in taking classes? Do you like learning to code? If the answer is yes, then try building your website. If you run into issues, you can always get a professional to help.

If you don't want to take classes, want to spend less time, and are comfortable with the drag-and-drop platforms, choose this option. New apps are designed every day to make the process simpler. Once again, if you have difficulties, you can hire a professional to help you finish.

3. CUSTOM BUILT WEBSITES

Web Design Agencies
Agencies cost you more but free up your time. Agencies employ Graphic Designers, Programmers, Copywriters, and other specialists. Their prices range between $10,000 and $50,000+ depending on the scope of the project.

Freelance Web Designers
Freelancers have a more personalized approach than an agency. Make sure budget and project specs are agreed upon at the start. Prices start at $2000.

If you dislike spending hours on your computer and want to leave it to the professionals, then hire a freelancer. It is important that you and the freelancer are compatible. Building a website is personal. Make sure it's the right fit. Don't make the mistake of using a friend or a family member who dabbles in website design. Find someone who builds websites as a business. You will get a better product and fewer headaches.

Off-Shore/Outsourced Web Designers
These have more disadvantages than advantages. Explaining your issues can be frustrating, and the time difference with the U.S. makes it difficult. There may be problems with licensing and copyright issues, quality of work, exposure of confidential data, system crashes, and fraud. The basic price will lure you in, but there are no guarantees. *Don't do it.*

4. E-COMMERCE

Most platforms have built-in e-commerce. I suggest using a more robust, third-party online shopping cart application like Big Commerce or Shopify. They are consistently rated high in reliability, have 24/7 support, and are easier to use than most. Perfect for small businesses that want to sell online.

MY ADVICE: For small businesses, go with one of the CMS systems or a Freelancer. It is cheaper, and you can customize later. Freelancers typically charge less to work on Drag-and-Drop systems than on customized platforms like WordPress. I have worked with clients who started on a CMS platform, got into trouble, and then called me. That is always an option.

"Thinking about design is hard, but not thinking about it can be disastrous." –**Ralph Caplan**

CHAPTER 5

WHAT MAKES A GOOD WEBSITE-PART I

BEFORE YOU BEGIN

"If you don't know where you are going, you'll end up someplace else." –**Yogi Berra**

There are millions of websites on the internet. How can you outshine your competitors? Sometimes, your website is the only thing about your business that your customers see. After you, your website is the most important marketing asset of your business.

There is much to think about when designing a website. Most businesses forget about the human connection. Don't get so involved in the technical aspects of building a website that you forget about your audience. You want to establish a relationship with your visitors. Website design can be awe-inspiring–and very cold. A good website establishes trust and generates a strong customer base.

You want to grab the viewer's attention and solve their needs. The information has to be easy to find, easy to understand (useful, clear, and uncluttered), and easy to navigate. The viewer shouldn't have to think too much to enjoy being on your website.

So how do you do it? Before you start to build your website, consider these 5 principles: Branding, Purpose, Audience, Structure, and Navigation.

1. DEVELOP YOUR BRAND

"Your brand is what other people say about you when you're not in the room." –**Jeff Bezos**

Branding is an ongoing effort to shape how you are perceived. It is one of the most important aspects of your business. It is your reputation and vital to your success.

Branding includes your name, logo, and tagline. It is made up of all the designs, images, slogans, and symbols associated with your company. It consists of many parts working together to promote one product.

Branding creates what is called brand awareness. When your brand is seen, you and your company come to mind.

Good Branding:

- Makes you easily identifiable.
- Distinguishes you from your competition.
- Creates trust with your customers.
- Supports your marketing efforts.
- Inspires your employees.
- What your customers remember about you.
- Why your customers return.

Good branding gives you an edge in the marketplace.

Defining your Brand

Branding is the focal point of your business. Everything revolves around it. Take some time to figure it out. Your choices will influence all your marketing decisions.
Ask yourself:

1. Why am I in business?
   Why do I get up in the morning and do what I do? What motivates me? Why do I like my business?

   Examples: Personal satisfaction, independence, making your vision a reality, you like to build things, you like cars, you like to help people, freedom.

2. What are my company's goals?
About what am I passionate? What is my purpose?
What is my mission?

Examples:

Google Organize the world's information and make it universally accessible.

Tesla Accelerate the world's transition to sustainable energy.

Honest Tea Create and promote great-tasting, healthy, organic beverages.

IKEA Create a better life for many people.

JetBlue Inspire humanity in the air and on the ground.

3. Who is my target audience?
Who benefits from my products/services?

First, determine lifestyle choices:
Examples: Single women, college students, retired people, children, CPAs, plumbers, etc.

Then get more personal:
Examples: Age, gender, location, income, education.

4. How am I beneficial to my customers?
How will they see me as important to them?
Do I "give back"? Do I support local interests?

Examples:

Target - Since 1946, Target has committed assets toward supporting communities in which there are stores.

Ben and Jerry's-Ben and Jerry support causes that affect its industry by opposing growth hormone usage in cows and supporting Farm Aid.

Levi Strauss-Levi Strauss is committed to reducing the amount of water used in the production of jeans.

5. What qualities does my company have?
   How am I different from my competitors?
   Research the competition. Is what I offer better?

Examples: More authentic, more service-oriented, more supportive, cheaper, more responsive, easier to operate.

6. How do I want my company to be perceived?
   What can I do to enhance my company values?

Examples:

Lego Lego uses sustainable materials and partners with the World Wildlife Fund.

Maes Beer Maes Beer offered a free barrel of their beer to everyone with the last name "Maes" on the condition that they share it with 20 of their friends.

Microsoft Microsoft is committed to enhancing education as a global human issue.

Sensu Sensu, a marketing firm, gave a free concert with free beer to promote an unknown artist. It was a big success.

Tweet Bra The Tweet Bra raised awareness about breast cancer by creating a bra that tweets every time it is unclasped.

Decide on a brand and then evaluate it by asking:

- Does it reflect my goals and values?
- Does it relate to my target audience? Do they "get it"?
- Will they see value in my services?
- Will people remember it?
- Will it generate repeat business?

Examples of good branding. There is no explanation included about the companies below, but you know them.

How many of you would like a coke right now–or perhaps a cookie?

These brands:

- Deliver their message.
- Make their company credible.
- Connect with their audience.
- Motivate sales.
- Create a loyal customer base.
- Generate new business.

Once you have a brand, be consistent. Stick with it and use it everywhere. You are its best advocate. Spread the word. Tell everyone about it.

BRAND COMPONENTS

Visual representation speaks volumes. It is what people remember the longest.

The fun part of building a brand is creating a logo and tagline. It is also the most frustrating. You might need help.

<u>LOGO</u>

The foundation of your brand is your logo. It should make an instant impression. Feeling the pressure?

It's all in the details:

- It has to be original. Generic is boring. Don't copy.
- Each part of the logo should relate to each other.
- It should be balanced in size and color.
- The fonts have to be supportive.
- It should be clear, simple, and in harmony with the company brand.

Examples of logos that work and why:

London Symphony Ochestra, LSO
Once you see it, you recognize the letters. It is also an elegant graphic.

Clever. Maintains legibility by manipulating the letters to make it easily readable.

Fun, smart, memorable.
by Action Designer

Simple. We get it.

Here are some other logos that need no explanation.

by Javoramirez on deviantART

by Alexander

by Nashifan

by Reghardt Grobbelaar

by Designabot

by Gal

by Mads Burcharth

by Sean Heisler

by Logo Diver

After deciding on your logo design colors, make sure they work well together. If they clash, your audience will disengage.

TAGLINE

A tagline is a memorable, meaningful phrase that adds to your brand. It is a way to connect the consumer to your business. It should be positive and upbeat. It doesn't have to be on your logo but should represent your philosophy.

Ads on television repeat taglines a lot. Sometimes you can't stop recalling them. Do you know these?

You're in Good Hands.
Good to the last drop.
Breakfast of Champions.
Think Different.
Can you hear me now?
The Quicker Picker Upper.
A Little Dab'll Do Ya.
Does She or Doesn't She?
All the News that's Fit to Print.

A Diamond is Forever.
Got Milk?
Mmm, Mmm Good.
Finger Lickin' Good.
I'm Lovin' It.
America runs on Dunkin.
Be All You Can Be.
Where's the Beef?

2. KNOW YOUR PURPOSE

"Efforts and courage are not enough without purpose and direction." –**John F. Kennedy**

Know what your website is going to do. It's fundamental. Make it succinct.

Websites:

- Provide information about your business.
- Promote who you are and what you do.
- Advance your beliefs.
- Interact with your customers.
- Sell products and services.
- Provide access to services.

A clear message on your home page is the best way to communicate your purpose. It will also help search engines like Google categorize your website.

EXAMPLES:

Welcome to Dove...

Dove does more than just sell soap. It sells self-esteem to women to build more confidence in their beauty. Women relate to it.

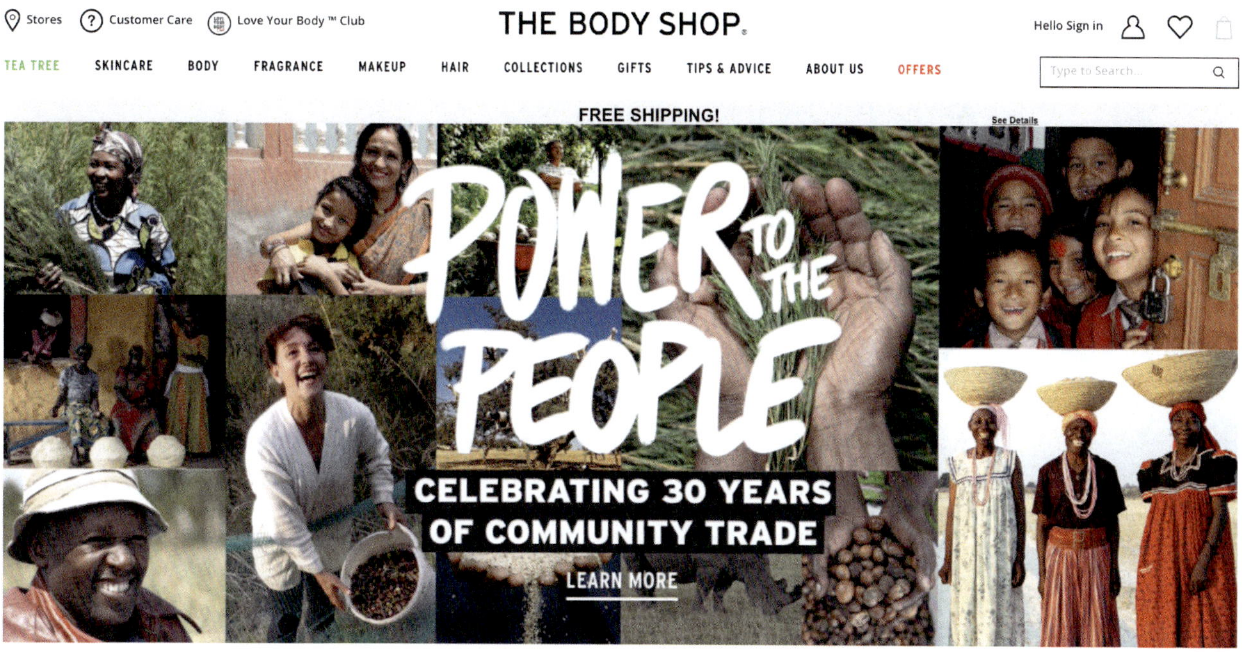

The Body Shop sells all-natural products. It is committed to enriching the environment and the lives of animals and people around the world.

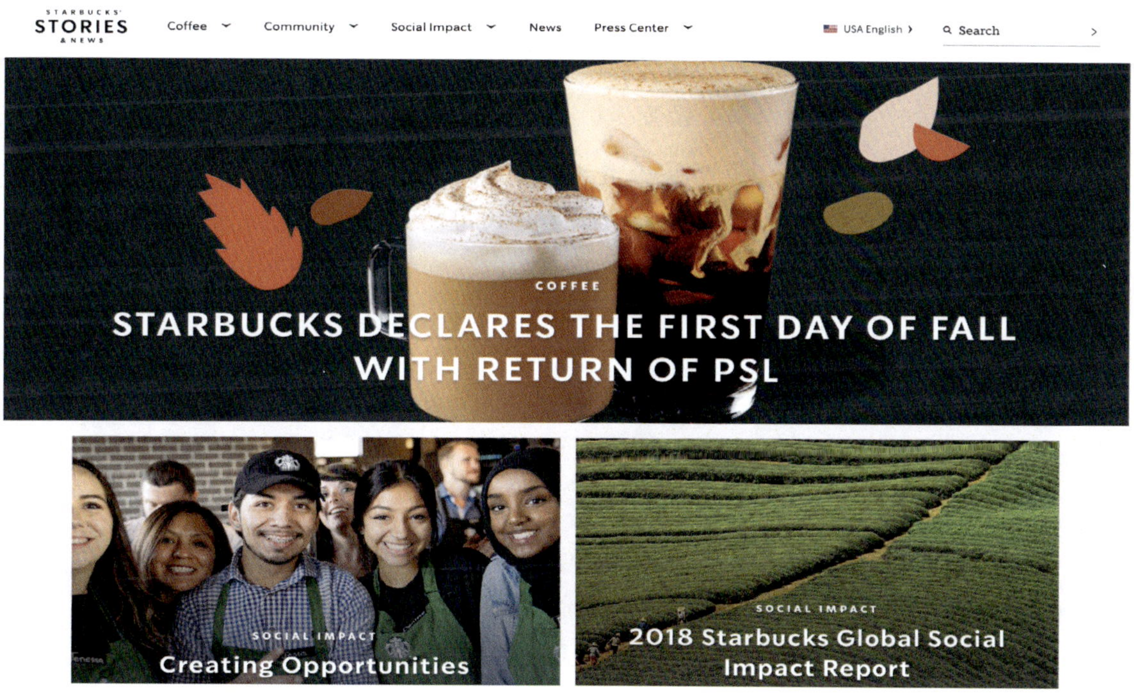

It's not just about selling coffee. Starbucks is committed to fighting hunger, promoting service, and helping the environment.

3. KNOW YOUR AUDIENCE

"Always make the audience suffer as much as possible."
–**Alfred Hitchcock**

This sounds simple, but it is a step that many people miss. Ask who you are trying to reach. Once you identify your customers, you can cater to their needs.

Aim your website at the people who can use your products and services. You need to know who they are so you can focus on them with your design, content, and imagery. Know their needs and offer them solutions for their problems.

Alfred Hitchcock identified his target audience. He knew who they were, what they wanted, and he always delivered.

- Who do you want to visit your website?

  Break them into groups:

  Age, gender, income, families, young singles, dog owners, children, empty nesters, travelers, tourists, locals–you get the picture.

- Check them out in the media (magazines, newspapers).
- Talk with family and friends.
- Subscribe to newsletters.
- Check out websites of companies similar to yours–to whom are they marketing?

EXAMPLES:

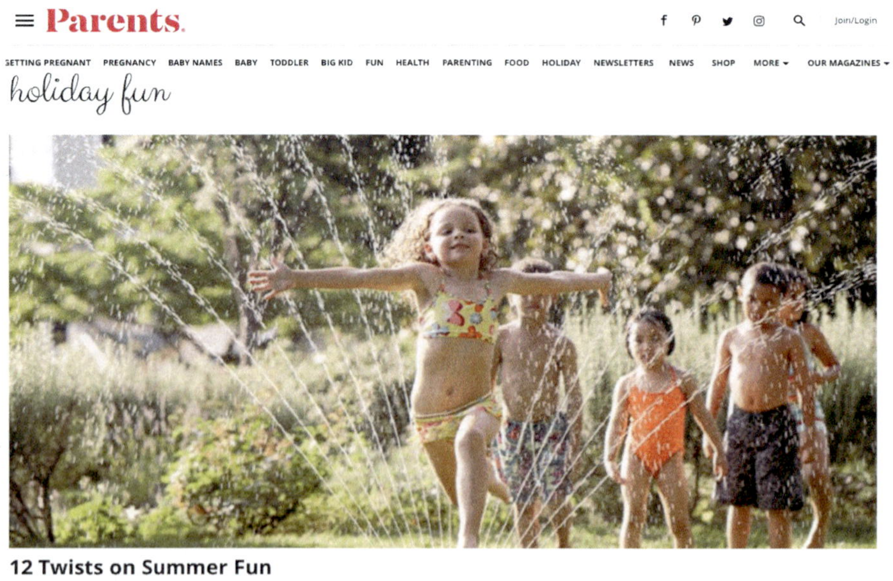

Search on dior.com
DIOR
WOMEN'S FASHION
MEN'S FASHION
FRAGRANCE
MAKEUP
SKINCARE
GIFTS
Sisterhood is Powerful
SISTERHOOD GLOBAL
Women's Fashion
NEW WINTER 2019 COLLECTION

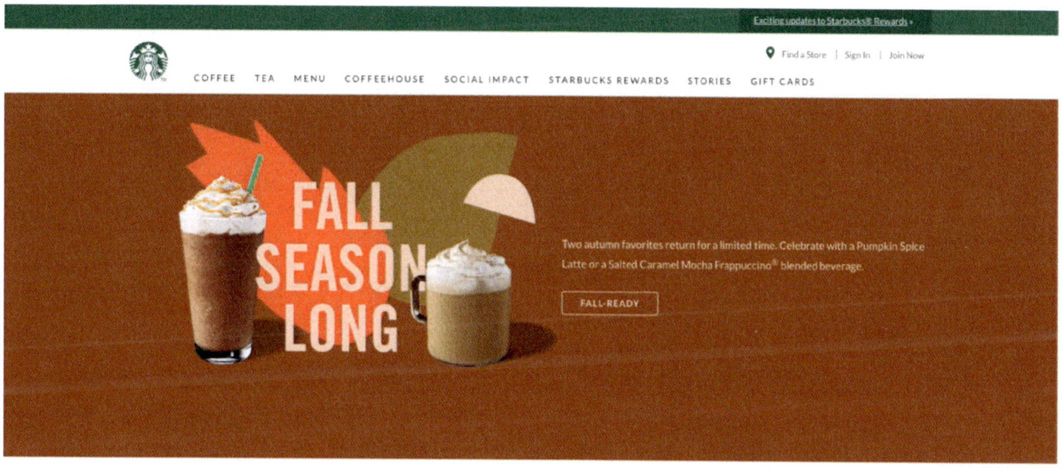
Exciting updates to Starbucks® Rewards »
Find a Store | Sign In | Join Now
COFFEE
TEA
MENU
COFFEEHOUSE
SOCIAL IMPACT
STARBUCKS REWARDS
STORIES
GIFT CARDS
FALL SEASON LONG
Two autumn favorites return for a limited time. Celebrate with a Pumpkin Spice Latte or a Salted Caramel Mocha Frappuccino® blended beverage.
FALL-READY

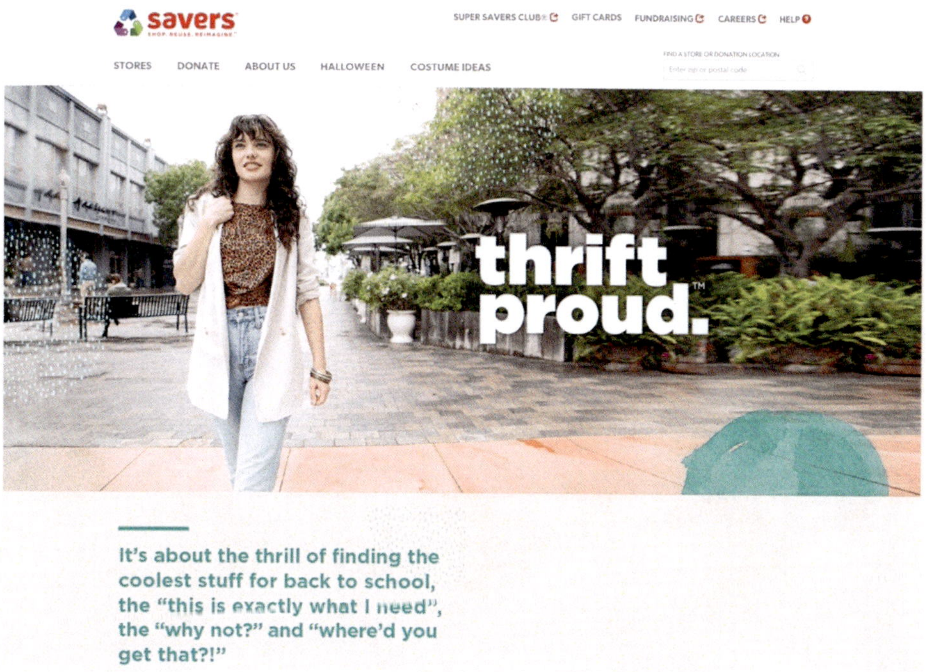
savers
SUPER SAVERS CLUB®
GIFT CARDS
FUNDRAISING
CAREERS
HELP
STORES
DONATE
ABOUT US
HALLOWEEN
COSTUME IDEAS
thrift proud.™
It's about the thrill of finding the coolest stuff for back to school, the "this is exactly what I need", the "why not?" and "where'd you get that?!"

I found this audience classification tool on websitecriteria.com

	Audience attributes	*Example characteristics and scenarios*	Your audiences' characteristics & scenarios	Impact H, M, L
Who	Age and age groups	*children, teenagers, baby-boomers, young adults, over 65, in their thirties*		
	Personal life-style	*resident, parent, single-parent, person with a disability, retired, tourist, Y-generation, school student, university student, migrant*		
	Gender	*mostly male, mostly female or both in equal numbers*		
	Language	*English as first language, English as a second language*		
	Education	*school, college, university, post-graduate*		
	Learning preferences	*practical demonstrations, learns by example, likes to know the theory, free-thinker, images rather than text, systematic learner, task-oriented, left-brain vs right-brain*		
	Work attributes	*employee, home duties, shift-worker, academic, professional, business owner, executive, carer, unemployed, volunteer, specific industry sector*		
	Expectations	*what they expect based on their experience with similar websites*		
	Existing knowledge	*how much they already know about the content, product, service*		
	Web and computer experience	*none, low, medium, high*		
How	On what device they will read it	*PC, handheld device, large monitor, small monitor*		
	Internet connection speed	*fast broadband, standard broadband, slow*		
Where	User's location	*local, national, international – urban, regional, remote*		
	Place where the page is read	*at home, school, work, public library, on the road, in the field, public places*		
Why	Why users seek the content	*to be informed, complete a task, seek an answer, buy something, entertainment, training*		
	Importance of the content to them	*vital, useful, interesting*		
	How they found the page	*Google, link from other site, word-of-mouth, enewsletter link, found it accidentally*		
When	When it is read	*at work between 9am and 5pm, during a lunch-break, after the children are in bed, weekends, at night, early morning*		

4. DEFINE YOUR STRUCTURE

"Structure is more important than content in the transmission of information." –Abbie Hoffman

Website structure is how you organize your content. To communicate visually, information must be structured and consistent.

Organization makes a website accessible and user-friendly. Websites are best when they are simple, uncluttered, clean, and professional. Pages are linked for easy navigation.

As your website grows, it will get more cluttered. You need to have a plan to keep it organized.

A good website organizational structure enables visitors to better navigate and find content. It has to be logical.

Clear organization allows Google to easily crawl and index your website, enhancing your SEO. You will be found online more easily.

How to structure your website:

- Be logical. Keep it simple.
- Rank what is most important.
- Categories – No more than seven.
- Subcategories are related to the categories.
- Clear Navigation path with internal links.

The Home page (*Amazing Websites!*) is at the top.
It is your hub and links to the other pages.

The Menu defines the sections of the website (Categories) and are links to the individual pages on the website.
(About/Projects/Web Design/Pricing/Blog/Contact)

Sub-categories further define the sections
(Branding/Design/Web Redo)

Examples of well-structured websites:

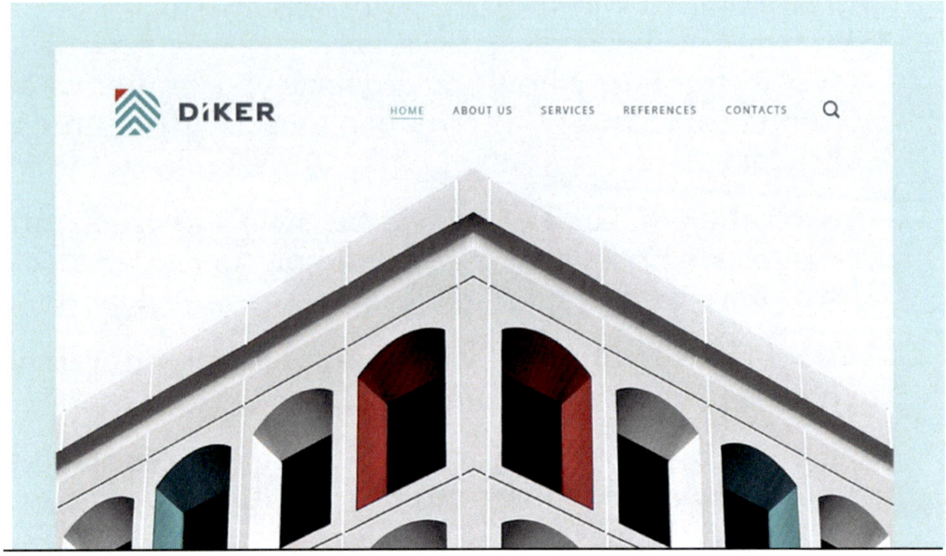

Diker Bau Design is clean and makes a strong statement. Focus is on the product. Menu is easy to use.

Kyle Steed is an artist. The menu is on the left and the choices are easy.

Tinker makes watches. It is obvious. The photo of the watch creates a strong impression. On the top right, the bar-style menu (hamburger menu) does not interrupt the spacial quality of the page.

You know what they do. It is easy to navigate. Simple. Strong.

<u>5. NAVIGATION PRINCIPALS</u>

"There's just something hypnotic about maps." –**Ken Jennings**

Navigation orients your website. The navigation menu is a map that guides visitors through your site. Everything must be found quickly and easily. If users have to wander around the site trying to find what they need, they will get frustrated and leave. *Don't make them think too hard.* PLAN IT OUT and KEEP IT SIMPLE.

<u>GUIDELINES</u>

1. <u>Navigation menus should have 4 to 7 choices.</u>
   Don't confuse the user with too many options. Keep it clean, uncluttered, and orderly. The most important items should be at the beginning and the end. The home page and the about page are viewed the most on a website. The contact page is usually last.

Apple has always stuck with 7 options–which fits nicely on the screen.

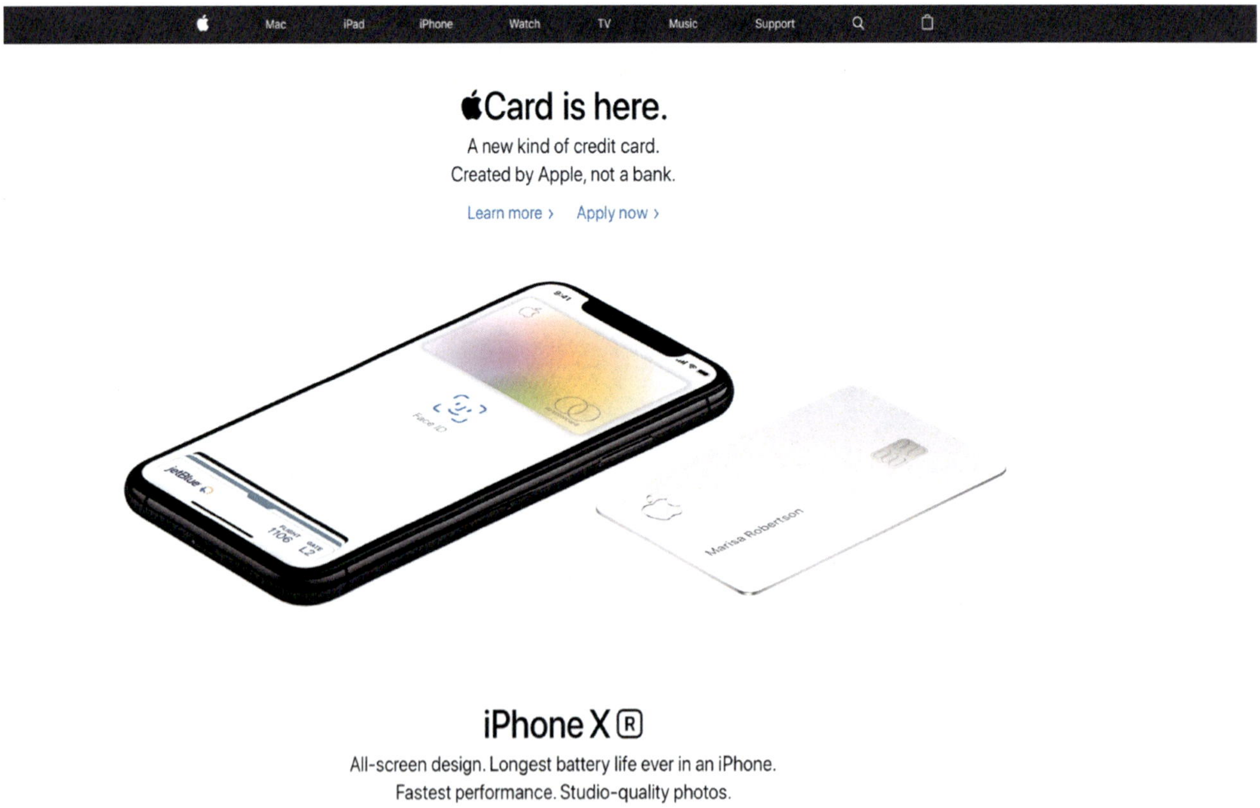

2. <u>Make the menu easy to find and obvious</u>.
Don't make the viewer have to guess. Typically, it will be on the top of the page or as a vertical sidebar.

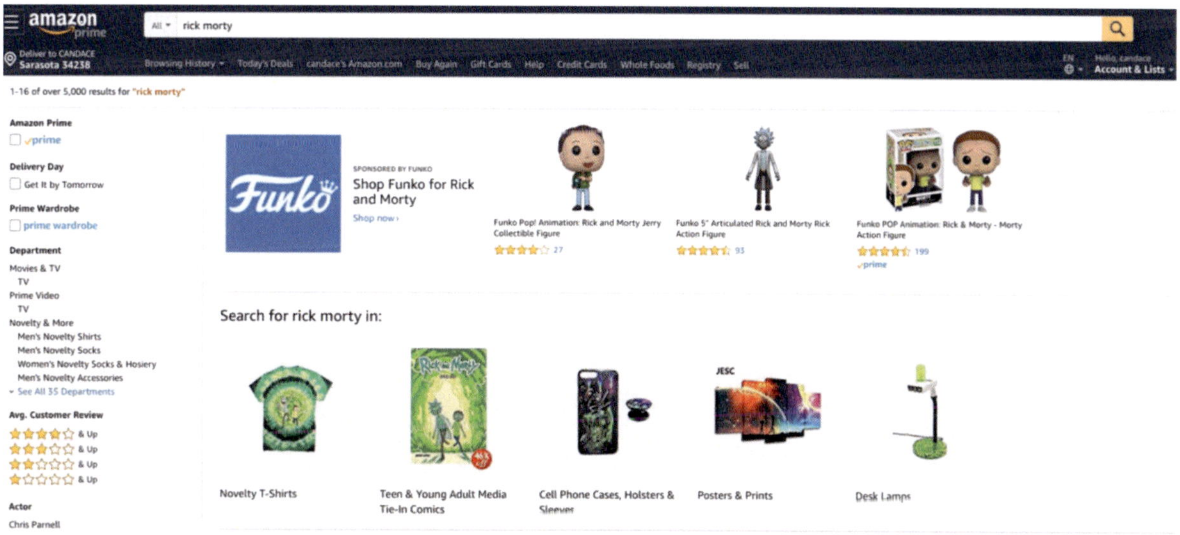

3. Use the same navigation model in the same place on all pages—be consistent.

4. Link your logo to the home page.
This is a no-brainer. The easiest, fastest way to return to the home page is to click on the logo.

5. Let users know where they are on your website.
Highlight, change the color, underline, or make the menu text bold when they are on the page. Use a hover color when your cursor points at a page title.

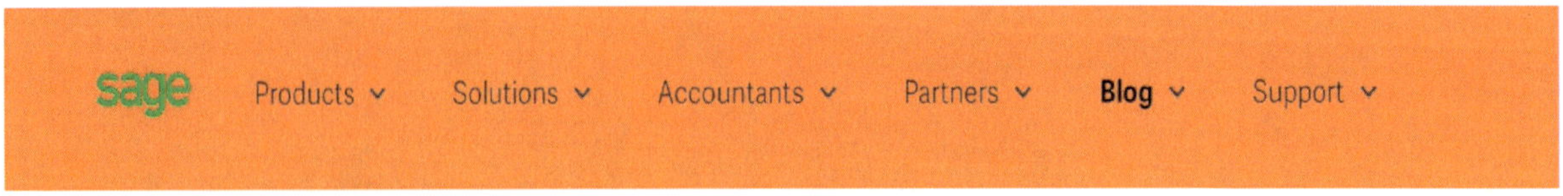

6. The Navigation Bar should be sticky/fixed.
   This means that it does not disappear when the user scrolls down the page. It is always visible. The navigation bar should not be too big–that would be annoying. Make your menu sticky.

7. Use simple, friendly, descriptive words.
   Don't use "Services" or "Products" in the Menu Bar. Use words that describe what you do. Google likes descriptive navigation, and we want Google to be happy!

8. Don't use phrases.
   Use 1 or 2 words and no more than a total of 12 letters.

9. Use words familiar to the viewer.
   Don't try and be clever or break with website conventional terms.

   Examples: Use "About" not "Profile"
   "Contact" not "Let's Chat."

10. Omit words that don't add anything.
    Navigation words should be concise.

    Example: "Contact" not "Contact Me."

11. Responsive Navigation.
    This makes your website look good on different devices. It's important. Google ranks sites higher if they are mobile-friendly.

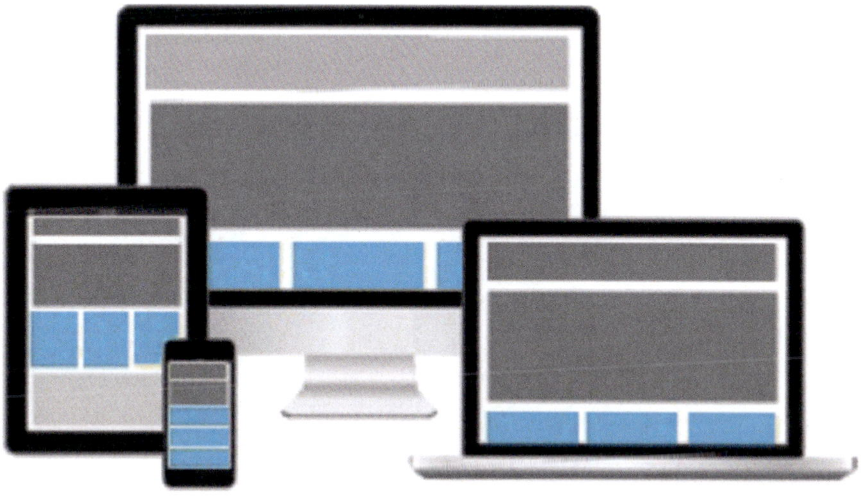

Note: The navigation bar usually turns to a "hamburger menu" on mobile devices. The icon is made up of 3 slightly separated horizontal lines. It is popular on websites that want to be more spacial. The lines open to show the menu.

12. Sub-Categories (added to "fill-out" a menu item). They clean up a busy website. If done correctly, they aid in the organization of your site; if not, they add to the confusion. Keep them at a minimum.

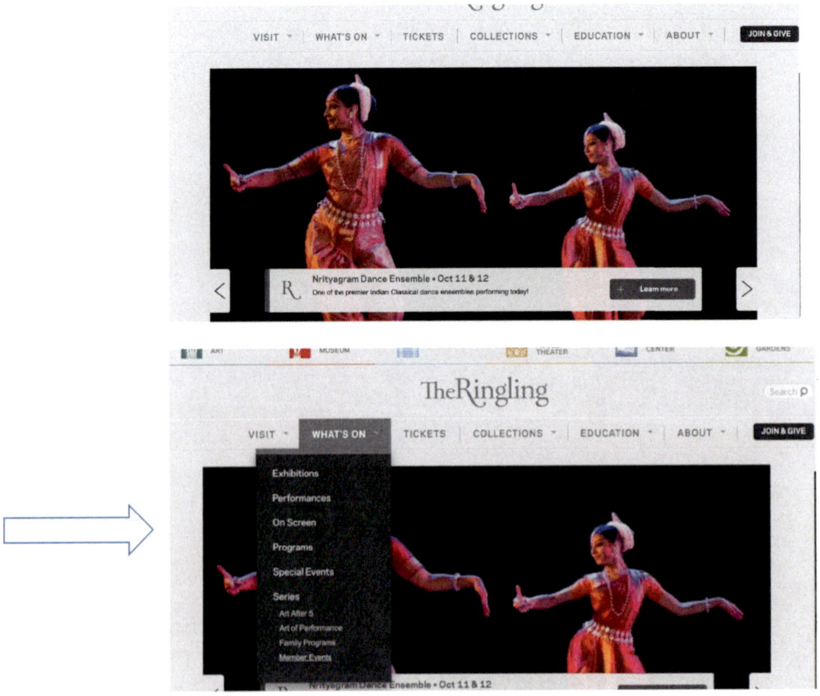

13. <u>Mega Dropdowns</u>

Mega Dropdowns are only for large menu panels. They are good for E-commerce sites with large category lists or businesses with a lot of services. They contain all the categories on one plane. Planning is essential before you begin. Google is not a fan. Many links on a page make it difficult to crawl the page. It doesn't work on mobile devices. Small businesses should not need Mega Dropdowns.

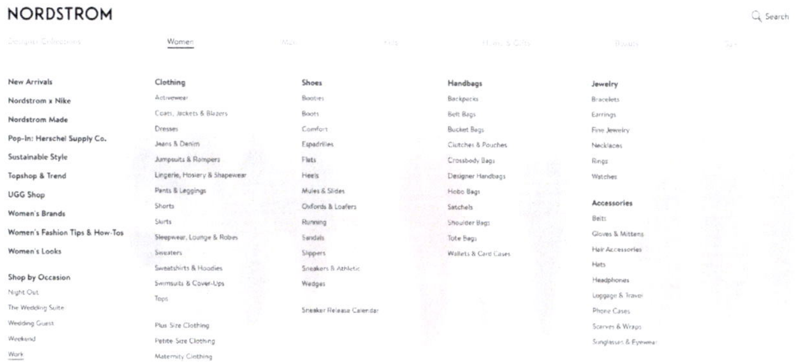

Navigation plays an important role in creating a good user experience. If done correctly, the viewer will get the information they want easily and stay longer on your website. They will engage with you–this is what you want. It's important to do it right.

CONCLUSION

You now understand the first steps in website creation:

- Branding - How you want people to perceive you.
- Purpose - What you want your website to do.
- Audience - Who you want to reach.
- Structure - How you will organize your information.
- Navigation - How viewers will access your website.

Now you are ready to build.

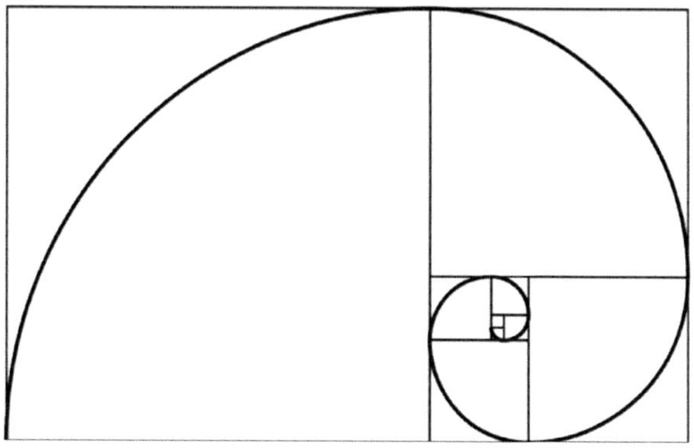

"Make it simple, but significant". —**Dan Draper**

CHAPTER 6

WHAT MAKES A GOOD WEBSITE-PART II

What you see.

THE 3 SECOND RULE

Three seconds is the average time a visitor will spend on your website to learn who you are and what you do. Fail this test, and your visitor will leave and seldom return.

Your website may be the only thing a customer sees about your business. It is an introduction to a prospective client and a way to relate to an existing client.

Websites must be clear, easy, and efficient. They should not require the viewer to think a lot.

In this chapter, we will discuss the aspects of good website design and review the differences between designing a custom website or using templates offered by website builders.

In Chapter 5, we listed important considerations to address before designing a website. Now we are ready to build our website. This is the fun part.

DESIGN

"Good design is like a refrigerator—when it works, no one notices, but when it doesn't, it sure stinks." —Irene Au

Web Design is the process of gathering ideas and arranging them aesthetically in such a way as to present content online so users can find and use the information.

75% of users admit to making judgments about a company's credibility based on its website design. (Stanford Web Credibility Research)

In designing a website, you decide the:

- layout design
- colors
- fonts
- content
- images
- structure

Design is about how your site looks and feels–and how effectively it communicates.

So, what do we look for in good website design?

Good design:

1. Has a purpose in mind.
   What do you want people to think when they see your website? How will you help them to find what they need?
2. Has an organized, balanced structure.
   Make it easy to engage. Don't make the viewer have to think. You aim to clarify, not to confuse.
3. Has visual appeal.
   Websites that are perceived as great looking are also perceived as usable and trustworthy. (Harvard)
4. Keeps it simple.
   Simplicity is key. Design themes that match your market and personality. Too many words, images, videos, fonts, and color will make you look confused and amateurish.

Note: Please no music—everyone has a preference and chances are, it is not the same as yours. It is annoying to listening to music that you don't like.

5. Has good content.
   Content is King. It must be organized, original, relevant, credible, and current. Use colors that augment your theme, professional-looking images, and text that is easy to understand. Don't try to impress by intimidating the viewer. Communicate clearly and honestly. Use fonts that are easy to read in complementary combinations.

6. Is consistent.
   Each page should be in the same format (colors, fonts, button styles, heading sizes, etc.). This makes your site look professional and gives you credibility.

7. Is functional.
   Navigation needs to be straightforward. Confusing, disorganized navigation frustrates. Make it easy for the viewer to locate pertinent information.

8. Has a responsive design.
   It adapts to all computer screens and sizes.

9. Is fast loading. No one waits for more than a few seconds. Google ranks sites on speed. If it takes more than 5 seconds, you lose your audience.

CUSTOM DESIGN

Custom web design caters to your specific needs. You can start from the ground up, using HTML, CSS, and PHP. Unless you have a lot of interest and time to devote to this endeavor—*don't go there*. Frankly, I don't understand why you would.

Remember the incident I related in the Forward of this book when an entire class of art students spent hours trying to draw a straight line? Rulers are an innovation that can assist in that endeavor. Templates solve website development problems.

MY ADVICE: If you want to go this route, take a class or do yourself a favor and hire a website developer/designer.

TEMPLATES

A website template is a predesigned framework to help make web design easier. Templates are professionally designed layouts with carefully selected complementary fonts, color schemes, graphics, and built-in functionality.

All you have to do is plug-in your information (text and images). They are flexible. You can make minor adjustments to the design or make major changes that further personalize your website.

Many templates are free, while others with more bells and whistles are offered at reasonable prices ($50-$150). Some templates only come with a home page. Choose a template package that has the home page and additional pages.

All website builders offer a variety of website templates. They vary extensively. Select a template enabled with features that coincide with your industry. You don't need a portfolio page if you are a plumber, and if you are an artist, you don't need a page describing plumbing problems. Many website builders categorize their templates by business type with specialized sections that are industry specific. This is your best option.

Templates are set up to be responsive on all devices. This is important. You want your website to look good on desktop computers, laptops, tablets, and smartphones. Choose a template that includes a responsive design.

You can customize templates so that they are unique to your business. There are many apps, plug-ins, widgets, forms, add-ons, backgrounds, sliders, and videos to personalize your website.

There are many choices. Try several out to see what fits.

Website Builder Examples:

Wix: Photography Templates – Category: Art Photographer.

Photography Portfolio

Urban Photography

Couples Photography

Outdoor Photography

Choose a Template.

Art Photographer

Travel Photographer

Check out the pages.

SquareSpace –Musicians and Bands Template: Miller

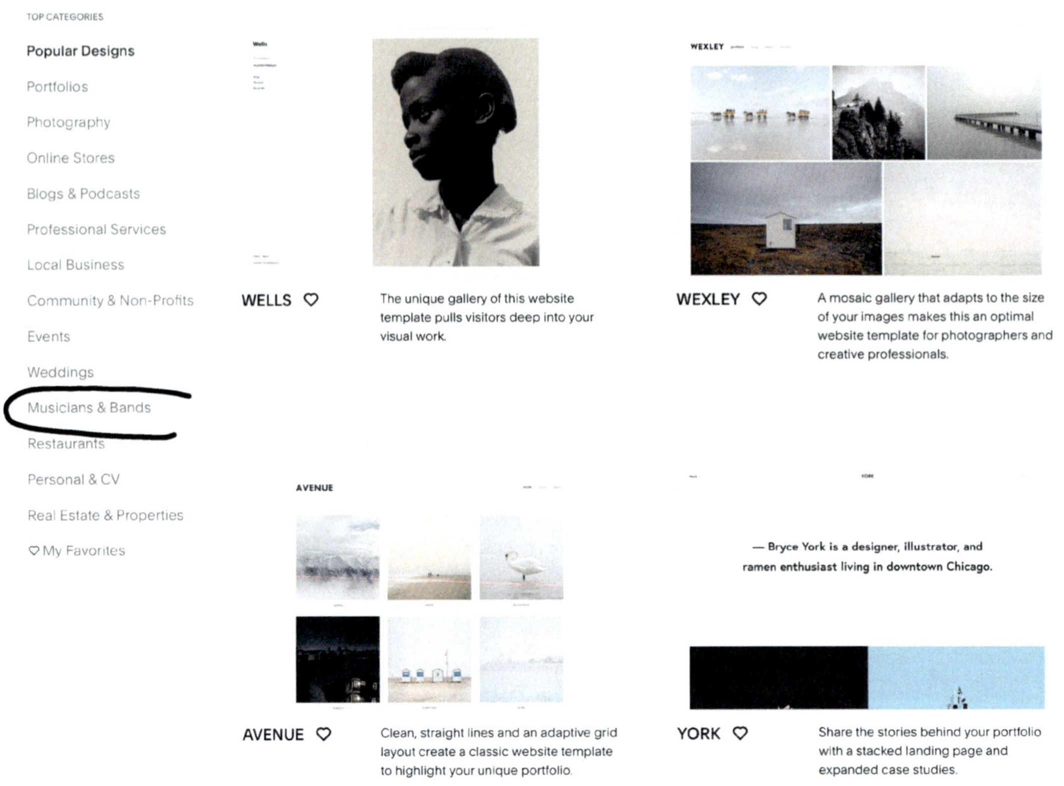

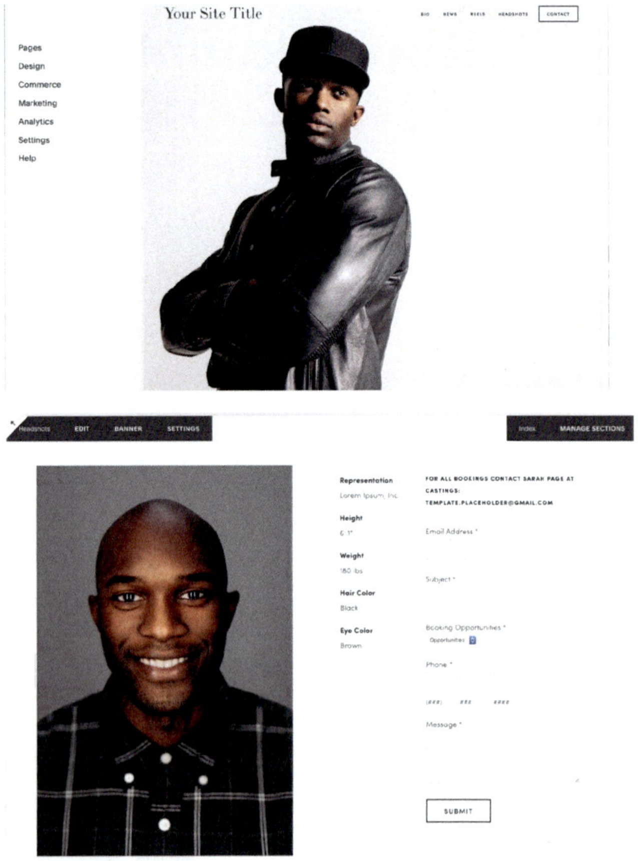

WordPress: Restaurant Templates: Gloria Food Restaurant

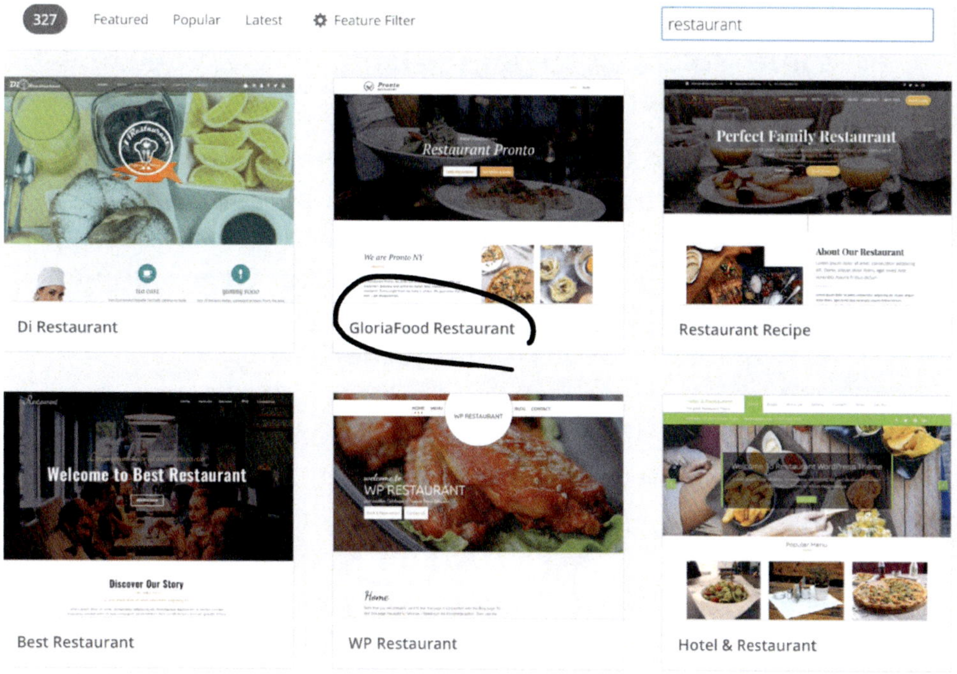

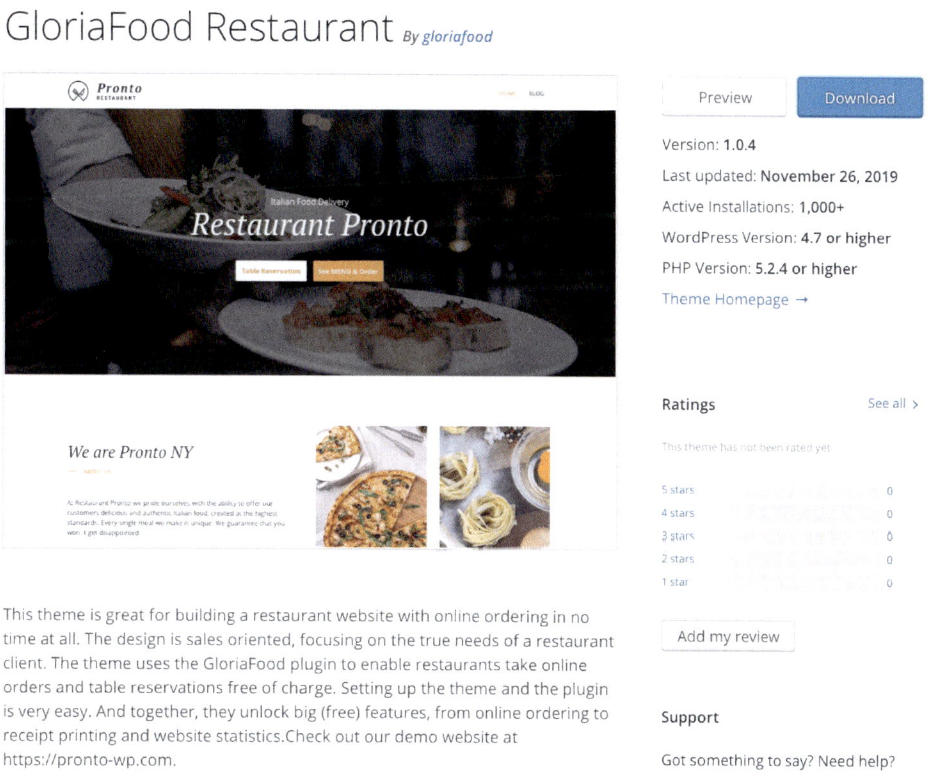

It will take some time to understand how the templates work but stick with it. Most templates are pretty much the same—so once you get the hang of one, you know how to use the others.

Exception: As you can see in the examples above, WordPress uses a different approach and is more complicated. All utilize drag-and-drop technology, but WordPress is far more sophisticated with many more options. Best to take a course to learn how, hire a freelancer, or avoid it altogether.

Wix ADI (Artificial Design Intelligence)
You can also opt to let Wix ADI choose a template that meets your specifications.

With just a few questions, Wix ADI designs a website based on your answers.

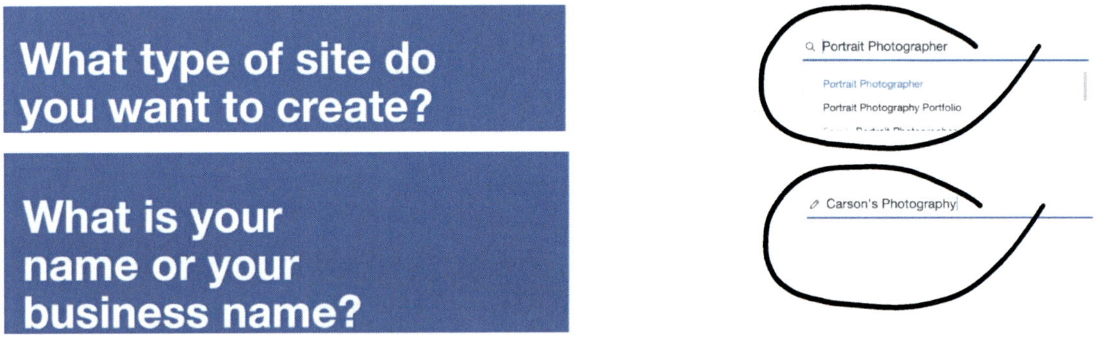

Wix ADI matches design and content elements to create a website design. You can customize it with colors and fonts and imagery.

Wix ADI will offer several formats from which to choose. Select one and then drag and drop images and text into the template.

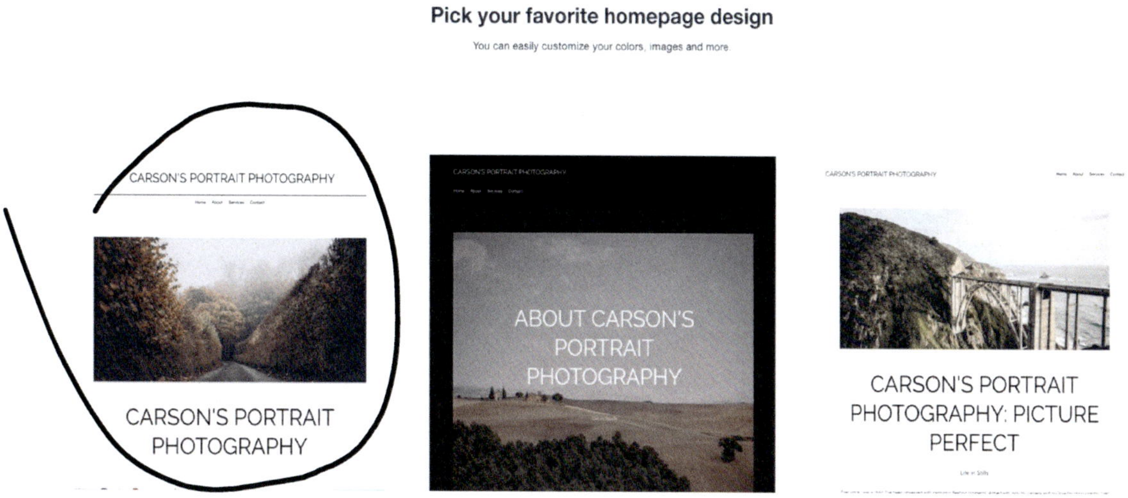

Website templates are cost-effective, easy to use, have built-in functionality, and come in many different designs. Look for a template that can be customized, is responsive to other devices, has several pages (not just the homepage), and can be updated.

Once you decide on a website builder, select a template.

Next, we will discuss the essential components used in building a good website:

Color
White Space
Contrast
Typography-Fonts
Content - Text
Content - Imagery
Alignment

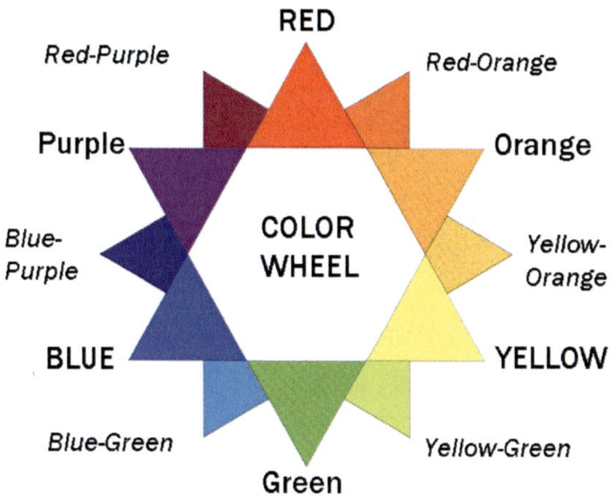

"Mere color, unspoiled by meaning, and unallied with definite form, can speak to the soul in a thousand different ways."
–**Oscar Wilde**

CHAPTER 7

COLOR

People make immediate, subconscious judgments based on color. Within seconds, 90% of viewers make up their minds about products based on their reaction to the product's color. Colors communicate on an emotional level, making them effective to use in your design.

Color is the most significant factor in the appearance of your website. You can use color to highlight important aspects of your business. You can create a mood with soft colors and make a statement with bold colors. It lends continuity and balance to your theme.

Color has aesthetic appeal, is pleasing to the eye, sparks interest, creates a sense of balance, and is imperative in the organizational structure of your website. When used correctly, *it will engage the viewer to stay on your site longer.*

The colors you choose must align with your brand and be liked by your target audience. It is the design component that your viewers will instantly relate to and remember the longest. The color scheme choice is not about your likes–it is about the likes of your audience. It should resonate with them. You want a positive response. Yellow appeals to children, while older adults prefer blue–and yellow is one of their least favorite colors.

MEANINGS OF COLOR:

Colors evoke different emotions in the viewer. By carefully selecting colors, you can reinforce the overall message of your design.

RED

Red is the most intense color and attracts the most attention. It activates the pituitary gland, which increases the heart and the breathing rate. It is the color of power, action, speed, danger, passion, romance, love, excitement, and energy. It is associated with anger, importance, and hunger. The darker shades are more elegant. (Signs, Clothing, Advertising, Fast Food)

YELLOW

Yellow is the color of the sun. It is a happy color associated with joy, optimism, cheerfulness, warmth, and summer. The eye sees yellow first. Bright yellow is energetic, medium shades are comforting, and dark shades symbolize curiosity. (Food, Sales, Childcare)

BLUE

Blue is the color of the ocean and the sky. It is the most liked of all the colors. It is the color of honesty, security, sincerity, trustworthiness, dependability, tranquility, and spirituality. Light blues are relaxed and friendly. Bright blues can be energizing. Dark blues are strong and reliable. (Corporations, Spas, Pharmacies, Airlines, Police, Science)

GREEN

Green is the color of nature. It is easy and relaxing on the eyes. It symbolizes growth, health, environment, nature, renewal, youth, success, harmony, good luck, wealth, and balance. Dark green is very stable and implies wealth. Bright green is vibrant. Olive green represents nature. (Nature, Recycling, Organic, Health, Finance)

ORANGE

Orange combines red's power and yellow's friendliness. It is a vibrant, energetic color. Orange is warm, fun, confident, friendly, enthusiastic, positive, creative and adventurous. The brightest shades impart energy. It is also associated with good value. (Sports, Home Improvement, Travel, Entertainment, Beauty Salons)

PURPLE

Purple is the color of creativity and imagination. It is associated with luxury, loyalty, royalty, courage, wisdom, spirituality, and mystery. Lighter shades like lavender are associated with spring and romance. (Magic, Spirituality, Massage, Yoga, Luxury products)

BROWN

Brown is the color of the earth, home, and hearth. It is a warm color associated with the outdoors, safety, stability, and dependability. When combined with green, it conveys recycling. (Home, Animals, Building, Coffee, Trucking, Chocolate)

GRAY

Gray is the most neutral color. It is unemotional and impartial. It is associated with stability, quietness, reliability, security, and intelligence. Darker shades are dramatic. Lighter shades are luminous (like silver). Gray is conservative, a bit boring when it is not matched with another color, but elegant and formal. (Tech companies, Automobiles, Appliances)

WHITE

White is the color of perfection. It is associated with purity, innocence, sterility, cleanliness, balance, and simplicity. It is neutral and goes with everything. (Weddings, Medical, Science, Dental, News, Infants)

BLACK

Black is the color of power and authority. It is classic and always in style. It is associated with strength, luxury, elegance, fashion, and sophistication. Too much is overpowering. (Luxury products, Limos, Cosmetics)

This book is directed toward the American market. Color has different meanings in other parts of the world. If you are selling to foreign markets, be aware of the deviations. Here are a few examples.

Red

China	Happiness
South Africa	Mourning
Thailand	Associated with the God Surya.
Russia	Communism

Blue

Korea and Iran	Mourning
Egypt	Wards off evil.
China	Feminine color (not pink!)

Green

Saudi Arabia	Wealth
China	Disgrace
Mexico	Independence
South America	Death
Indonesia	Forbidden color

Yellow

Japan	Courage
Egypt	Mourning
Greece	Sadness
China	Associated with pornography.
France	Jealousy
African nations	Used by people of high rank.

White

China	Death
India	Unhappiness-widow's color

Purple

Japan	Denotes wealth.
Brazil	Worn at funerals.

Orange

Netherlands	Represents the Dutch Royal family.
Egypt	Mourning
China	Courage

CHOICES OF SUCCESSFUL COMPANIES

Coca Cola - Before 1900, tax officials checked trucks for alcohol. Coke chose red to distinguish its product from alcohol. It is one of the strongest brands in the world.

Google wanted to be playful, hence the primary colors. The "l" broke the primary color scheme to emphasize they don't "follow the rules".

BMW used the colors of Bavaria, Germany–blue and white.

Facebook - Mark Zuckerberg is color-blind to red and green. Blue was the richest color for him.

Shell - Designed in 1915. The colors were chosen because the company had strong ties with Spain. The Spanish flag is yellow and red.

UPS - In 1916 brown was the color of luxury and class. Today it means dependability and solidarity. It is a grounded color.

McDonald's uses red because stimulates hunger and yellow to imply happiness.

Subway uses green for health and yellow to stand out.

Chanel - is noted for its "little black dress" design. Black is for sophistication.

Hermes is the world's second most valuable luxury brand. Orange exudes confidence and extroversion. It was the color of the only paperboard available during WWII.

Merck - (pharmaceuticals) green is associated with health.

Lufthansa uses blue for trustworthiness and yellow for happiness and optimism.

Home Depot chose orange because it is associated with good value. Low cost for quality products.

Land-Rover is green because British racing cars used to be green.

JAL - (Japan Air Lines) Red is power and symbolizes good luck in Asia. They share the same colors of the Japanese flag.

The chart below was created by "The Logo Company".
It shows color choices made by different companies. What colors appeal to your target audience?

HOW TO CHOOSE YOUR COLORS:

Check out your competition; it will give you a starting point. Remember, you do not want to look like them.

Experiment with several color schemes to see what fits. Think about your target audience. Go with colors that set you apart from others but keep it simple.

Be careful. Too many colors will confuse the viewer. Use no more than 3: base, accent, and neutral.

Dominant Color

This color is your brand color. It reflects your most dominant personality trait and will subconsciously affect your target audience. It gets their attention and makes your brand memorable.

Which color best matches your business or how you want your viewers to see your brand?

Example: If you own a spa, you want to use calm colors (greens and blues, not red!).

Use your base color sparingly. It is supposed to highlight your focus. If you use it too much, your message is missed.

Accent Color

The accent color pairs visually with the base color and your target audience. It gives your page appeal. It creates a mood. Use only 1 or 2.

Background Color

A neutral color is chosen to avoid attention. White is the best because it is uncluttered, easy on the eye, and shows off the colors. Tints work well. Artists may choose bold colors. Black is also an option, but too much is “so yesterday”.

WHITE SPACE

"Whitespace is like air: it is necessary for design to breathe."
—Wojciech Zieliński

Whitespace, or negative space, is the portion of a page left blank. The empty space on a page. It is associated with elegance and sophistication. It is a way to organize text and images and direct the user to areas of importance.

Even though we call it white space, it doesn't have to be white. The blank space may be filled with any color as long as it is free of text or images.

EXAMPLES:

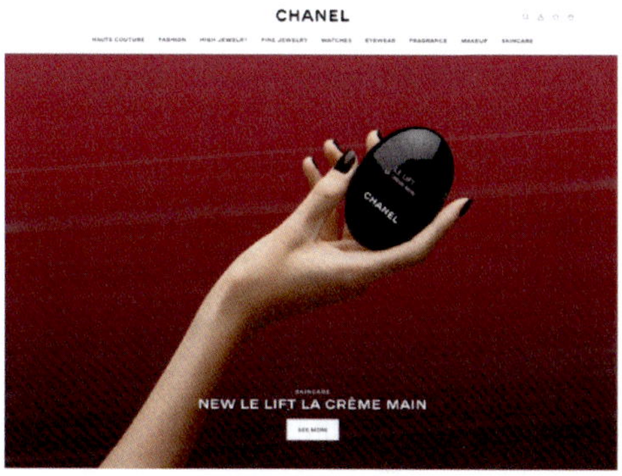

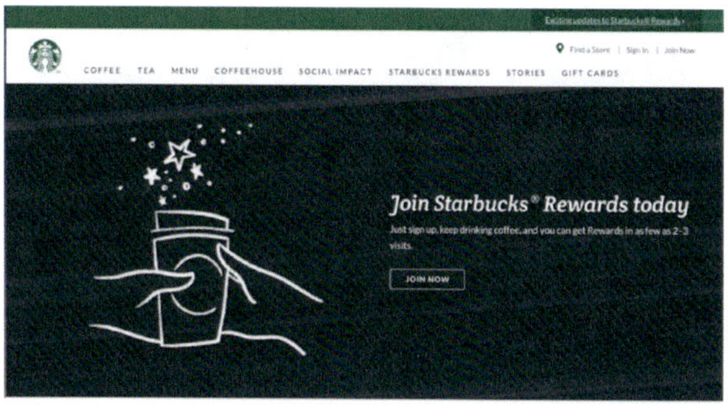

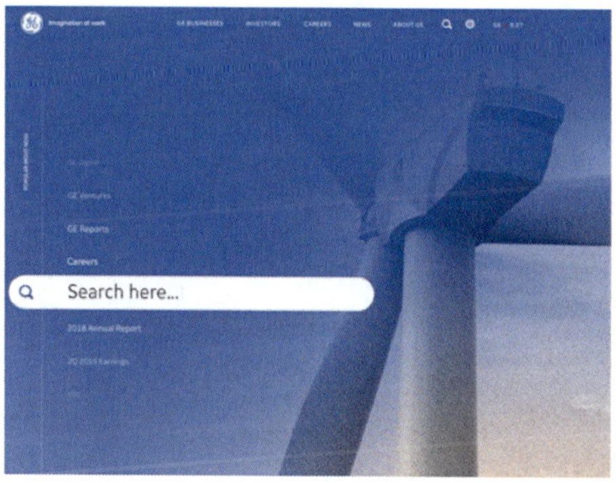

THE COLOR WHEEL

"All colors are the friends of their neighbors and the lovers of their opposites." – **Marc Chagall**

PRIMARY, SECONDARY AND TERTIARY COLORS

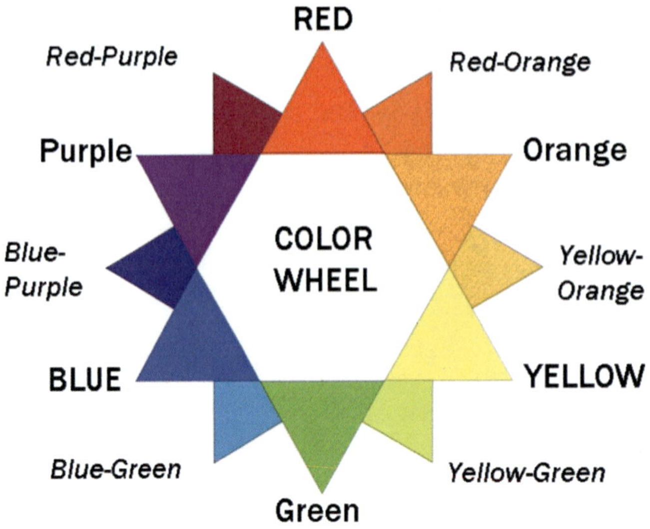

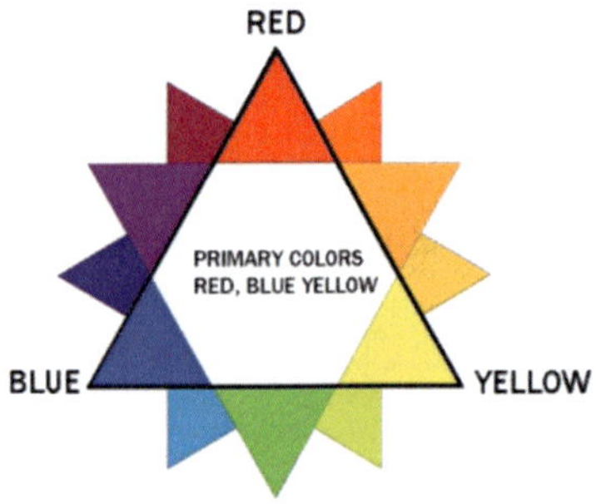

Primary colors

Red, Blue, Yellow

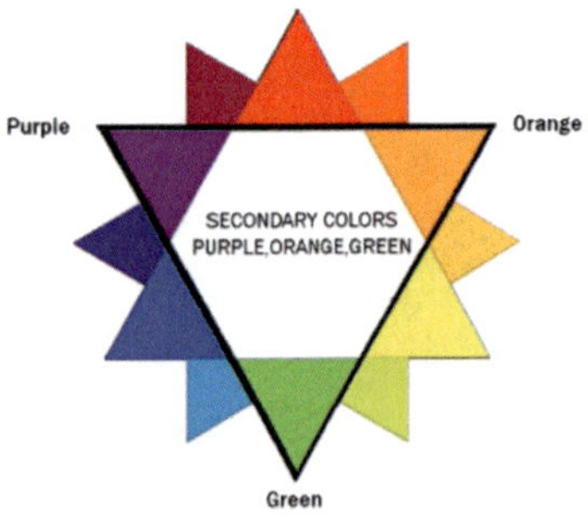

Secondary colors

Mix 2 primary colors

Red+Blue = Purple

Red+Yellow = Orange

Blue+Yellow = Green

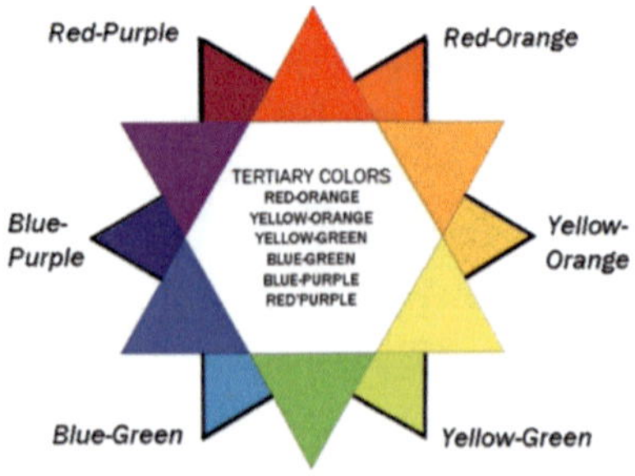

Tertiary Colors

Mix 1 primary + 1 secondary color

Red+Purple = Magenta

Red+Orange = Vermilion

Yellow+Orange = Amber

Yellow+Green = Chartreuse

Blue+Green = Teal

Blue+Purple = Violet

Primary colors are the base for all other colors. They cannot be derived by mixing with other colors. There are 3:

Red Blue Yellow.

Secondary colors are mixtures of 2 primary colors in equal parts. There are 3:

Purple Orange Green

Tertiary Colors are mixtures of 1 primary and 1 secondary color. There are 6:

Magenta Vermilion Amber Chartreuse Teal Violet

COMPLIMENTARY AND ANALOGOUS COLORS

Complimentary colors are on opposite sides of the color wheel. Placing a cool color with a warm color creates balance, contrast, and harmony. They make things "pop".

Purple and Yellow Green and Red Blue and Orange.

Analogous colors are 3 colors next to one another on the color wheel. Usually primary + secondary + tertiary. One color usually dominates, and the others are supportive. They are pleasing to the eye, nature colors, subtle, and harmonious.

Blue Blue/Green Green Orange Yellow/Orange Yellow

WARM COLORS AND COOL COLORS

Warm Colors are on the right side of the color wheel. They impart a sense of boldness, passion, energy, and aggressiveness. Objects seem larger and closer.

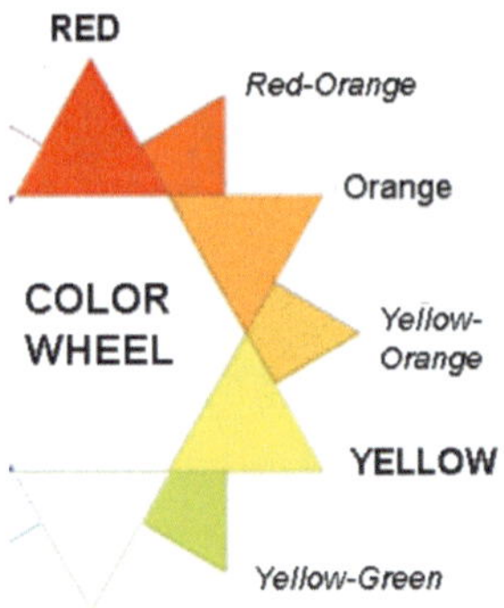

You would not want to use warm colors for a Spa. You want people to "chill". You would choose a more relaxing, cooler color like blue or green.

Cool Colors are on the left side of the color wheel and are more soothing, more detached, and less aggressive. Often used by professionals in the cosmetic and medical fields.

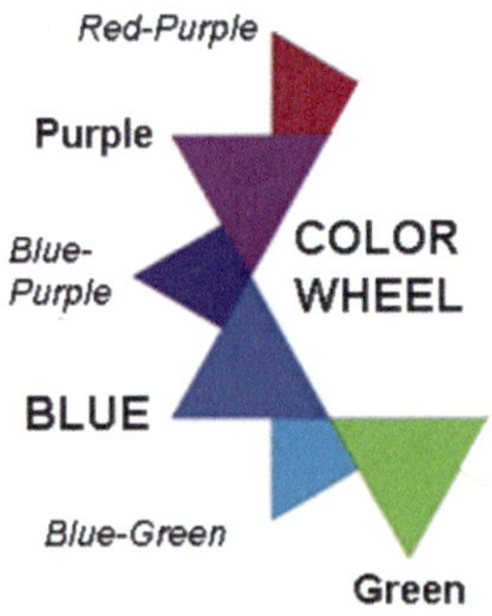

You would not use cool colors for Fast Food. Cool colors don't stimulate the appetite like warm colors. A better choice would be red or yellow.

COLOR PROPERTIES

TINTS AND SHADES

Tints are colors that are mixed with white. Tints lighten a color and lessen the intensity. Pastels are tints. Tints are more feminine.

Shades are colors that are mixed with black. It darkens a color. Shades are more masculine.

SATURATION AND DESATURATION

Saturation is used in digital imaging. It amplifies the intensity of a color. It makes it more vivid. If you over-saturate a color it looks unnatural, which can be a nice effect if you want to add vibrance.

Desaturation makes the color duller, less pure. It is softer. Too much desaturation will make colors look washed-out.

Saturation Desaturation

BLACK AND WHITE

At opposite ends of the color spectrum are black and white. They help the viewer focus on the essential elements.

Black absorbs color. It is the color easiest to read.

White reflects color. It is balanced and perfect for backgrounds.

CONTRAST

Contrast

Contrast is how colors work together. It is an important visual tool because it is what attracts the eye to the page.

High Contrast

High-contrast is when colors easily stand apart from each other. It makes it easy to read and scan. Use if you want to emphasize something important.
Think of it as a “highlighter.” ("buy" or "sale")

If everything is in high contrast, nothing stands out.

Low Contrast

When colors do not separate visually from one another, they are in low contrast. It is harder to read but more attractive. Think of it as a “mute”.

If everything is low contrast, nothing stands out. It's boring.

Contrast enables text to be read easily.

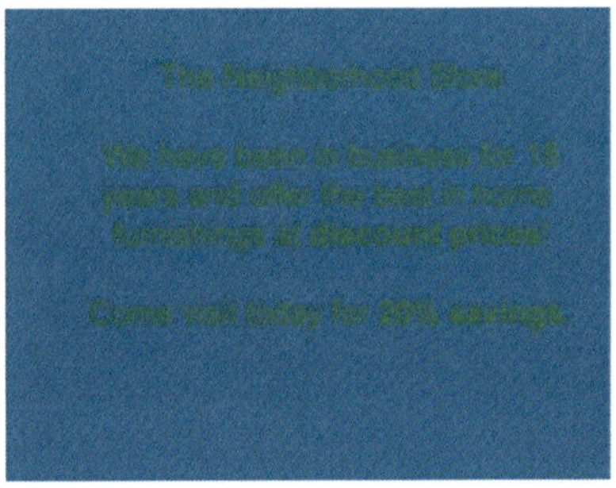

BAD

STILL BAD

GOOD

Black is the easiest color to read.

Sometimes you can use white on a dark background.
Use it sparingly because it can cause eye strain if there is too much text or if the text is too small.

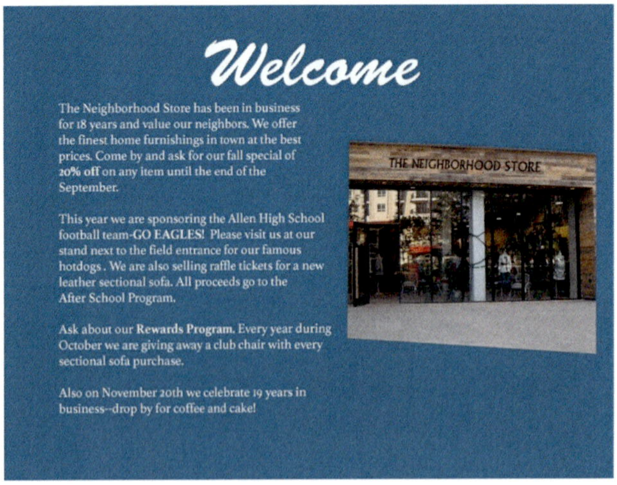

The title works well but the body of text is too lengthy and too small to be read easily.

COLOR SCHEMES

Monochrome- One-Color Scheme

All colors used in the design of the website are derived from one color. Contrast makes the colors stand out. The color decisions are minimal, which gives a sense of harmony and focus. You can also choose a black and white scheme and add an accent color. If you use a strong color, it will spark interest and make a strong statement.

https://shibui.com

https://www.raymondloe

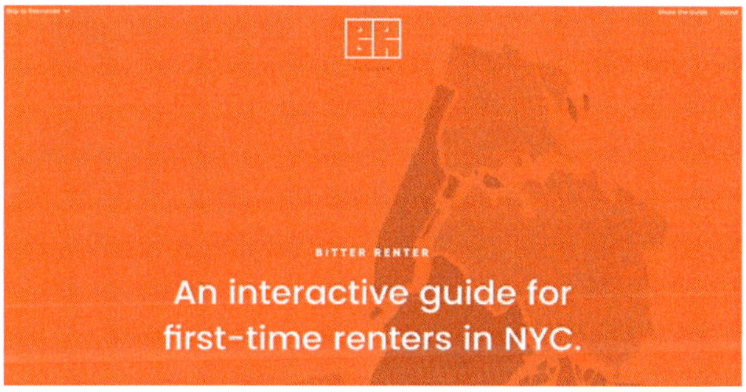

http://www.bitterrenter.nyc

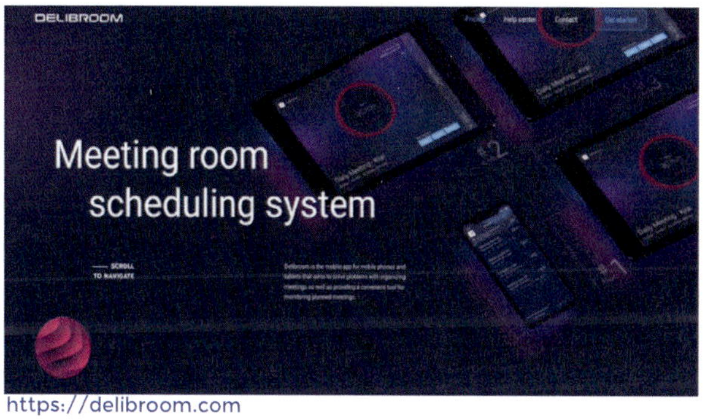

https://delibroom.com

Complementary - Opposite Color Theme

The colors used in the design of the website that are opposite one another on the color wheel.
Purple and Yellow, Green and Red, Blue and Orange

Complementary colors are a memorable combination and attract attention. By working together, they balance emotions (ex: red for impact and green to calm), make the text easier to read and make a positive impact on the viewer.

https://www.violetta.ch

https://ubisoft.com

https://naturestable.com

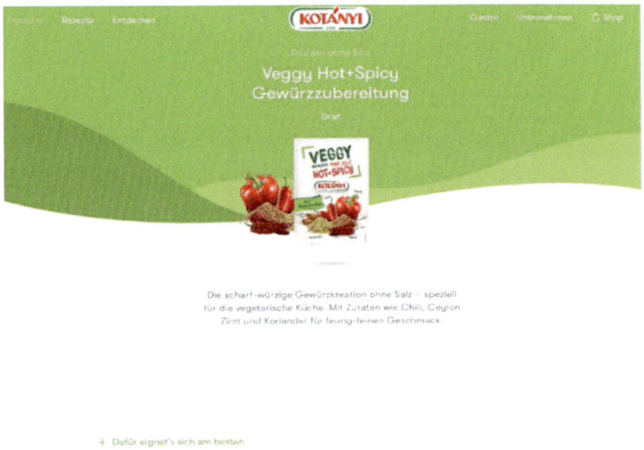

https://www.kotanyi.com

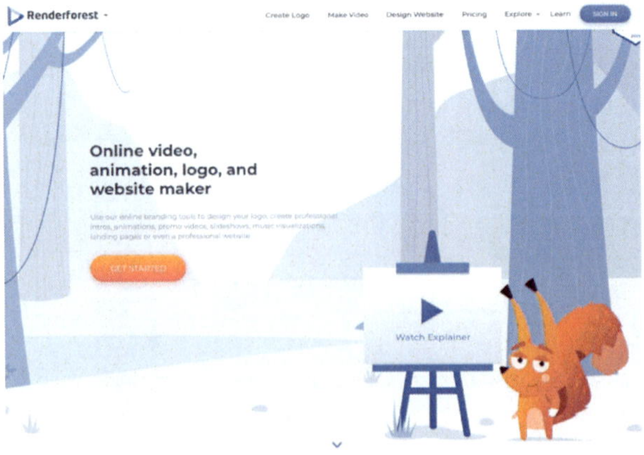

https://www.renderforest.com

https://www.ososphere.org

Analogous -Next To One Another Color Theme

The colors used in the design of the website that are next to one another on the color wheel.

Usually primary + secondary + tertiary. One color usually dominates, and the others are supportive.

Analogous colors convey a sense of simplicity, are pleasing to the eye, subtle, and harmonious. They have richer nuances than the Monochromatic Color Scheme but don't have the "pop" of the Complementary Color Scheme.

https://ourhabitas.com

https://www.expedia..com

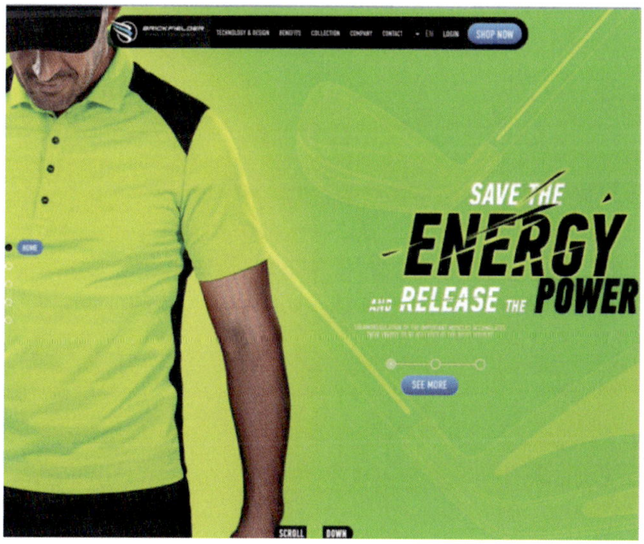

https://brickfielder.co.uk

https://www.michelbergerhotel.com/en/rooms

NOW, WHAT?

For most of you, you have now learned all you want to know about color. Use your new-found knowledge to determine:

- Color Scheme
  Monochrome, Complementary, or Analogous.
- Dominant Color
  Use this color to attract attention.
  Which color works best for your target audience?
  Don't choose the same color as your competition.
  Avoid color cliches (pink is not just for girls).
- Accent Colors
  Use this color as a call-to-action. Choose 1 or 2.
  What colors support your dominant color?
- Background Color
  What color best promotes your content as the focal point of your design?
  White, neutrals, and tints are popular. "Less is more."
  (E-commerce, Information, Banks)
  Bold colors are creative but can overwhelm.
  (Artists, Fashion, Design, Beauty, Restaurants)
  Logo color variations promote your brand.
  (Corporations, Banks)

WEB COLORPICKER

Use the WebFX Colorpicker tool at https://www.webfx.com/web-design/color-picker/

Click on "Color Chart" below the color square to select your color and write down the Hex Color#.
Hex colors are coded in 6-digit numbers and letters. They represent all the colors on the web.

Spread the Word   Quick Tips   CSS Examples   Feedback   Color Chart

Examples: Catalina Blue is #062A78
White is #ffffff
Black is #000000

Go back by clicking on "Return to ColorPiker.com" on the upper left side of the page.

Color Chart (HTML Color Codes, Color Names, Colors)

Return to ColorPicker.com

Type in the hex color# in the top box on the right side of the large square and click Complementary Color on the top. The chart selected the color Blue #0081ff.

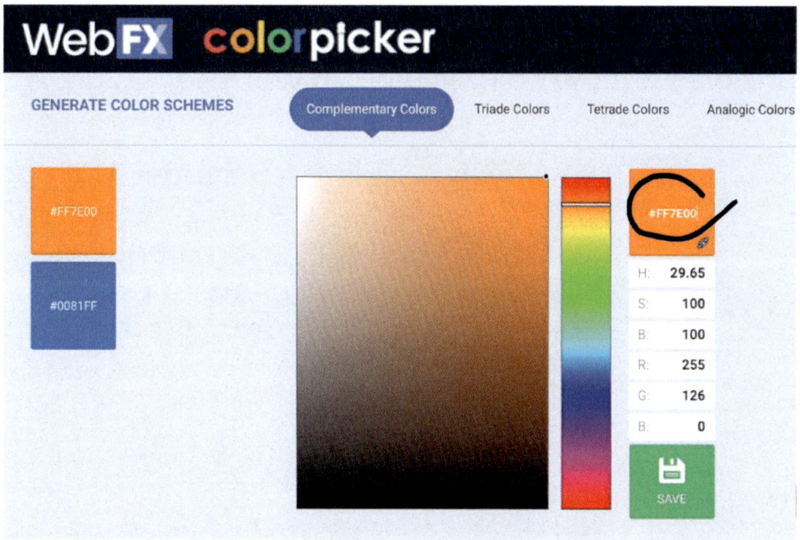

Click on The Triade Colors at the top and you see #00ff7e and #7e00ff are selected on the left side.

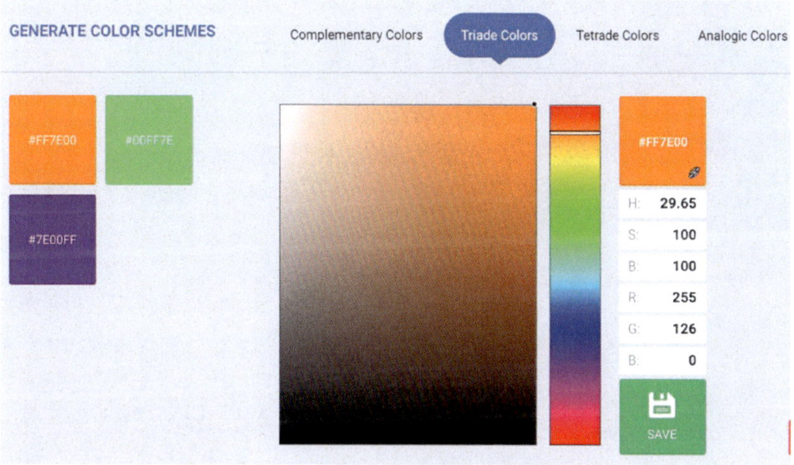

Click on Analogic Colors and the chart assigns: #ffff00, #80ff00, #00ff00, #ff8000and #ff000

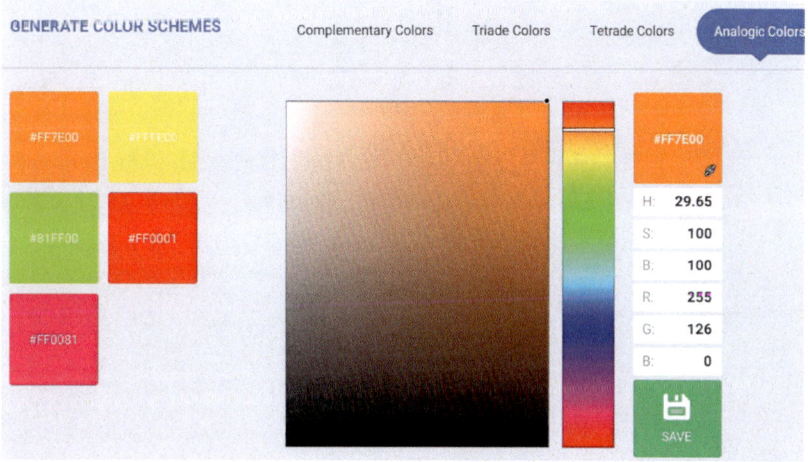

Experiment with the chart. Try different colors until you find the ones you like. It is only a guide. You can alter the results by using tints, shade, contrast, etc. It is just a tool to point you in the right direction. Don't be intimidated–have fun with it.

Examples of how color is used in website design:

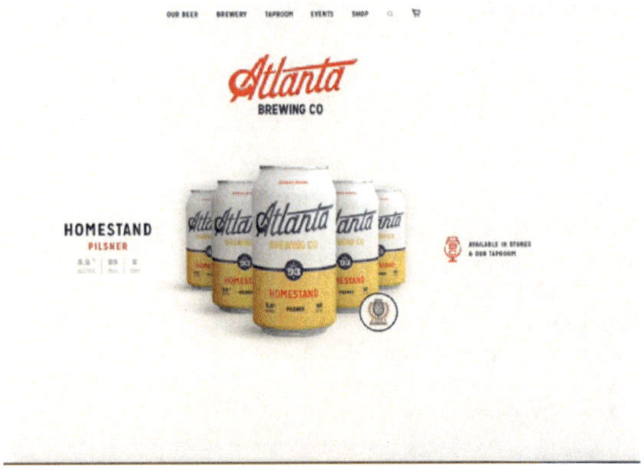

Scheme: Analogous:
Red +Orange/Yellow
Dominent Color: Red
Accent Color: Yellow
Background Color: White

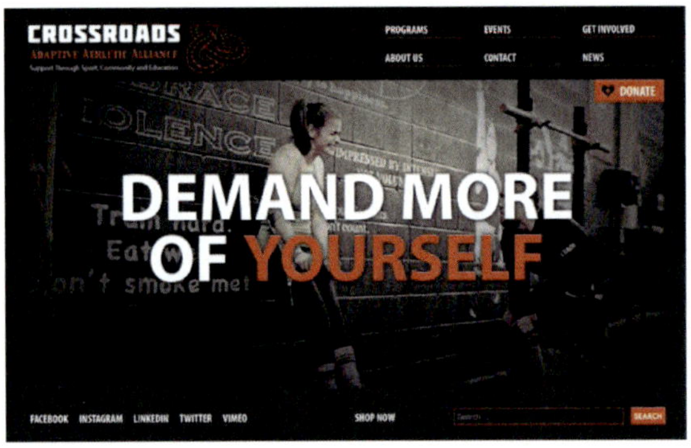

Scheme: Monochrome
Dominent Color: Orange
Accent Color: White
Background Color: Black

Scheme: Complementary
Yellow + Purple
Dominent Color: Purple
Accent Color: White
Background Color: Yellow

Scheme: Analogous
Blue+ Green+Lt. Blue
Dominent Color: Blue
Accent Color: Green
Background Color: White

Scheme: Complementary
Red + Green
Dominent Color: Red
Accent Color: Green
Background Color: Lt Green

Scheme: Monochrome
Dominent Color: Blue
Accent Color: Lt. Blue
Background Color: Blue

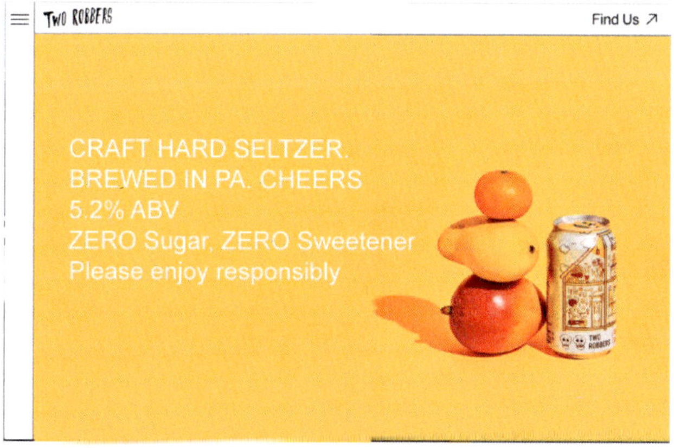

Scheme: Analogous:
Red+Orange+Yellow
Dominent Color: Red
Accent Color: White
Background Color: Yellow

Scheme: Complementary
Blue + Orange
Dominent Color: Red
Accent Color: White
Background Color: Blue

“FONTS
Turn Words
into
STORIES”
Sara Hyndman

“Type is like the air; we need it to live and don’t notice it, until someone farts.” –**Fabio Maag**

CHAPTER 8

TYPOGRAPHY - FONTS

Typography is the art of arranging type. Most people don’t think about it, but the type of font you use has a profound effect on your brand identity.

Fonts deliver your brand message and are integral to your image. They not only communicate your name but your personality. They give your brand cohesiveness, evoke interest, and add to the design. Choose the wrong font, and you don’t connect; you lose your audience.

Your font choice must be readable, should evoke a positive response, and be industry-specific. The font you choose should reflect the expectations of your target audience.

- If you are targeting children, your fonts will be more fun.

Highlights™ kids

- If you are targeting financial companies, your fonts will be more professional.

BERKSHIRE HATHAWAY INC.

FIVE CATEGORIES OF FONTS

1. SERIF

This font is one of the oldest typefaces. It has details, which are small lines attached to the ends of the letters called flags or tags.

It is more formal and evokes trustworthiness, reliability, and professionalism. It is bold but can feel old fashioned and lack-luster, which is perfect if your target audience wants to feel you are traditional and dependable. It is used by newspapers, financial services, insurance, academia, etc.

Prudential

UnitedHealthcare®

2. SANS SERIF

Sans means "without." The letters don't have tags or flags attached. The font is clean, modern, and easy to read. It is straightforward and contemporary. Sans serif is popular with digital design companies. It is often used as a headline when serif is used for text.

Google

Walmart

3. SCRIPT

Script fonts mimic handwriting and tend to be more personal. It is creative, casual, and has a carefree quality. It can be hand-drawn. Sometimes script can be difficult to read. It is often used by artistic companies.

Amazing Websites!

Walgreens

4. DECORATIVE/DISPLAY

This type of font gets attention. It is big, bold, and unusual--meant to be noticed. Entertainment companies love it for the impact it generates. Never used in text–used in logos and headings.

WALT DISNEY

METALLICA

5. MODERN

Modern fonts are trendy and eye-catching. A favorite of tech companies for their futuristic appearance.

VIACOM®

NASA

HOW TO CHOOSE YOUR FONTS

1. Know your target audience.
   Different fonts appeal to different audiences. Teens like decorative/display fonts while older adults like serif and sans serif. Women tend to like script.

2. What is the personality of your target audience?
   Are they witty, serious, realistic, playful, aloft, etc.? Children are playful, while adults might be more serious.

3. Does it match your message?
   Does it support your brand? If your brand is creative, you don't want to use a formal font that is traditional. If your brand depicts traditional concepts, you don't want to use a fun font.

4. Is it readable?
   You are trying to communicate clearly. If the font is too complex, it will confuse the viewer. It should be at least 16pt in size, should have adequate space around it to give the eye a rest (white space), and contrast with the background.

Examples of fonts and the emotions they elicit:

Charley's Seafood Shack	Fun, lively, a little retro. (Lobster)
High Fashion	Sophisticated, refined, Elegant. (Alex Brush)
Tech Studios	Contemporary, clean, fresh. (Anton)
Spa Splendor	Calming, relaxed. (Allura)
Kids Corner	Fun, child-like. (Sniglet)
Amazing Websites!	Creative, hand-brushed, artistic, fun. (RofiTaste)

FREE FONTS

Many fonts are licensed. You will have to pay for them. *Read the fine print.* I thought my font was free, but it was free for personal use and demos only. I like the RofiTaste font because it is original, different, and unique. I don't regret paying for the license, but I wish it was free!

Three good sources online for free fonts are:

1. **Font Squirrel** offers free fonts that are licensed for commercial use. https://www.fontsquirrel.

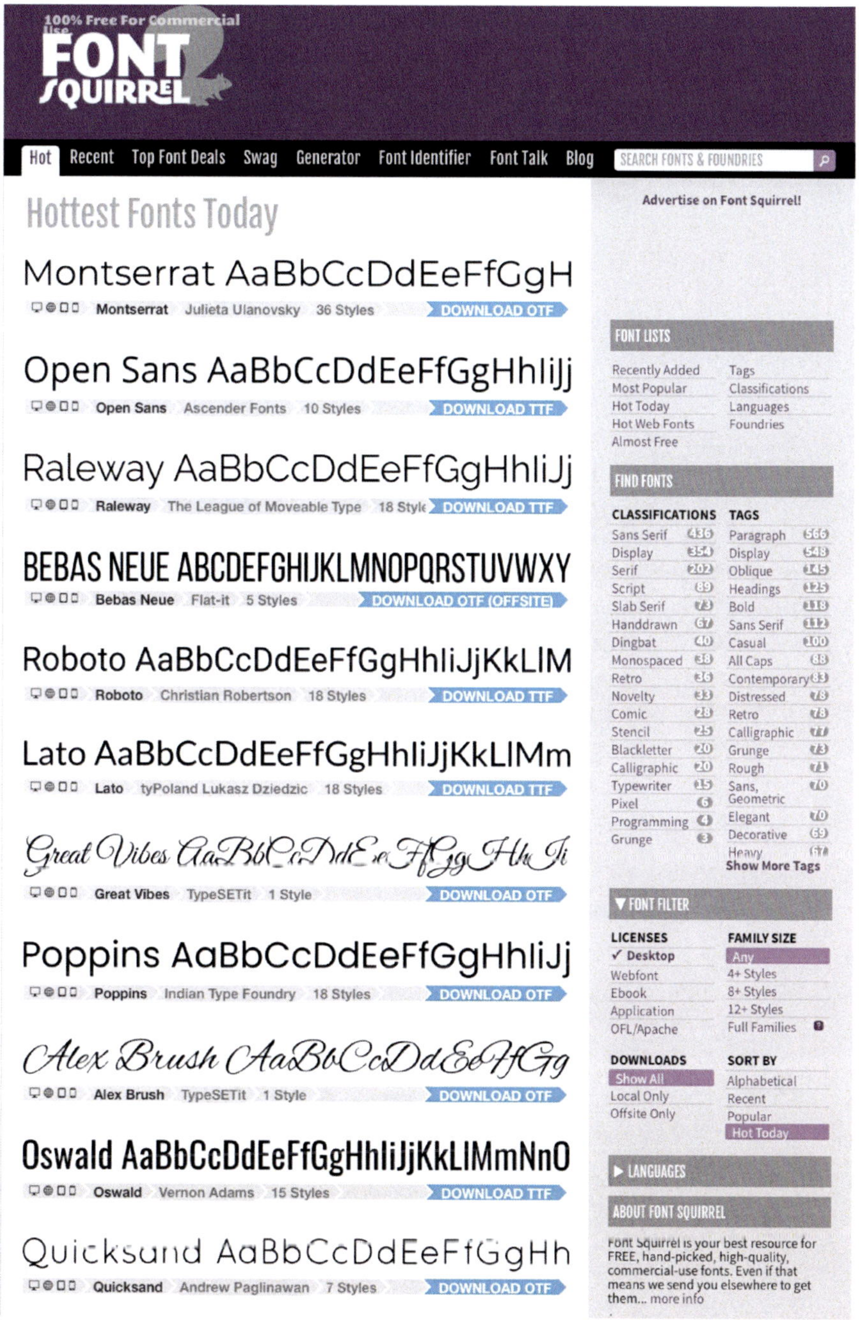

2. **Google Fonts** are fonts created to use on websites. All the fonts are "Open Source" which means they are free and can be shared and customized. https://fonts.google.com

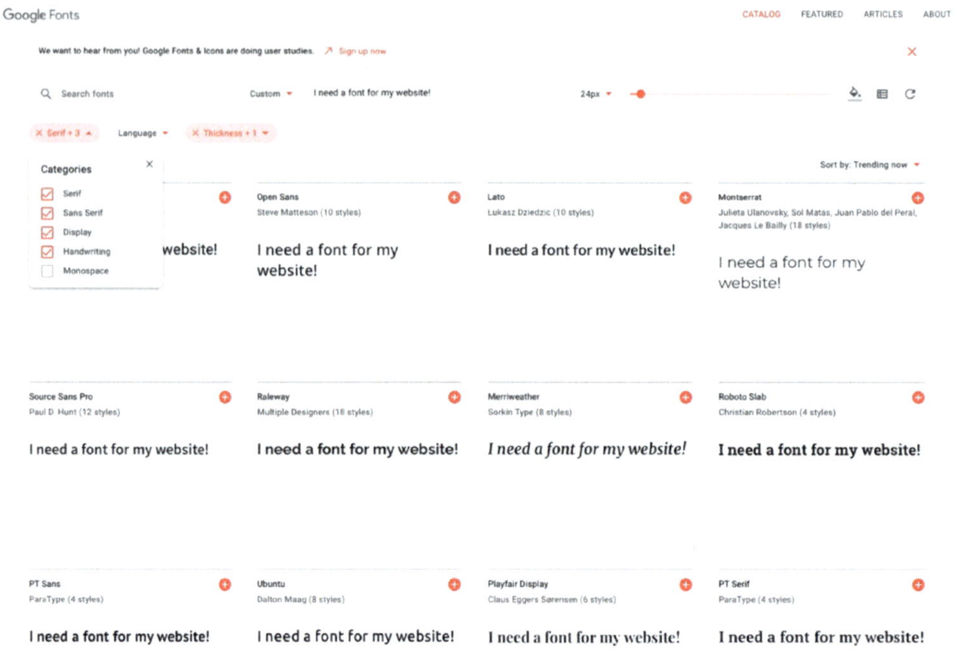

3. **1001 Fonts** – Fonts are free and for sale. Choose the "Free Fonts for Commercial Use" category in the drop-down menu. https://www.1001fonts.com/free-fonts-for-commercial-use.html

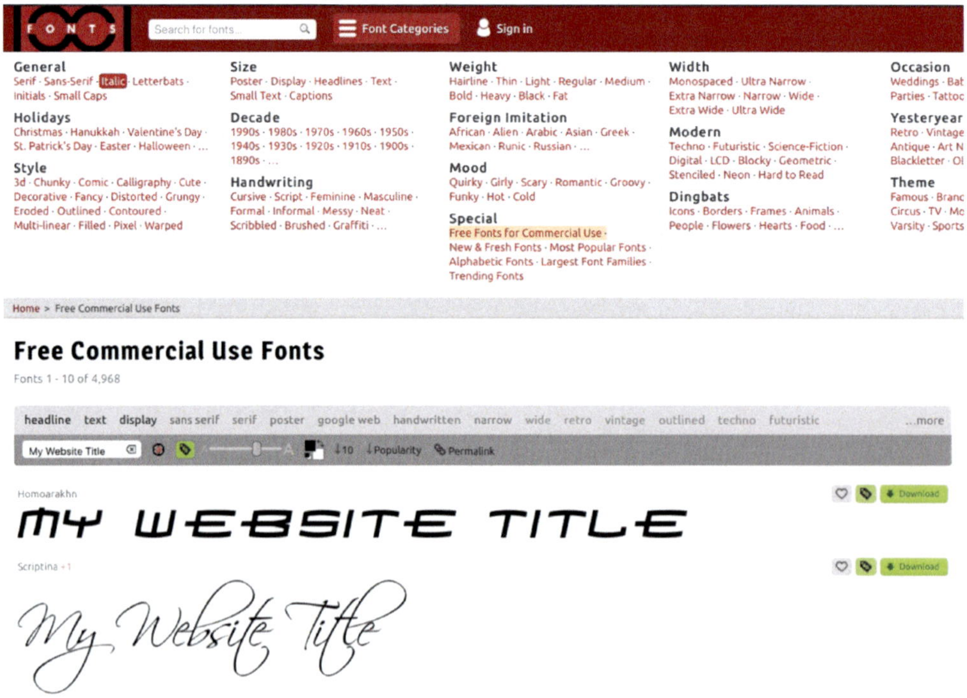

HOW TO USE FONTS

HIERARCHY

Hierarchy is a system used to organize type in a way to communicate data effectively. It is visual. It breaks up the dialog so the type is not all the same, which would be boring. It makes it easy to scan for information. The hierarchy needs to be clear and consistent throughout the website design.

The type is layered by using different font sizes, boldness, style, colors, contrast, italics, location, and capitalization.

> Header - (Primary) The most important element is the header. It has the most impact. Use fonts that are big, bold, and attract the viewer's attention.
>
> Sub-Header - (Secondary) These fonts support the header fonts. They are smaller than the header fonts but larger than the text fonts.
>
> Body Text - (Tertiary) The body text contains the main content in easy-to-read fonts not smaller than 16pt. Keep it brief. No one reads long columns of text.

Spacing is important. Empty space eliminates the clutter, allows the page to breathe, and gives the viewer a positive experience.

Siesta Key Drum Circle

Sponsored by
Sarasota High School

November 3, 2019
at 6:00 pm -8:00 pm

The Drum Team
789 Tamiami Trail
Sarasota, FL 34231

thedrumteam.com

DRUM CIRCLE - Primary font (Roboto)
Siesta Key - Secondary font (Snell Rd)
Text - Tertiary font (Montserrat)

www.awwwards.com is a website that selects the best websites. Here are some examples of good typographic hierarchy:

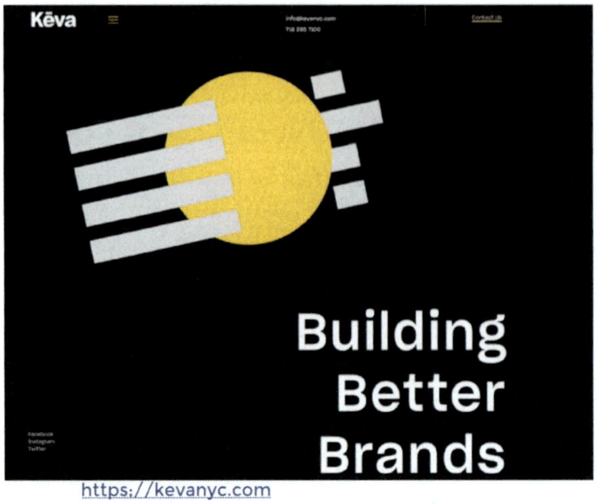

https://kevanyc.com

https://www.amsterdamferryfestival.nl

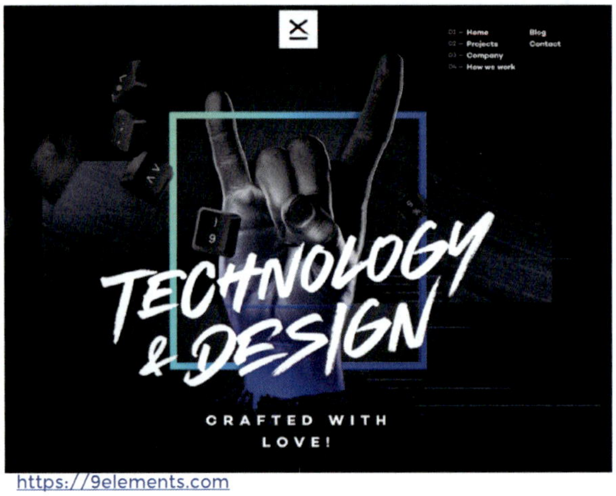

https://9elements.com

https://culture.pl/en

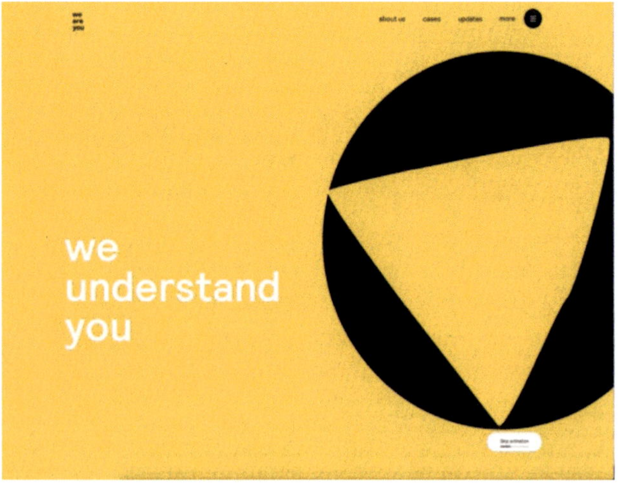

https://www.fondationstejustine.org/en/

https://www.weareyou.com/en

FONT COMBINATIONS

There are thousands of fonts; how do you choose? It can be a challenge. Fonts have to harmonize and still have an impact.

Superfamily Fonts

Superfamily fonts share identical features and have a similar appearance (example: serif fonts). They have been designed to work together. Using a superfamily is perfect if you are looking to appeal to a traditional, conservative market.

Examples: Lucida Superfamily

Lucida Bright	*Lucida Calligraphy*
Lucida Grande	Lucida Fax
Lucida Sans	*Lucida Handwriting*

Non-Identical Fonts

Non-Identical fonts contrast and do not have identical features, but still work well together. They usually consist of using a serif font paired with a sans-serif font. You can use a bold serif font with a light sans-serif. These combinations tend to be more creative.

Examples:

Bembo + **Gill Sans**

Roboto + Montserrat

Minion Pro + **Brandon Grotesque**

Only use two main fonts. (A third font can be used for accent.) You can use the same font in different ways. One way is to make the title bolder and larger and the subtitle lighter in italics. Add a complementary font for the text.

Example: Use **Roboto Black** for the header, *Roboto Light Italic* for the sub-header and Montserrat light for the text

LIBERATION BANK

New Money Give-Away

Free Money, Free Money
Free Money, Free Money
Free Money, Free Money
Free Money, Free Money
Free Money, Free Money

Rule: Similar or Contrast but never Conflict. You can avoid conflict if you select two fonts. The more fonts, the more conflict.

Basics

- Try to use only 2 fonts.
- Use fonts that compliment.

    Superfamily Fonts
    Script and Non-Script
    Serif and Non-Serif
    Size: Bold and Light

- Be consistent throughout the website.

The good news is that there is a lot of help online. Dozens of sites will show you pairings that work and explain why. Remember to reflect your industry type. Bold fonts are appropriate for construction companies while beauty salons might prefer script fonts.

I have included some popular Google font combinations. All are free. Look at the pairings. You will begin to see how they complement each other.

Decide what appeals to you and what fits your target audience. There is no one "right" choice. Apply the basics and you will succeed in selecting the right combination.

JULIUS SANS ONE
Archivo Narrow

Montserrat
Merriweather

Raleway
Lato

Playfair Display
Source Sans Pro

Amaranth
Open Sans

Cooper
Patrick Hand

Merriweather
Oswald

Oswald
Lato

Dancing Script
Josefin Sans

Sansita Open Sans	Josefin Slab Patrick Hand	Franklin Gothic Sabon
BEBAS NEUE Montserrat Light	Sign Painter OPEN SANS BOLD	ROBOTO Lora
Minion Pro Brandon Grotesque	BAUHAUS 93 OPEN SANS	Garamond Quicksand
League Spartan Libre Baskerville	Bodoni Josefin Sans	SIX CAPS Daun Penh
Corben Nobile	Elsie Roboto	Spirax Open Sans

Content

"Content is king." –**Bill Gates**

CHAPTER 9

CONTENT - TEXT

Content is the visual information on your website. It includes text, images, videos, etc. It is the way you communicate your values. You only have a few seconds to connect with your viewer, so it must be engaging.

The main components of website content are:
Text and Imagery

TEXT

Creating a text can be a challenge. So what else is new? You'd probably rather have your appendix removed than write text. It's a process and can be much easier than you think.

Aim to satisfy your target audience. You are writing for them, not yourself. You need to catch their eye and reel them in.

The second thing you need to remember is to be brief. As I said earlier, no one reads. Websites are scanned, not read, which is good news for you when considering what to write.

Text should:

- Offer useful, practical information.
- Be brief, easy to read, and well-organized.
- Engage the reader to stay and return later.
- Entertain–never bore your reader.

TEXT GUIDELINES

Think of Your Target Audience

Why are they on your website?
What information are they seeking?
What do you want to say to them?
What do you want them to do?

Be Brief

Viewers scan, they don't read. The average American reads on an 8th-grade level. Use as few words as possible in your content. Keep sentences short.

Don't be "wordy". Don't ramble, be concise, clear, and direct. Get to the point and try not to bore people.

Simplify: Eliminate useless words. Eliminate adverbs. (~~Completely~~ sold out - "sold-out" is enough)

"I believe the road to hell is paved with adverbs."
-Stephen King

Be Readable

Use clear fonts, text that is not too small (16pt+), and color that is easy to read. The contrast between the background color and the text color is vital for readability. *Which of these works?*

Our fall collection has arrived!

Our fall collection has arrived!

Our fall collection has arrived!

Use a Conversational Tone

Avoid jargon, trite phrases, overly formal language, or highly technical terms. Use terms your visitors will know and understand. You don't need to impress them. Think of them as friends.

Use an Active Voice

Use the first person (I and we). Never use the third person (he, she, it, they). First-person is clearer, more engaging, and personalizes your website.

Example: On Sue Adam's website:

✓ 1st Person: "I will serve our community."

3rd Person: "She will serve our community."

Write as though you are talking to someone standing in front of you.

Write with Authority

You know your products and services better than anyone else. They are looking for an expert–that's YOU!

Make the Text Valuable

Don't confuse people. Information should be relevant and current. Give them your "hook-line" at the beginning. That's what they want–don't make them hunt for it. They will appreciate it and return.

Use Keywords

Keywords identify your business to Google. People use popular words when they look for information online. Identify what those words are and use them so Google will recognize them. It will improve your Search Engine Optimization (SEO). Use them throughout your website: in headers and sub-headers and text.

Example: You own Simone's Bakery. In an online search, keywords would be bakery, pastry, cakes, pies. Use those words repeatedly on your website.

Simone's **Bakery**

Cakes for Every Occasion

Pies Made from Scratch.

Fresh **Pastries** Daily

More about Keywords in Chapter 14.

Organize your Information.

- Content Hierarchy

    Prioritize by putting important content upfront.
    State the facts clearly. Don't try to be clever.
    Newspapers use the inverted pyramid style.

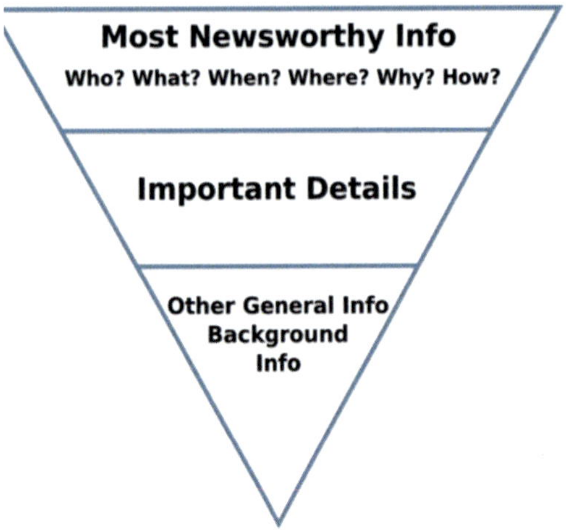

- Segment information into visual areas.
    - Focus on one topic per area.
    - Use sub-headings.
    - Make it easy to spot and easy to read.

Make Text Scannable.

Make lists, not long sentences.
Lists are easy to scan—no one reads full paragraphs.

Below are examples from awwwards.com

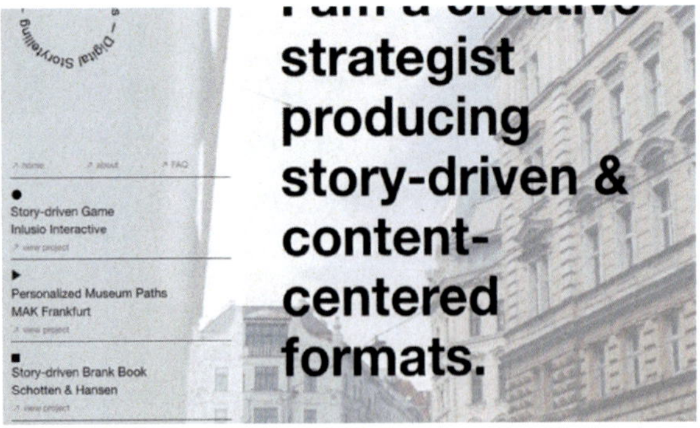

https://www.robinburgauer.com

https://www.anticafe.eu

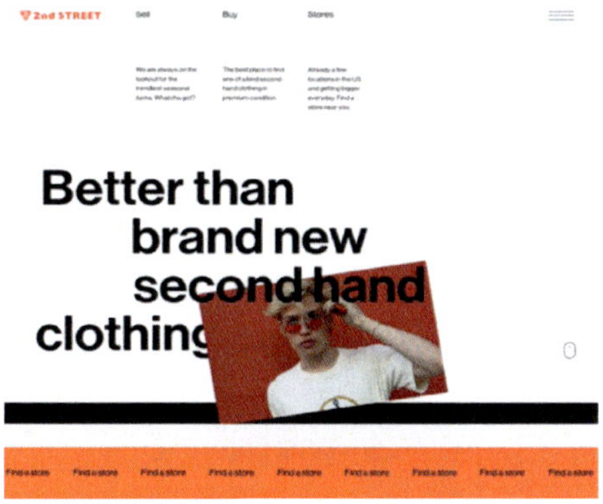

http://2ndstreetusa.com

https://www.operanationaldurhin.eu/en

Use White Space.

Don't crowd your content–let it breathe. Use white space to break up bodies of text, around paragraphs, and around images. This makes reading easier and relaxes the eye.

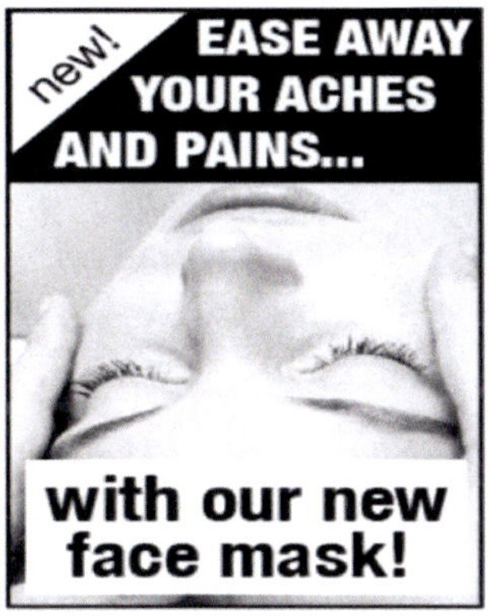

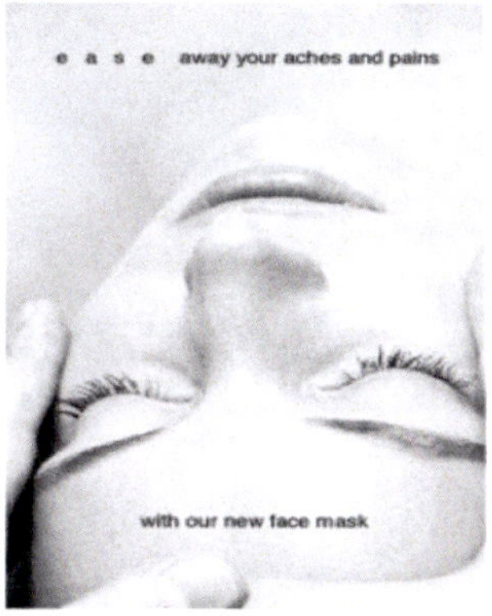

Mike Boulton
"Whitespace" 2004

Published in Graphic Design, Layout & Grids

Heading

Be specific, don't generalize. Heading should be no more than five to seven words, compelling, simple, and straightforward. This is your attention-grabber. Be positive and authoritative.

Which heading grabs you?

CLOSEOUT–EVERYTHING MUST GO!

or

JANUARY SALE

Sub-Heading

Sub-headings make scanning easier by dividing up the information. They support the heading and transition to the body of the text.

Use Images

People like pictures. We process imagery 600,000 times faster than words. Written information is retained longer when paired with an image. Nothing makes your point better than adding quality images. More about imagery in Chapter 10.

Use Links

Don't use lots of words, use links. Incorporate links within your text to elaborate on another page. We delve more into links in Chapter 13.

Be Consistent

Stay focused. Keep size, fonts, and spacing the same throughout.

Be Current

Don't offer something that is no longer available, like out-of-date coupons or discontinued services.

Proofread

Proofread, proofread, and then proofread again. Check your facts and your spelling. Get someone to help you proofread. Nothing is more unprofessional than text with spelling or grammatical errors.

Copyright

All information, images, and intellectual properties are protected by law. Do not copy from another site. Use your own words. Be real.

Readable.com has a FREE tool to score text readability.
https://app.readable.com/text/

Copy and paste your text in the textbox. The results will automatically grade it on the left.

Example: I pasted in the textbox:

> Do you want your website to look like everyone else's?
> Do you want a CUSTOM WEBSITE?
>
> Your website should capitalize on what makes you better.
> I can make your presence on the web SPECIAL.

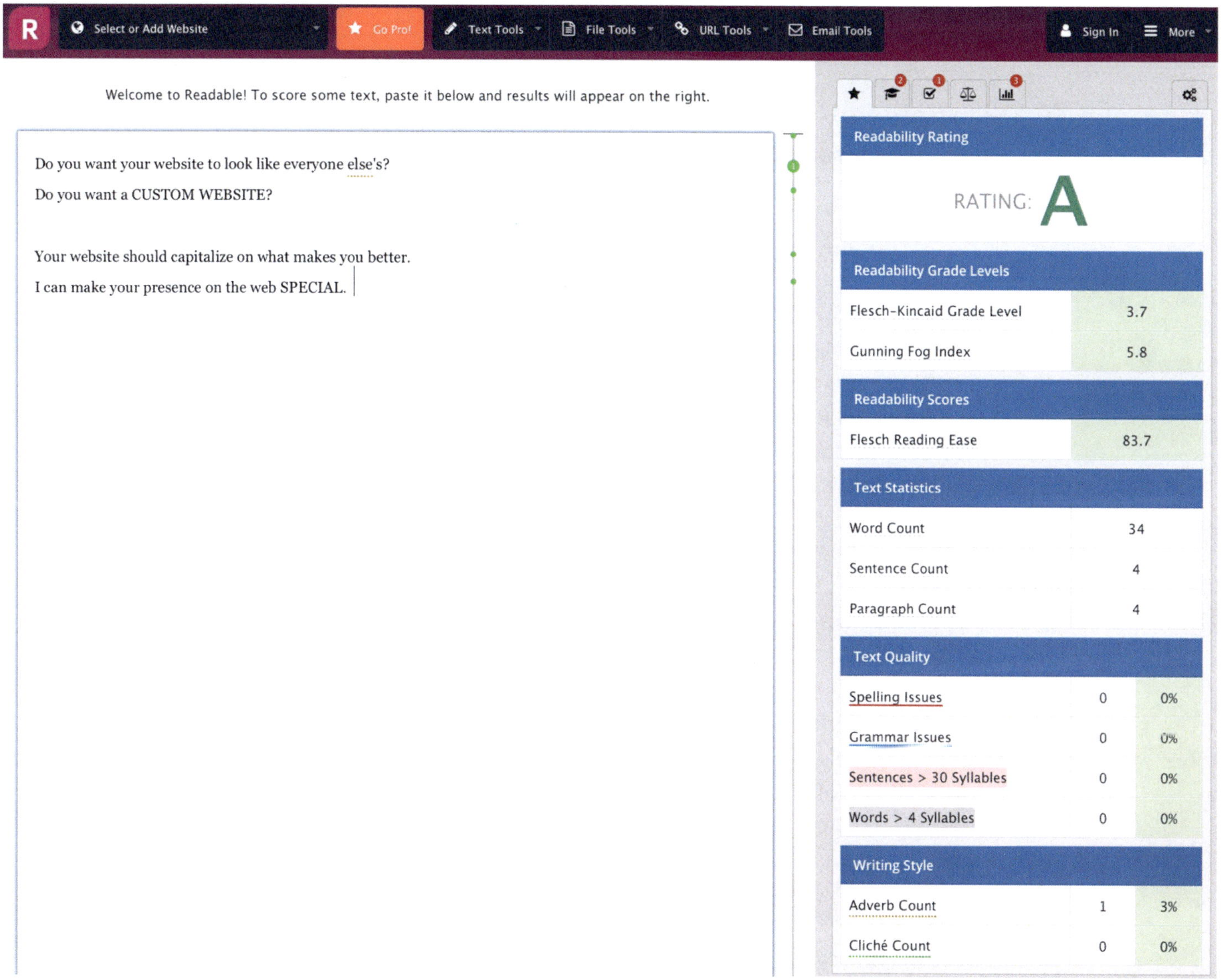

My overall readability score is an A.

Readability Grade Levels (low is best)
Flesch-Kincaid (general reading) is grade 3.7
Gunning Fog Index (business reading) is grade 5.8

Readability Score 83.7 (high is best)
Scores are 0-100. A score of 60 is considered good.

Text Statistics give word, sentence and paragraph counts

Text Quality
Spelling Issues - underlined in red: likible
Grammar Issues -underlined in blue: websites is
Sentences > 30 syllables
Words > 4 Syllables

Writing style
Adverb Count -adverbs are not as strong as active verbs
Underlined with a yellow dotted line: else's

I used "else's" at the end of the sentence and decided not to change it because it seemed more conversational.

Cliché Count - overused, trite phrases

Once you know the weak areas in your text, you can make changes to make it better.

CONCLUSION:
Think about issues that are important to your target audience. Get ideas by checking your competition. This is just to get you started. Don't copy–your ideas need to be your own. The way you get customers is by offering something different.

Write down your ideas. Review the guidelines above and put them into a few short sentences. Pretend you are telling a friend what you do, what excites you about your business, and how you are better than your competition.

Work with it until you think it is right and then type it into the textbox on Readable.com. Get your readability score.
Make changes–clean it up and go with it. What you write is not etched in stone–you can always change it later.

Try not to fret over it and remember to KEEP IT SIMPLE.

"A picture is worth a thousand words." –**Napolean Bonaparte**

CHAPTER 10

CONTENT-IMAGERY

John Storr - Three zebras drinking. Taken on safari in Tanzania. Wikimedia Creative Commons, the free media repository

Appearance is everything.

First impressions are made within seconds. Since humans are visual, those impressions are primarily based on what they see. Images can grab attention, trigger emotion, create trust, and drive a viewer to action.

Imagery is one of the most powerful elements on your website. Visuals reinforce the power of your text to convey your message. Information coupled with an image is retained longer. A website without images would be boring.

Images highlight your products, services, and business. They impart information instantly. They are an invaluable selling tool.

People love pictures, but they must be of good quality. A blurry image makes you look unprofessional.

What is Imagery?

Imagery refers to any content which is not text; examples include:

- Images: Photos, clip art, graphics, line drawings.
- Animation: Pictures manipulated to appear as moving.
- Video: Recorded moving imagery - very trendy.
- Audio: Sound files can be added as part of the web content.

Reasons for using images on your website:

- Your website is more visually appealing.
- Text with images gets 94% more views.
- Readers process information faster with images.
- Information is retained longer when images are used with text.
- Images give credibility to your website.
- Images boost SEO (Search Engine Optimization).
- Google ranks websites higher when they have good images.
- Images encourage return visits.
- Viewers stay longer reducing the bounce rate (the amount of time before they leave your site).

IMAGERY GUIDELINES

1. Images must have a purpose.
    - What is the benefit of the image?
    - Does it enhance the product and/or service?
    - Is it easy to understand quickly?
    - Does it appeal to your target audience?
    - Does it relate to your brand?
    - Does it support the text?

2. Types of Images that relate to viewers.
    - Those that draw attention to your message.
    - Bright, vibrant colors grab attention.
    - Happy, smiling human faces are more personal.
    - Looking directly at the viewer seems more honest.
    - Real people connect. Use real people images.
    - Natural, candid, unstaged images.

3 Use high-quality photos.

Sharp images are appealing, professional, and grab attention. Images must never be out of focus. If you chose a small image, it might be blurry when you enlarge it. If it is, dump it. You look amateurish if your images are not good quality.

The best format to use is JPG because the files are small, and the loss of detail during compression is minimal. PNG formats can be used, but the file size is larger, which reduces website speed.

4. Name the image.

Include author, descriptive titles, or captions to inform and help with google searches.

5. Resize and Optimize.

Images take up load time. Smaller images should be 30 kb and larger ones no more than 100 kb. The more images you have, the more it affects load time.

Summary: Images should be relevant, relate to the viewer, of good quality, descriptive, and optimized.

WHERE TO FIND IMAGES

A FEW WORDS ABOUT COPYRIGHT

Assume that all images are protected by copyright.
Copyright infringement is illegal and carries with it potentially significant consequences.

There are tens of millions of free, high-quality graphics and photos available. Use them or create your own.

PUBLIC DOMAIN

There are many websites with images that are in the public domain, free to use and modify because:

- The image was never copyrighted.
- The copyright has expired.
- The copyright has been released to the public domain.
- The copyright usage is given without restrictions.
- The image was published before 1924.

Find public domain images on
https://commons.wikimedia.org/wiki/Main_Page
https://www.flickr.com/commons/usage/

CREATIVE COMMONS

Many people are happy to share their photos. One caveat is that an owner may change the license after you use the image, which may trigger a request for removal. It is important to know that a Creative Commons license is non-revocable.

Photo-sharing sites allow others to download and use images while still retaining some control over how they are used. *Only use images that allow commercial use.*
There are three types:

- Attribution
  Use the image however you wish but credit the creator.
- Attribution-ShareAlike
  Change the image, credit the creator, and license the new work under identical terms.
- Attribution-ShareAlike-No Derivatives.
  Use the image unchanged and credit the creator.

They all have one common element: *Credit the Creator.*

STOCK PHOTOS

Stock photos are professional, high-quality images that are offered for free or a fee. When you purchase the license, you can use the photo anyway prescribed by the licensing agreement. Always credit the creator and follow the license guidelines for each photo.

Read the fine print. Some images may be only used privately.

Note: Using pretty stock images feels fake. Your audience won't relate to them and might ignore them because there are so many similar photos on the web. The more you use genuine images, the more trustworthy you seem.

Free Stock Images:

https://morguefile.com

Photo by Sean R Watson

https://unsplash.com

Photo by Rebeca G. Sendroiu on Unsplash

https://www.flickr.com

Photo by Gnuckx

https://commons.wikime

Charlie Marshall - Woman with Red Headscarf
Creative Commons Attribution 2.0 Generic

https://www.rawpixel.com

Photo by Markus Spiske

https://pixels.com

Photo by Brett Sayles

https://www.canva.com

Photo by Elle Hughes via Canva

Other sites that offer free images:

https://pixabay.com
https://picjumbo.com
https://www.publicdomainarchive.com
https://publicdomainpictures.net
https://freeimages.com

Good Quality Stock Images for Purchase

Professional images are of high quality, work well for all types of businesses, and you don't have to worry about copyright issues. Use them to make your home page exude professionalism. Getty Images is my favorite because it has a good selection of "real-looking" photos that are easy to access.

https://www.gettyimages.com

John Lund/Blend Images via Getty Images

https://www.shutterstock.com
https://www.istockphoto.com
https://www.bigstock.com

USE ORIGINAL IMAGES
Original images create a more personal relationship with your viewer, and you avoid copyright issues.

Tips for taking pictures.

- Use Natural Light
  Avoid full sun or cloudy days.
  Morning or an hour before sunset is best.
  Don't use a flash.
  Keep the light source in front of you to avoid shadows.
- Use a Tripod
- Focus
  35mm - Use lens control.
  Smartphone - Tap the viewfinder screen.
  iPhone - Hold down the spot on the viewfinder.
  A yellow box means the focus is locked.
- Don't use the zoom. Get closer to the subject.
- Think about composition.
  Don't clutter the scene.
  Cleanup background.
  Choose landscape or portrait.
- Edit -
  Apps for iPhones:

  Camera+Legacy ($2.99)
  https://apps.apple.com/us/app/camera/id329670577

  VSCO: Photo & Video Editor (free)
  https://apps.apple.com/us/app/vsco-photo-editor-and-community/id588013838

  Snapseed by Google (free)
  https://apps.apple.com/us/app/snapseed/id439438619

  Prisma Photo Editor -add filters and effects (free)
  https://apps.apple.com/us/app/prisma-photo-editor-art-filters-pic-effects/id1122649984

HOW TO SEARCH FOR IMAGES ON YAHOO

Example: **Type in the search bar "miniature schnauzer" or "public domain miniature schnauzer".**

Click on **Images**, Size: **L**, and Type: **Photo**.
On the right side open **Any License** and drag down to
Free to modify, share, and use commercially

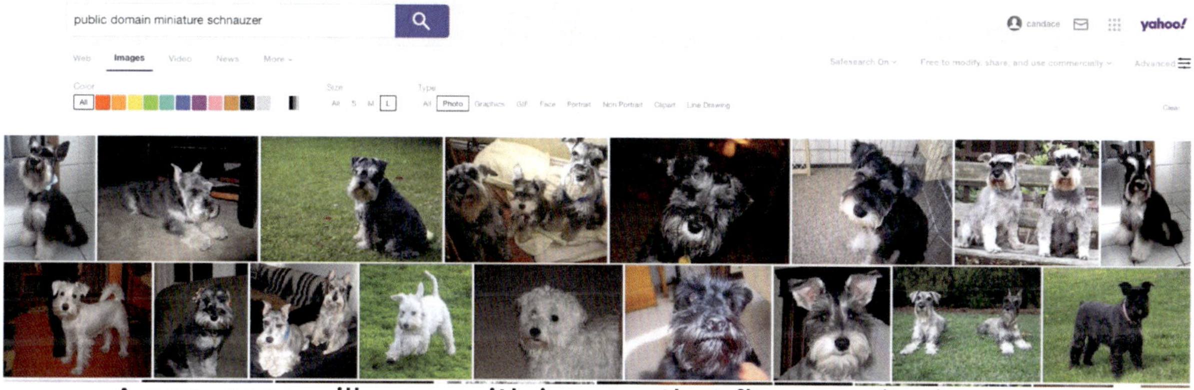

A new page will open with images that fit your criteria:

Chose the image you like and click on **View Page** on the right-side.

The page gives information about the image and licensing.

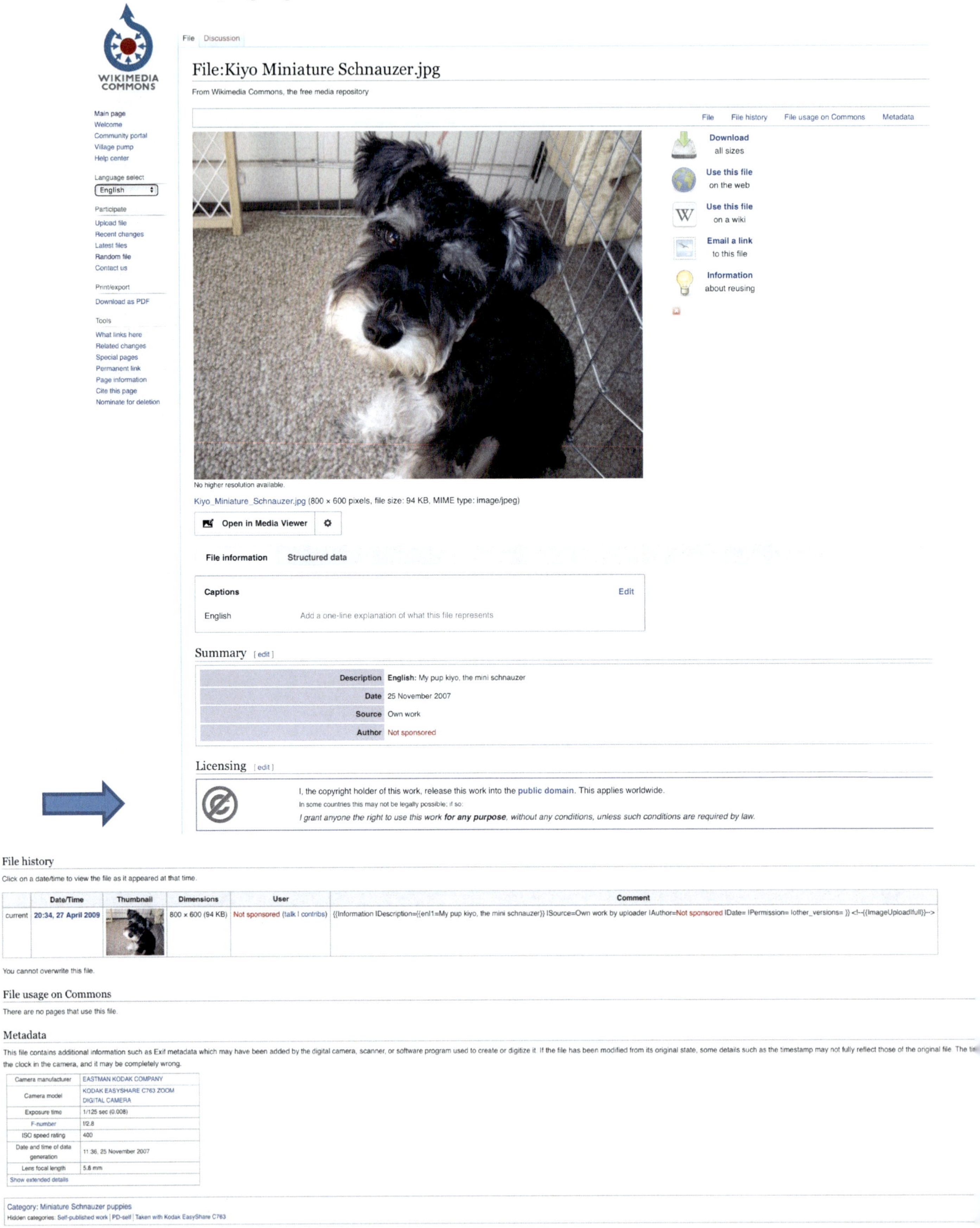

IMAGE OPTIMIZATION

It is always best to compress your images before uploading them to your website. Images reduce site speed, especially on mobile devices. The average web page is 1.28 MB, and 61% of that is taken up by images.

Use photos in JPG or PNG format and reduce the size by 70-80%. If the photo is of good quality, the change will not be significant.

STEPS

The photo should be in JPG/JPEG format at 72 dpi resolution.

Free tools to use:

https://shortpixel.com My favorite. Easy to use.

1. Copy the URL address of the miniature schnauzer picture you found online:

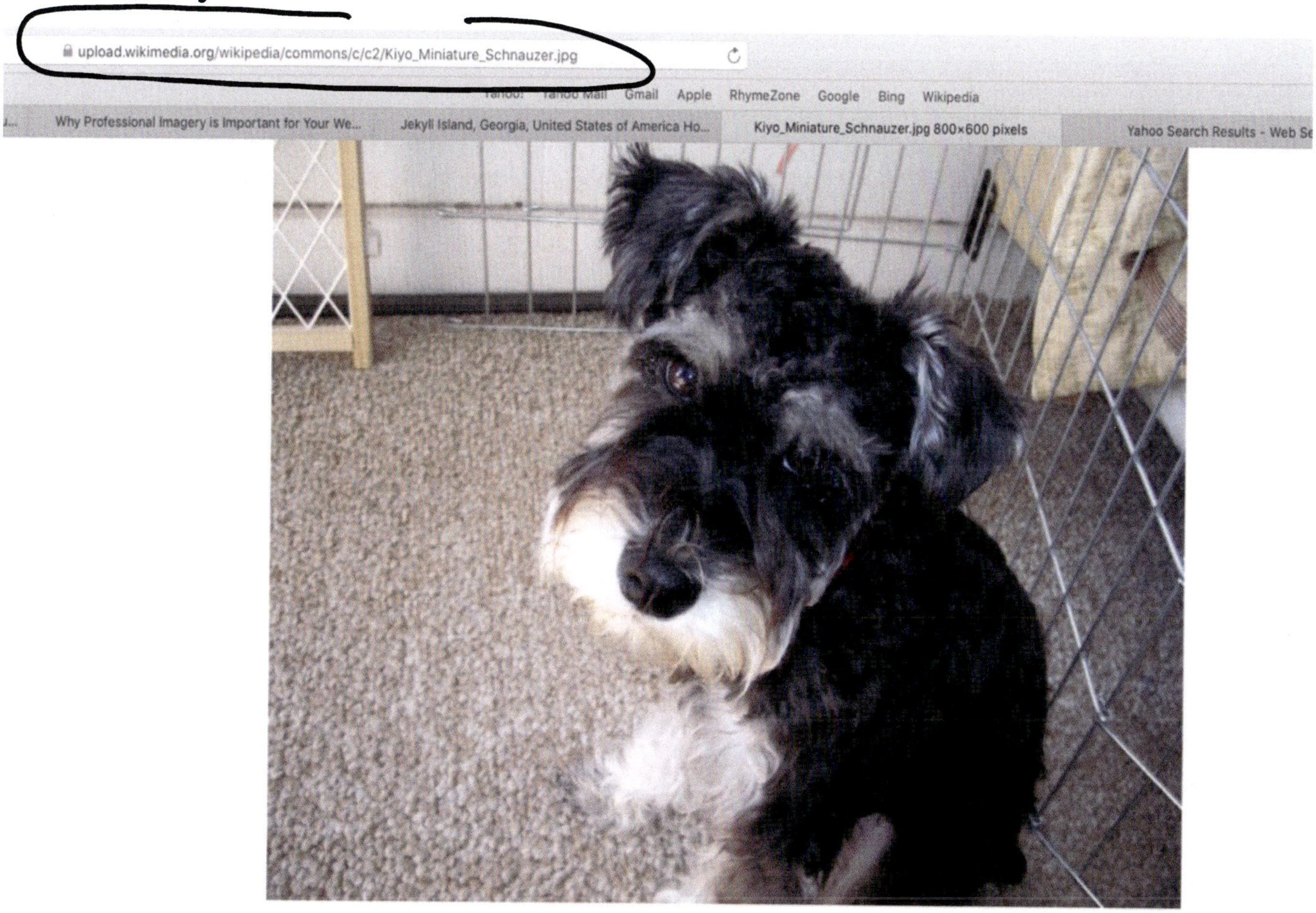

2. Open shortpixel.com, paste the URL address in the box, click on the arrow on the right.

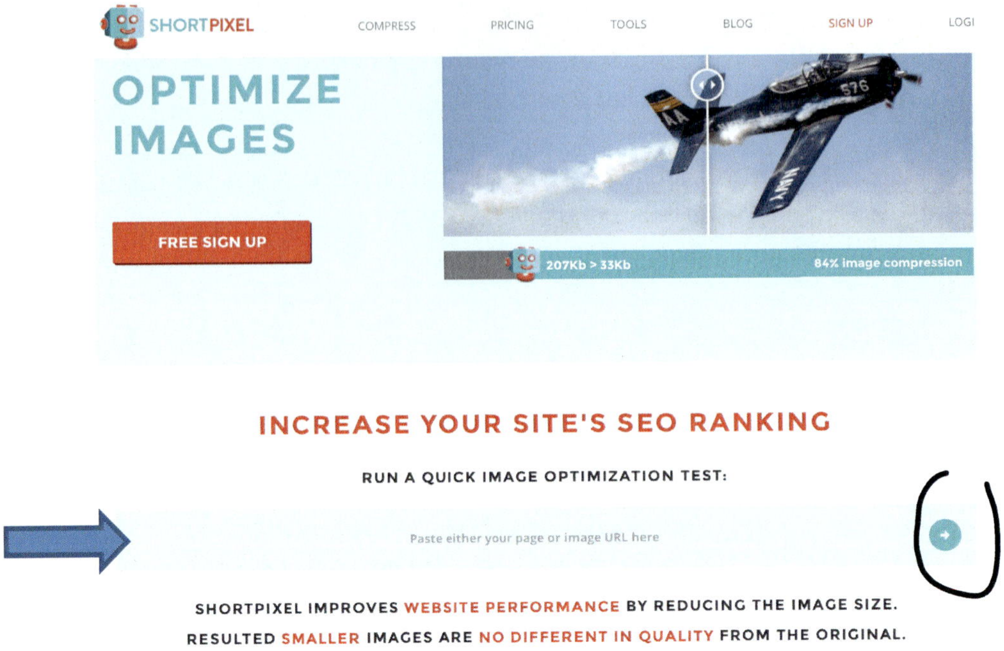

3. Results: Compression was 36%. The line in the middle can be moved left and right to show the difference between the original on the left and the compressed on the right.

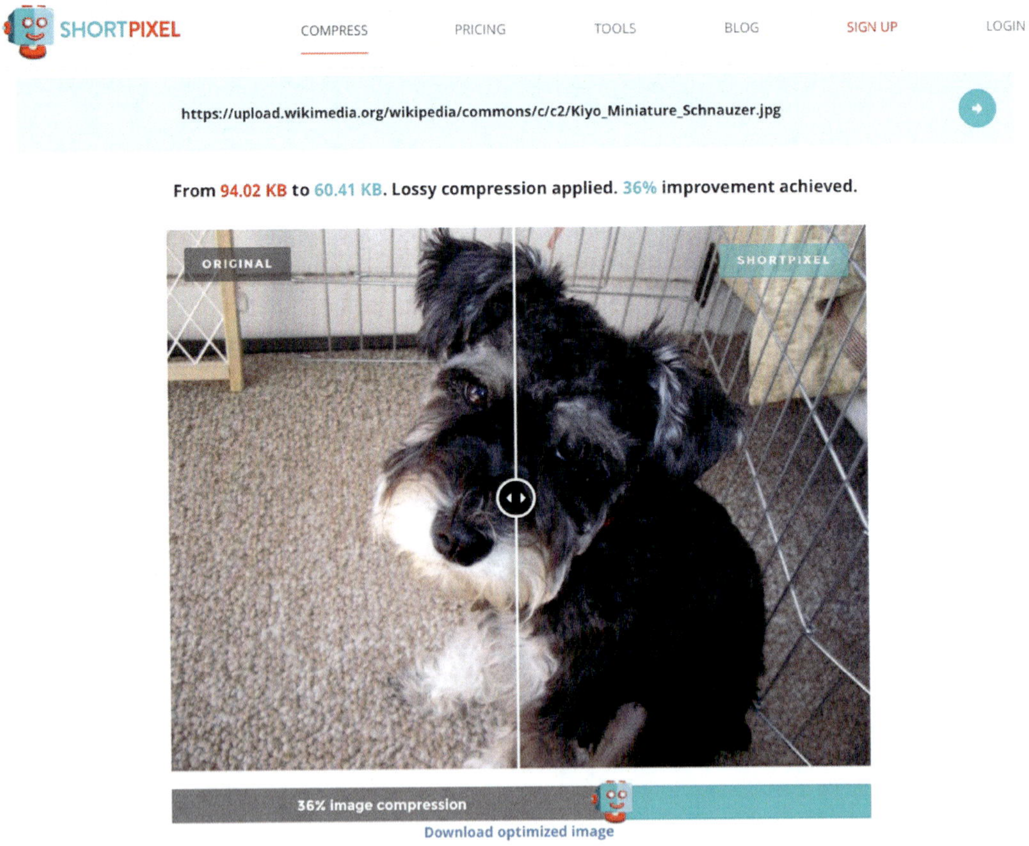

Other recommended compression tools work much the same way:

https://imagecompressor.com
https://compressjpeg.com
https://compressor.io/compress
https://www.iloveimg.com
https://imagecompressor.com

Other things to consider:

- Don't put text inside images. Text is not searchable when embedded in an image.

- Use words in bold and italics sparingly. Too much slows down web page speed.

- Use the right file format:

  - GIF for animation.
  - PNG if resolution is important.
  - PNG-24 if your image has a lot of colors.
  - PNG-8 if your image has few colors.
  - JPEG if you resolution is not important.
    This is the most used file format.

SLIDERS

Sliders are slideshows on your website. They can be anywhere on your site, but most often they are at the top (above-the-fold; what you see before you scroll down).

Sliders make it easy to showcase products and services without taking up space on the page. Advance the images manually or advance them automatically.

Etsy and eBay use sliders to show product items. *Example:* Baskets on Etsy.

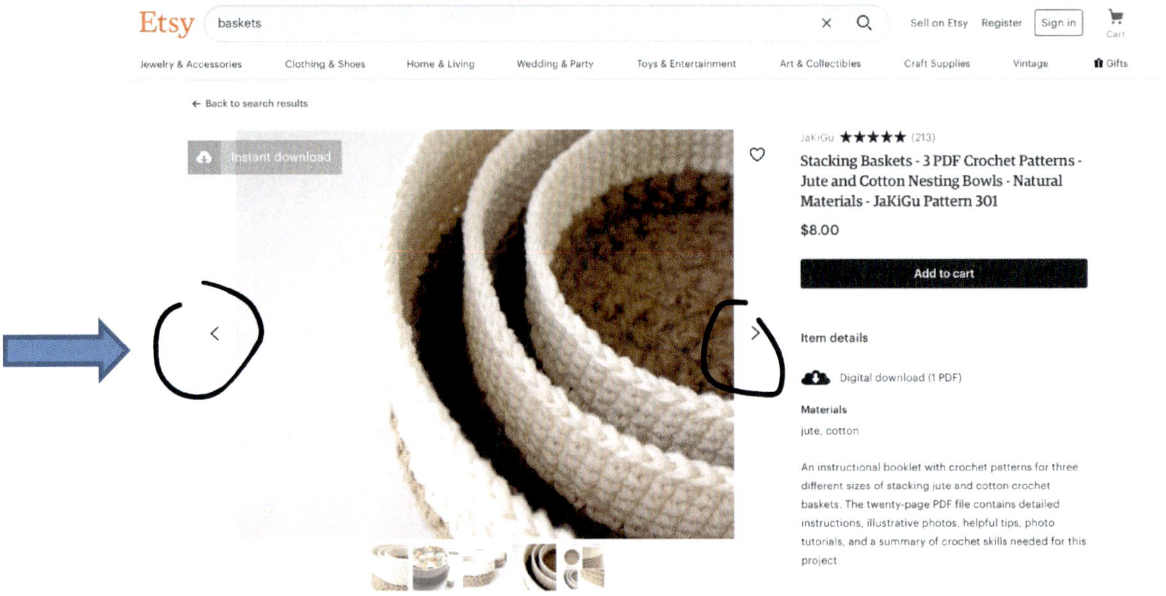

Real Estate companies use sliders to show property details.

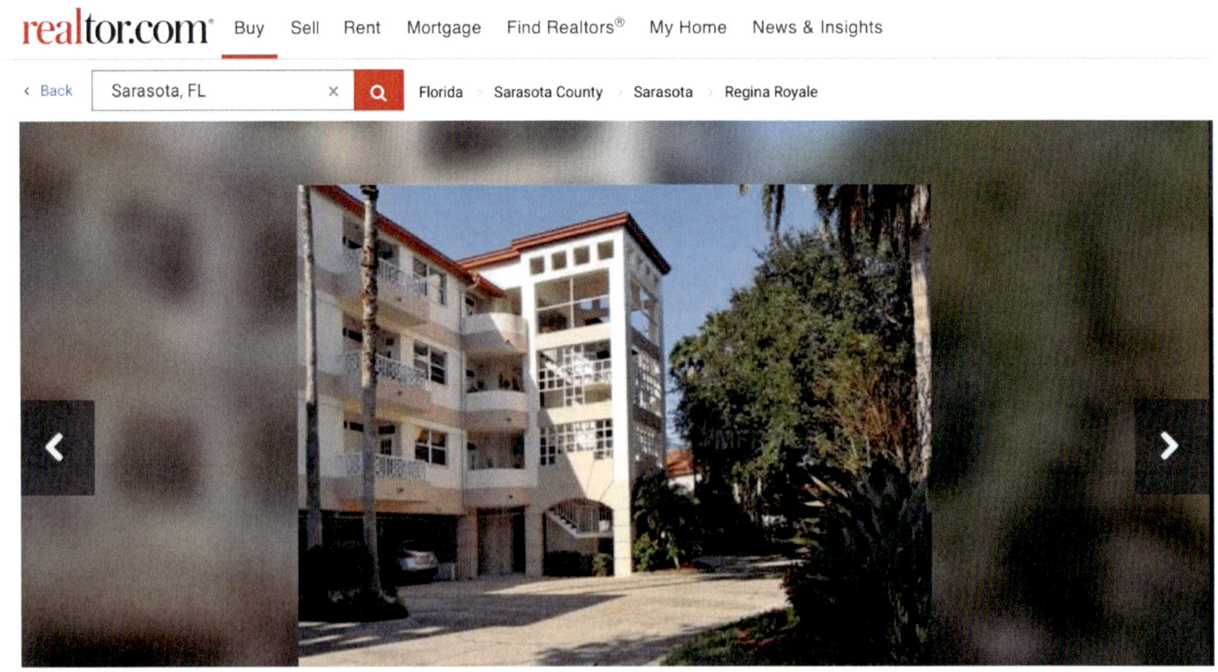

Automobile companies also use sliders.

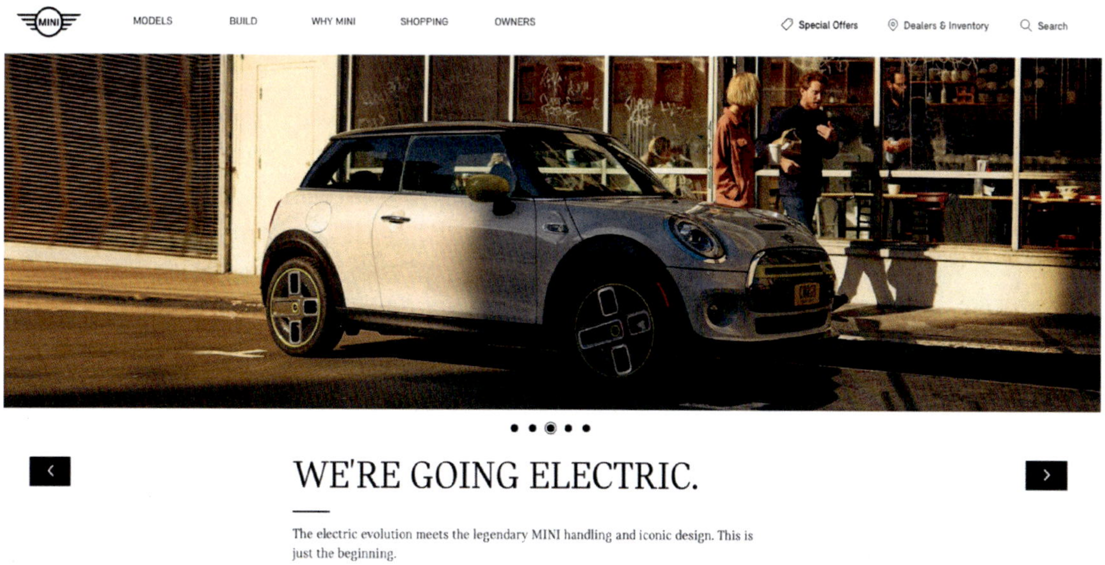

Apps are available for sliders on all platforms. They are popular and use less space than videos.

When you use a slider, you can stretch your image to full-screen size. Use quality images that retain clarity when they are enlarged.

VIDEOS

Video marketing is here. It is one of the fastest-growing and most in-demand forms of marketing.

Videos are a great way to get your visitors engaged. Viewers are distracted by movement. A quick introductory video explains what you do, shows your products, your workplace, and introduces your team. A background video gets attention and piques interest.

Some website builders are more receptive to video than others:

- WordPress has templates that support videos and plug-ins for add-ons.
- Wix, SquareSpace and Shopify support video addition.
- Weebly does not make it easy to add a video.

Pros for using videos:

1. Viewers better understand what you do.
2. People stay longer. Google likes that.
3. 46% of people who watch a video take action.
4. 80% of users will recall a video a month later.
5. You stand out from your competition.
6. Video boosts sales.
7. 1/3 of all time spent online is watching videos.
8. Mobile users prefer videos to reading text.

Cons for using videos:

1. It is more expensive and requires more expertise.
2. It must interest your target market, or they bounce.
3. It is annoying if it starts automatically.
4. Load time can be affected.

Homemade videos are the best. They personalize your website. They make it real but be aware of the pitfalls. Problems with custom videos:

- Files are large and must be compressed - 6MB or less.
- Files must be converted for HTML5.
  Two formats are used, MP4 and WebM.
- You are going to need a Video editor and learn how to use it. Adobe Premiere Pro CC is my favorite.

There are many "how-to" videos online to assist you with all the techniques you need to compress and convert your files. Technology is making it easier each day.

If you want help, hire a video editor from:

Fiver.com
https://www.fiverr.com/categories/video-animation/video-editing

Upwork.com
https://www.upwork.com/search/profiles/?q=video%20editing&user_pref=2

Points to Remember About Videos

1. They should be relevant and have a purpose. If not, videos are a distraction and will confuse your viewer.
2. They should reinforce your message. Don't let the video interfere with readability. If the video is dark, use white text; if it is light, use dark text.
3. Use an overlay screen to soften the video and make the text easier to read. You can use dark or light overlays in black, white, or your brand color.

https://www.wix.com/website-template/view/html/1737?utm_source=affiliate&utm_medium=paid_referral&utm_campaign=af_websitebuilderexpert.com&experiment_id=cake_56566917-57

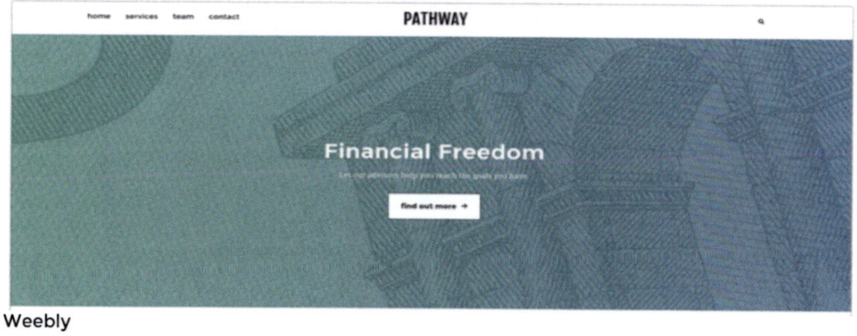

Weebly

4. Make the video short and on a loop. Videos affect loading speed time because the files are large. It should be 5-10 seconds and 6MB or less.
5. *NEVER* add audio to your video. In short, it's annoying. If you purchase a video with sound, *mute it.*
6. Don't show the video controls. You might think it looks cool, but it isn't.

FREE VIDEOS

There are lots of free videos available. The quality is very good, but they may not work on all devices. Choose 4K clips.

Many stock video sites charge a subscription fee, but there are still some good sites available. Try not to use clips with identifiable people because there might be copyright issues even if it is in the public domain.

Check out the videos from some of the best sites:

https://coverr.co

Video: Wild Horse. Coverr.com

https://www.pexels.com/videos

Video by Tyler Francis on Pexels.com

https://pixabay.com/videos

Video by Engin Akyurt on Pixabay.com

Other sites to check out:

https://www.videezy.com
https://www.videvo.net
https://mazwai.com
https://www.stockfootageforfree.com

VIDEOS TO PURCHASE

https://videohive.net $10-$50
https://vimeo.com subscription

AUDIO

"Sound is invasive, intrusive, and irresistible."

–**Bryan and Jeffrey Eisenberg**

The accepted thought on using sound on websites has always been a resounding, NO...but the times are changing.

Sounds are remembered, and if something is remembered, it is a good marketing tool.

Think about how your target audience will respond. There is plenty of information online to help you put audio on your website if you want to give it a try.

Windows Movie Maker and iMovie are easy to use video and audio editing programs.

Example: Snowfall video with music added.

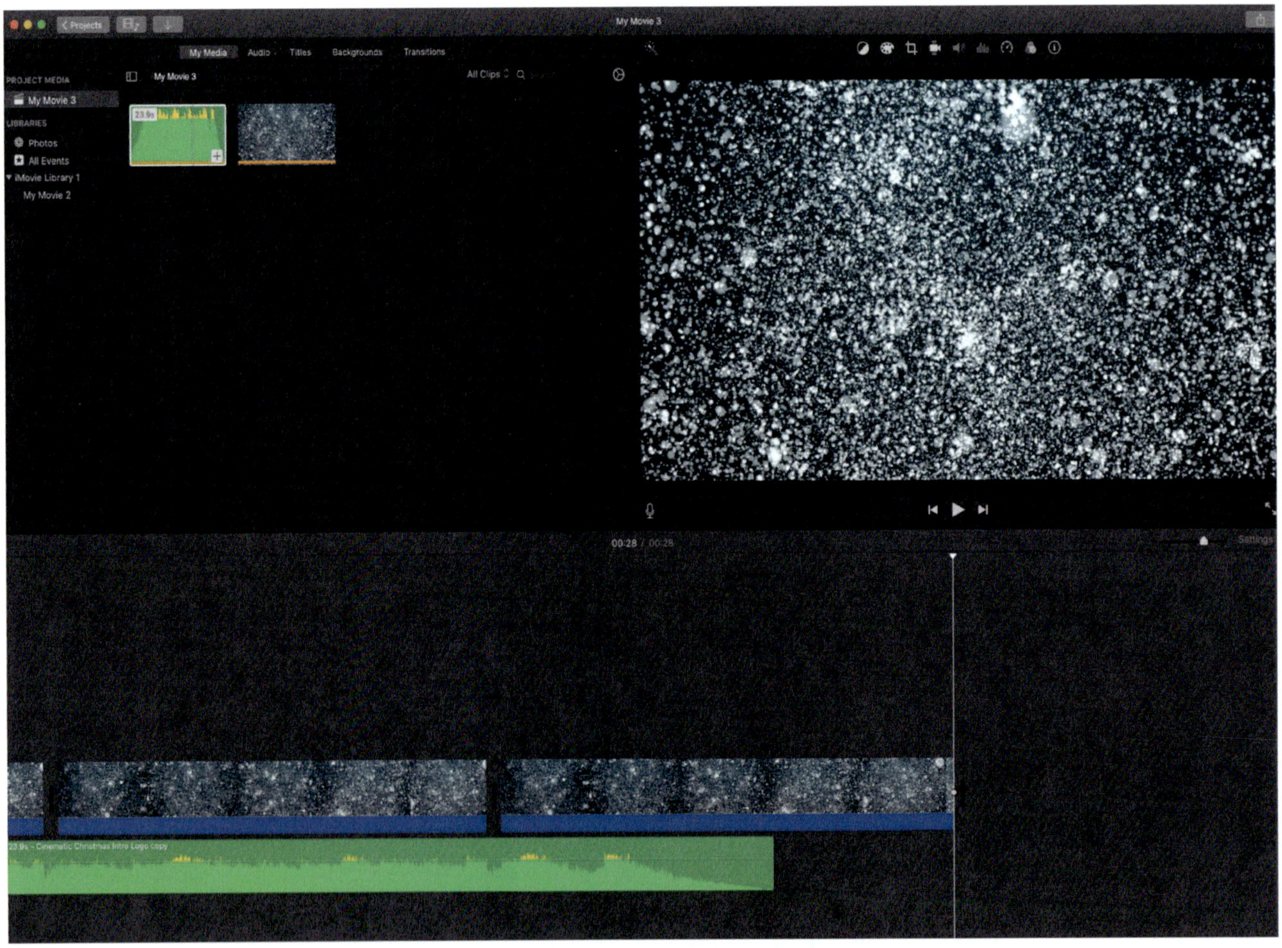

SoundSnap has high-quality, professionally produced sound clips, but they charge a fee.
https://www.soundsnap.com

If you want audio clips for free, go to:

https://freesound.org
https://www.audiomicro.com

Background music is still not recommended. Everyone has different tastes in music. You don't want viewers leaving at the sound of music they don't like. (Of course, disregard my advice if you are a musician!)

Tom Corson-Knowles

"Alignment trumps everything." –Abraham Hicks

CHAPTER 11

ALIGNMENT

You have chosen your text, headings, subheadings, and images. Now you must make decisions about where you will place them on the page.

Alignment is used to organize and group elements to create a balanced, connected structure. The result is a design that is clear, concise, and visually appealing.

Elements on the page interact with each other. To make sense, you need to create relationships between them by setting up a structure.

The majority of the information you arrange will follow the structure you set up, but not everything. You can set the pattern and then introduce an item outside the pattern to emphasize its importance. This creates another level of interest.

You can also mix alignments. Mixing keeps the viewer interested by introducing a different focus to the design. Your Headline may be aligned to the center, but your text is aligned to the left.

Alignment should never be arbitrary. Whether the design is simple or complex, there must be order. A good way to achieve this is by using a grid. Grids create structure and ensure accurate alignment.

GRID

TREES FOR OUR FUTURE
MISSION FELLOWSHIP GET INVOLVED NEWS ABOUT DONATE
TREE PLANTING
OUR APPROACH
We support bold ideas for forest regneration. Climate Change is here and reforestration is the key to saving our planet.
Pruning in India
Fruit retrival in Tanzania
Tree planting in Kenya
Trees For Our Future
World Wide Progress
914-896-0087

Wedding Bouquets
Wedding Designs by Andrea Blusque
Whether your wedding is informal or formal, we create bouquets that are unique to you. Rated the best in all of Seattle.
Ochid Festival Elegant Orchids for the sophistocate, formal wedding.
Garden Spledor Roses for the garden wedding.
Red Spendor Romantic and elegant. Nothing says love like red roses.
Rose Delight Red roses with white orchids. Perfect for a formal wedding.

TEXT ALIGNMENT

The way text appears on the page affects the readability. It makes a difference.

Alignment options for your text are:

LEFT ALIGNMENT

SHOE FASHION

Boots are the fashion
statement of the fall
season this year. They
can be worn to the
ankle, knee or thigh.
Invest in a pair or two,
you won't regret it!

RIGHT ALIGNMENT

SHOE FASHION

Boots are the fashion
statement of the fall
season this year. They
can be worn to the
ankle, knee or thigh.
Invest in a pair or two,
you won't regret it!

CENTER ALIGNMENT

SHOE FASHION

Boots are the
fashion statement
of the fall
season this year.
They can be
worn to the
ankle, knee or thigh.
Invest in a pair
or two,
you won't regret it !

JUSTIFIED ALIGNMENT

SHOE FASHION

Boots are the fashion
statement of the fall
season this year. They
can be worn to the
ankle, knee or thigh.
Invest in a pair or two,
you won't regret it!

Left Alignment

Left Alignment text is the strongest, most popular, and the easiest to read. Each line starts at the same place on the left. In Western cultures, the eye reads left to right. Google uses left side alignment along with a lot of other large companies. It also fits mobile phones and tablets better.

https://reininghausgründe.at

https://edesigninteractive.com

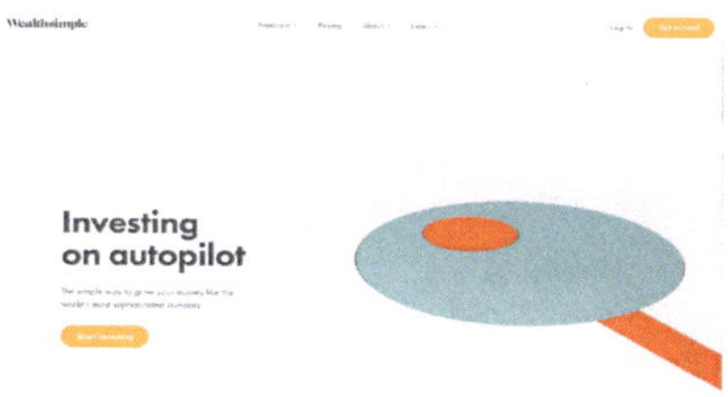

https://www.wealthsimple.com/en-us/

Right Alignment

Text is difficult to read and can be confusing when on the right. The lines end on the right margin but start at different places. It has a creative appeal and is appropriate for numbers within columns, shortlists, and often call-to-action buttons.

Photo: James Green/Printwand.com

https://www.csswinner.com

Center Alignment

Titles, headings, short lines of text are centered to call attention to something. For large chunks of text, use left alignment because it is easier to read.

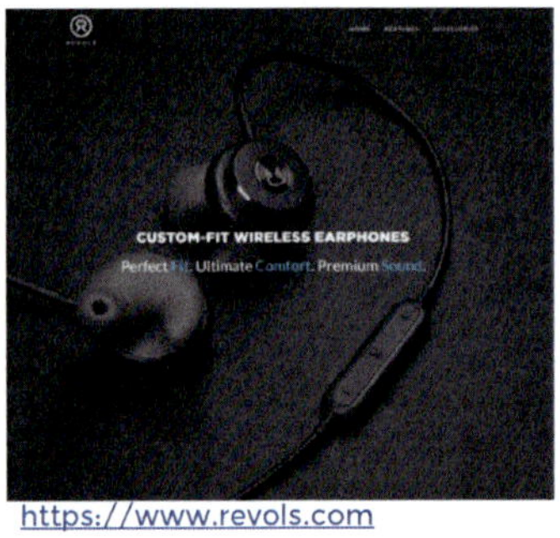

https://www.revols.com

https://whoamama.com

https://olympp.fr

Justified Alignment

The alignment of text that has an even left and right margin. To achieve this effect, extra space is added between words. It is neat but looks unnatural because the spacing is off. It works as a shape, but it is hard to read, renders differently on different screens, and does not flow evenly. Many people with cognitive disabilities have trouble reading justified text. It does not fit on other devices.

Justified Alignmnet is not a good form to use on websites. Don't use it.

MY ADVICE: **Stick to left-sided and center alignment. Make it easy to read and understand.**

IMAGERY ALIGNMENT

Align imagery according to size and relationship to text or other images.

Two basic types of alignment principals are:

Edge Alignment

Element edges are aligned against a margin. Everything is on a grid. Edges line up.

Center Alignment

Elements line up with one another in the center vertically or horizontally.

Right-Margin Alignment

Left-Margin Alignment

Center Alignment

No Alignment

You may think the example on the far right above is interesting, but you are designing the web page for your target audience. You want them to be able to get information quickly without having to think too much.

Aligning images to the left of text is easier to read because it is aligned to a straight line.

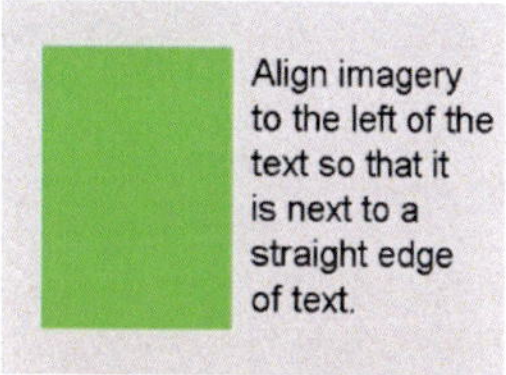

Aligning images to the right of text places it next to a "ragged" text line.

DO NOT:

Do not align an image in the middle of text. Text has to be read without interruption.

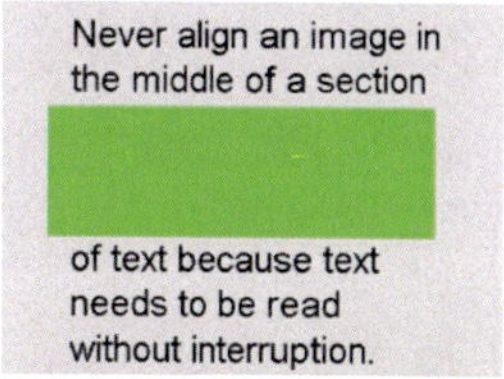

Do not use justified text on Your website. It is hard to read. Google won't scan it.

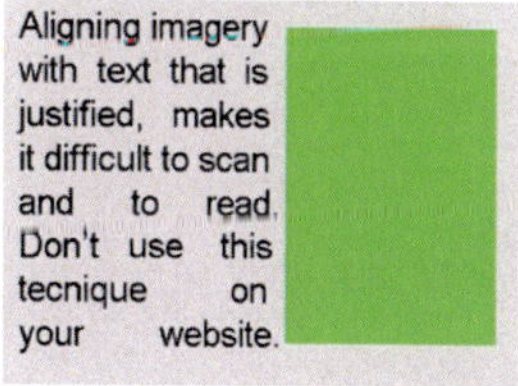

MIXED ALIGNMENT

Not everything has to be structured the same way. Mixing alignment styles can make the page appear more radical, free, playful, and creative. The elements are aligned properly, just in different ways to create more visual interest.

https://manipine.com via https://awwwards.com

Title is larger.

Text is in a different font.

Text is horizonal and vertical.

Images are different sizes and on different planes.

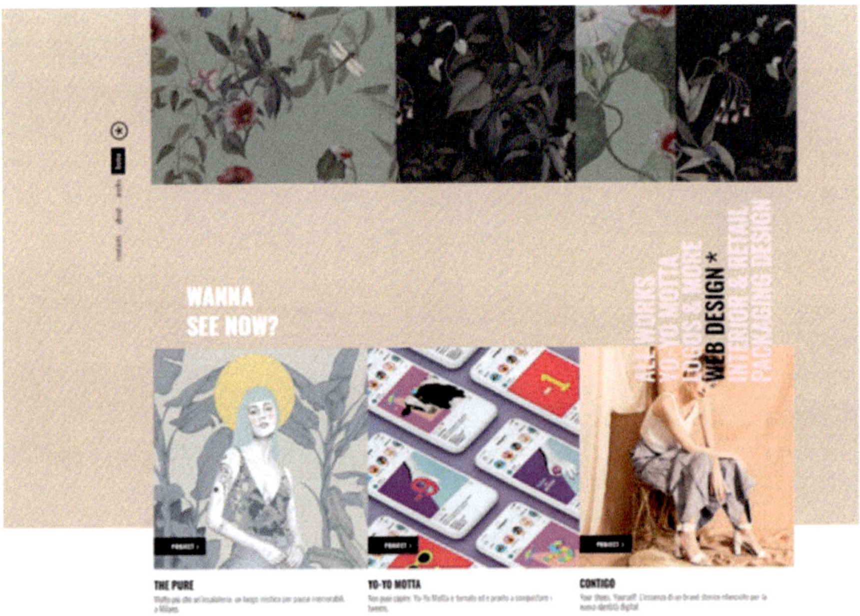

https://asteriscocreativeagency.com via https://awwwards.com

Text is horizontal and vertical.

Top images are different widths.

Bottom images are larger and aligned beneath the top.

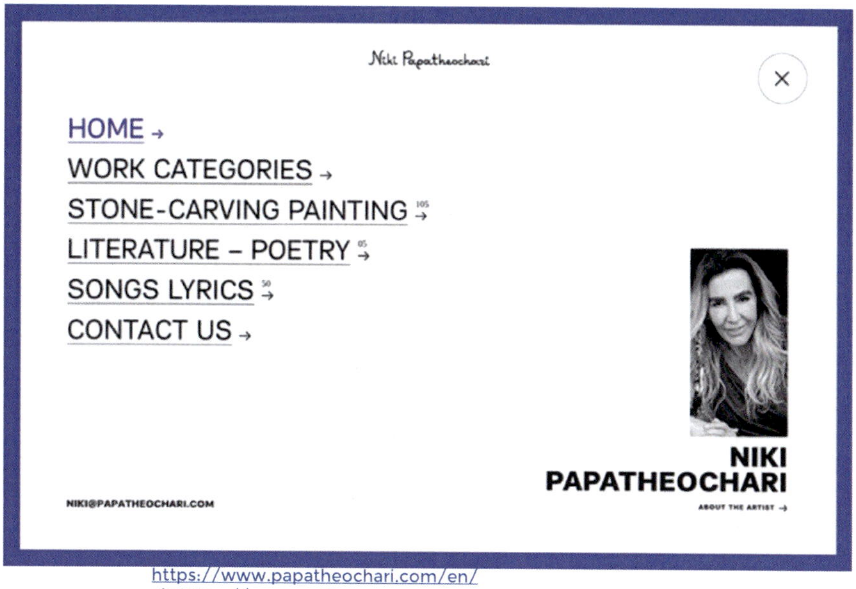

Text is:

center-aligned,

left-aligned and

right-aligned.

https://www.papatheochari.com/en/
via https://awwwards.com

Keep mixing at a minimum to avoid a visually cluttered and confusing page.

"The whole is greater than the sum of its parts." –**Aristotle**

CHAPTER 12

PUTTING IT ALL TOGETHER

WEBSITE BUILDERS

So many choices. Where to begin? There are over 50 website builders on the market, and new companies join in every day.

My suggestions based on a review by PC Magazine, 8/15/2019 https://www.pcmag.com/roundup/334639/the-best-website-builders

Wix	Easy to use, customizable, 600+themes, free plan.
SquareSpace	Easy to use, beautiful templates, good support.
GoDaddy	Easy to use, limited customization.
Weebly	Easy to use, no mobile customization, free plan.

WordPress.org Free, customizable, offers lots of themes, and plug-ins. Free, but requires a hosting plan (Bluehost), hardest to learn.

Shopify and **Big Commerce** are my picks for retail E-commerce sites. They are both easy and offer POS (Point of Sale) options and support.

Browse the website builders above. If you are interested in others, check them out, too. Look at their plans, themes, and support structure.

Take some time and browse the templates. Website builders offer hundreds of templates from which to choose. It can be daunting, and after a while, they begin to look alike.

Read the advice in this chapter and then take another look. Narrow your choice to two website builders and try using a template on each site. *Make your decision*.

HOW TO CHOOSE A TEMPLATE

Your choice depends on:

- Industry (example: business vs photography)
- Target Audience (example: mechanics vs stylists)
- Attractive Clean Design
- Ease of Use (Drag-and-Drop)
- Features and Add-ons
- Support Structure
- Cost: Free vs Paid - There are many quality free templates available. Paid templates offer more upgrades and support.

THREE TEMPLATE CONSIDERATIONS:

1. Boxed Width or Full-Width

- Boxed width -All page elements are arranged the same way with a set margin around the page. Very effective in directing the viewer's attention toward important elements on the website. It is easier to construct, offers a structured, more uniform look, and works well on all devices. It has a traditional, classic look, and designed for professional business websites.

SquareSpace

Avenue Template

Clean lines
Grid Layout
Classic

GoDaddy

Happy Fox Template

Vivid Colors
Simple design

- Full-width -Images are stretched to the full width of your computer screen. Images appear bigger and fuller. Very popular and works well on all devices. It requires experience to modify the images to look good on all devices but is more creative and contemporary.

Wix

Mechanic Template

Big, Heavy

Weebly

Urban Dine Template

Trendy

2. Above-the-Fold Design

Newspapers are printed on large sheets of paper and folded in half before being delivered to news-stands where they are stacked for sale. The top half is seen first and contains the attention-grabbing headlines.

On websites, it is the screen area first seen by visitors, under the menu bar, and contains information to interest the viewers. It communicates your message. All other information is obtained when scrolling downward.

There are 4 main Above-the-Fold template types:

- Static with No Content Design
  Dynamic, dramatic, and creative. It has a "wow" appeal. The image says it all. Words are not necessary. Used by artists, photographers, hotels, restaurants.
  Examples on Wix and Squarespace.

- Static with Content Design
  The most popular. It has a headline, supporting text, and images. There is no confusion about the message.
  Examples on Wix and Weebly.

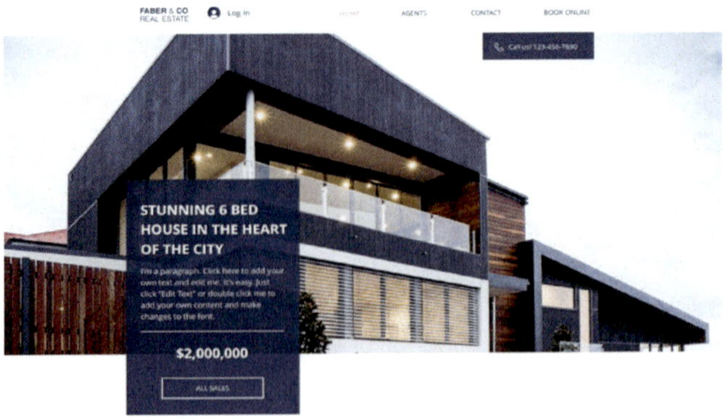

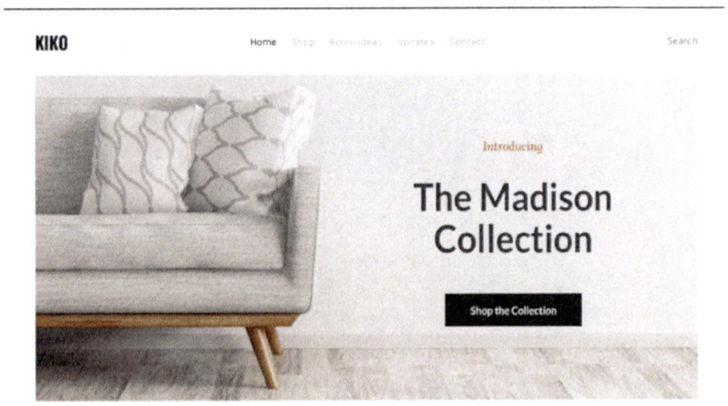

- <u>Slider Design</u>
  A slideshow is used to showcase your work. This design works well if you have many products, provide other services, or want to reach different audiences.
  Examples on **Wix and Squarespace.**

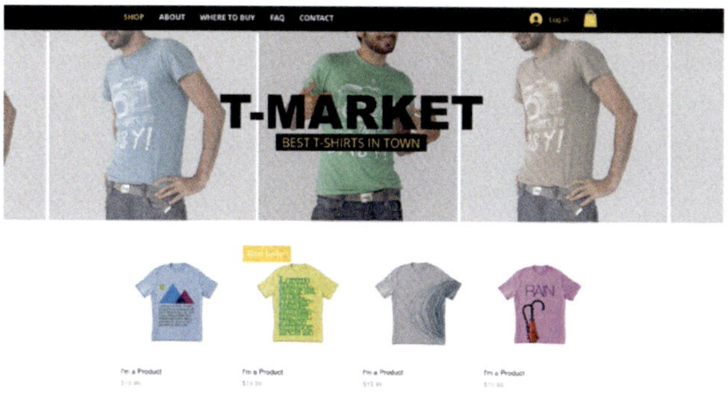

- <u>Video</u>
  Background videos are trendy. They are attention-grabbers and, when done well, work extremely well. Best to use a high-quality video that is original and below 6MB. Google ranks sites with videos higher.

Trux Studio via awwwards.com

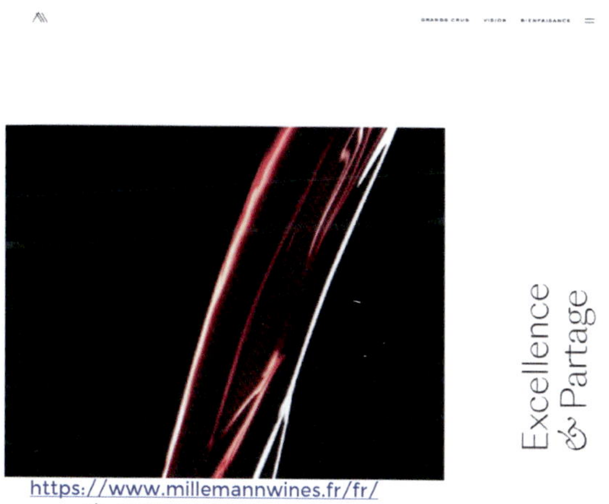

https://www.millemannwines.fr/fr/
via awwwards.com

3. **Menu or Navigation Bar**
The menu bar is the website road map to guide visitors throughout a website. It contains your name or logo and the titles of your pages.

It should be:

- Clean, simple, in a readable font on a plain background.
- Ordered by importance (ex: Home, About, Work, Contact)
- One color with a highlight color
- 1 or 2 word page titles
- Contain no more than seven page titles

There are 3 Menu Bar Positions

- Horizontal on the top is the most popular and effective. Visitors are used to seeing menus on top. It is easiest to find, saves space, and is the most efficient. *Example:* Wix

- Side Vertical is used by artists, restaurants, salons, and other graphic-intensive websites. It is a good option if you have a lot of menu tabs to display.
Example: Wix uses the hamburger menu, which opens the vertical menu when clicked.

- <u>Bottom Horizontal</u> is used when the focus is on the image, not the menu. The least used menu position because the eye always drifts to the top first. *Example:* **SquareSpace.**

Name/Logo Placement

<u>Right-Side</u> - Statistics confirm that right-sided logo placement never works as well as left-sided or centered placement. Brand recall is significantly weakened (89%) when a logo is placed on the right-side. Viewers scan left to right. Do not choose this option.

Which header is easier to view below?

<u>Left-Side</u> - The left side is the best place to put a name or logo because we read left to right. In correspondence, logos have always been positioned on the left side of the page. It communicates location, reinforces the brand, and is better for navigation. Left-side placement is used by business-to-business.

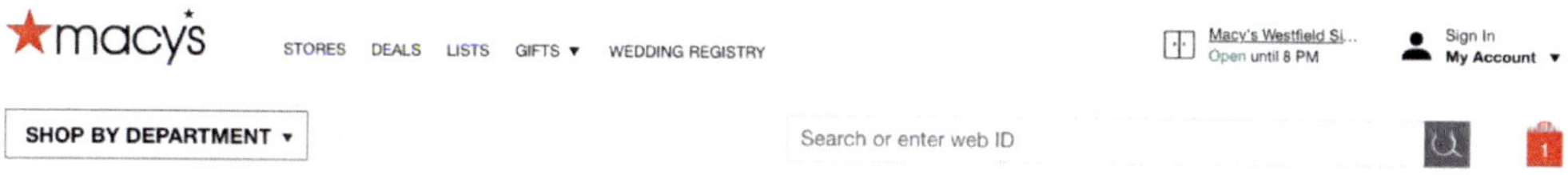

__Centered__ - Navigation suffers with centered placement because it hampers the ability to return to the home page. Users are more comfortable clicking the logo when it is on the left side. Only use centered placement if you have a strong, recognizable brand name. You might think it looks better, but logos on the left *work* better. Example: Wordpress

HEADERS AND FOOTERS

The header (or menu bar) and the footer have largely been ignored. They are important sections of a website. Both contain valuable information. They should:

- Have a simple, clean design in a readable font.
- Be on a solid background for legibility.
- Be organized and easy to navigate.
- Be consistent on all pages.
- Have a page designation that is underlined, in bold type, or a different color.

__HEADER OR MENU BAR__

The header bar is the strip across the top of the web page. It is important because it is where visitors find links to pages on your website. You should include:

1. __Name/Logo__ This is your identity. It should function as a home button on the other pages. Example: Wix

2. <u>Menu</u> The menu contains the categories of your website. Use no more than 7. Sub-categories are dropdowns from the main categories. *Example*: SquareSpace

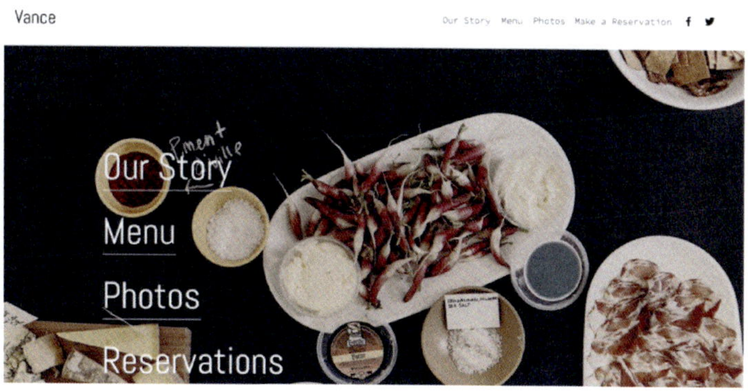

3. <u>Page Title</u> The title of the page you are on should be designated for the viewer. It can be in a different color, highlighted, underlined, or in bold text.

OTHER MENU BAR ITEMS:

<u>Search Bar</u>- The template must support a built-in search bar.

Shopping Cart - The shopping cart or handbag icon is in the upper right corner of all E-commerce sites.

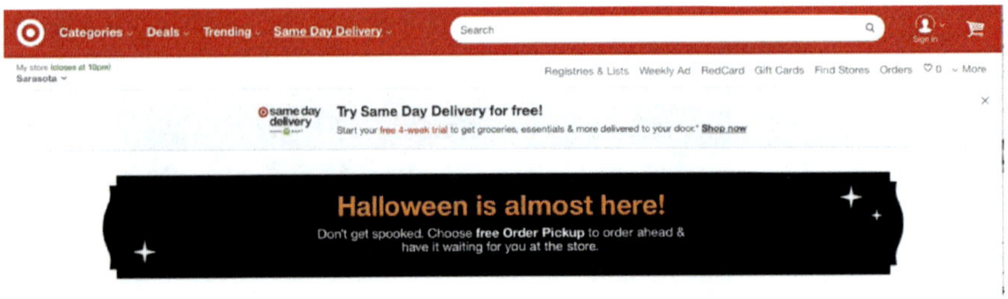

Login/Logout - The login is on the upper right corner. It gives access to select viewers.

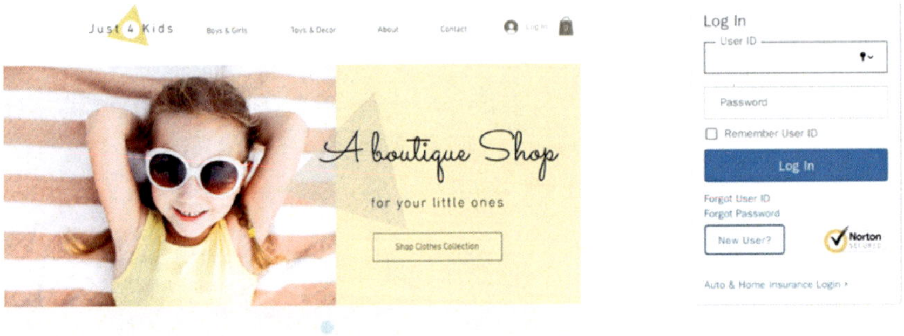

FOOTER

The footer is the strip across the bottom of the web page that contains important information. It is usually the last thing a user will see.

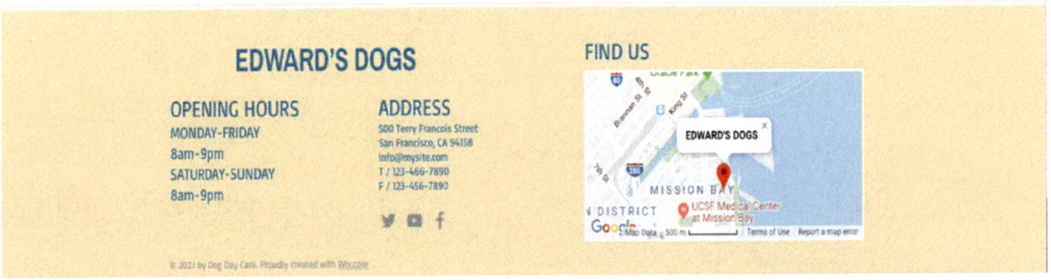

You should include:

1. Copyright - © symbol, the year and the name of the copyright owner:

   © 2019 Amazing Websites!

2. Contact Information - Name, physical address, email address, and phone number. You can also include hours of operation and a map.

3. <u>Social Links</u> - Social media links in the footer encourage visitors to stay on your site longer.

https://fernandomastrangelo.com via www.awwwards.com

Other additions:

<u>Widgets</u> - Widgets are apps embedded in a website that add functions that link to another page: Calendar, Archives, Posts, etc.

<u>Subscription Signup</u>- Apps for emails or newsletters.

<u>Call-to-Action</u> -<u>*Examples:*</u> Buy Now, Signup, Gift Cards, etc.

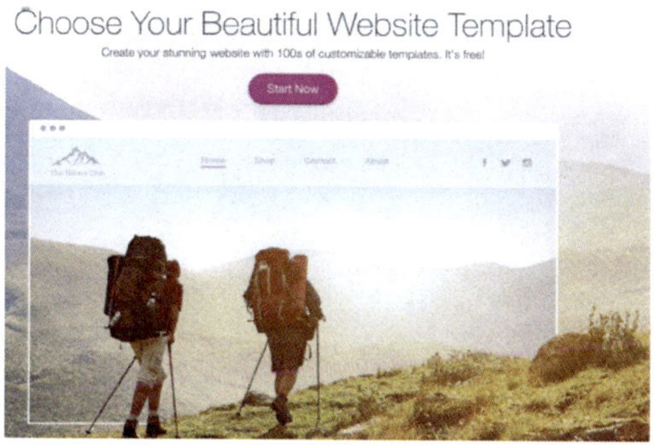

Privacy Policy is a link to a page that explains the type of information the website collects and how it is used.

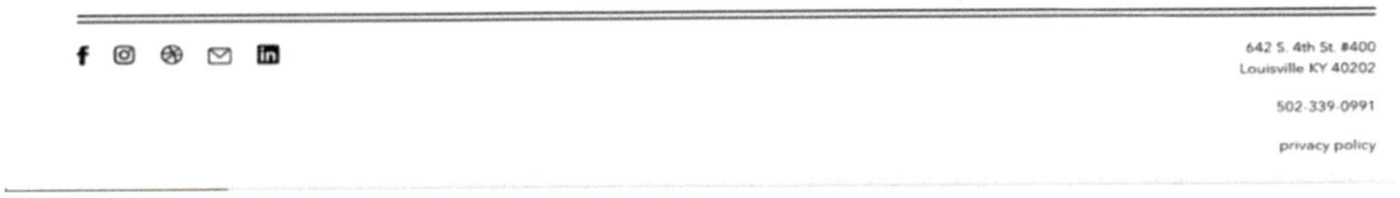

Footer design has been pretty straightforward in the past. It has been organized and standardized. Times are changing.

Just remember not to clutter. Here are some examples.

https://www.okalpha.co

https://tworobbers.com via www.awwwards.com

https://www.srqmagazine.com

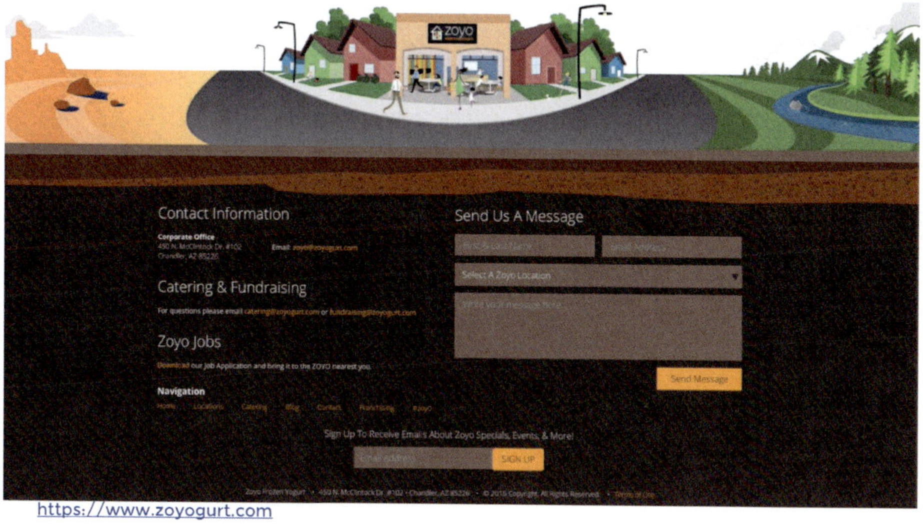

https://www.zoyogurt.com

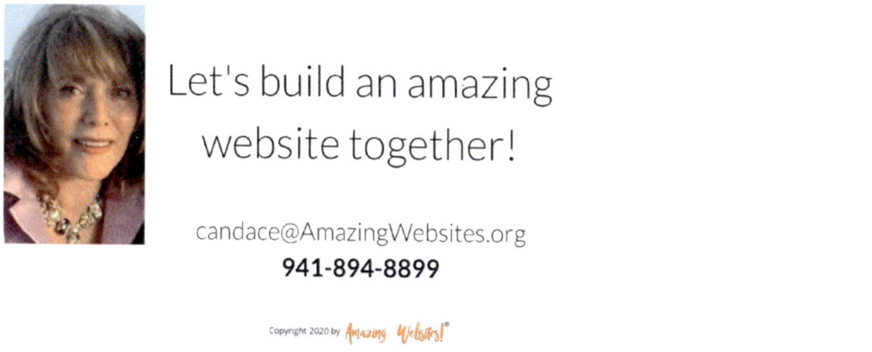

https://amazingwebsites.org

https://technolex.com

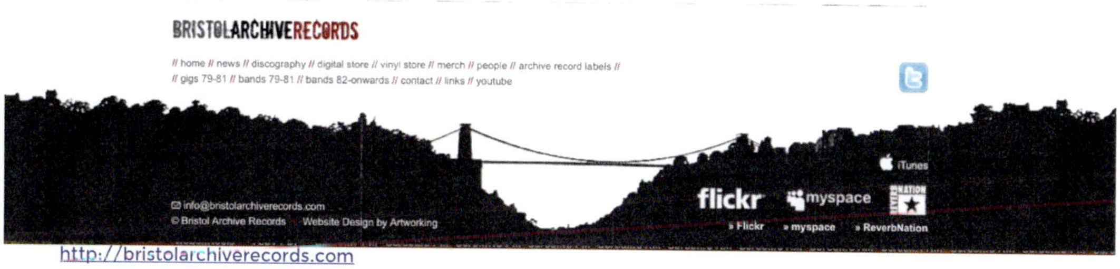

http://bristolarchiverecords.com

CALL-TO-ACTION (CTA)

A Call-to-Action is a piece of content or a button that encourages the viewer to take action. CTAs are an essential web technique in encouraging a prospective customer to sign-up for something, subscribe, make a purchase, etc.

If someone walks into your store, you greet them, establish a rapport, learn their needs, show them products, and sell them merchandise. You convert them into being a customer.

You cannot personally be with them on a website. In internet marketing, Conversion Rate Optimization (CRO) is a system for converting the number of people who visit your website into customers. CTAs get the viewer to engage and bring them closer to buying your products or services.

CTAs must be clear and concise. They can be a sign-up for a newsletter, a contact form, a purchase button, etc. Viewers choose to click on a CAT because it fulfills a specific need.
Examples:

Sign up	Try for free	Buy
Subscribe	Get Started	Join
Learn more	Try for free	Share
Support	Free Estimates	Register
Free Trial	Donate	Start

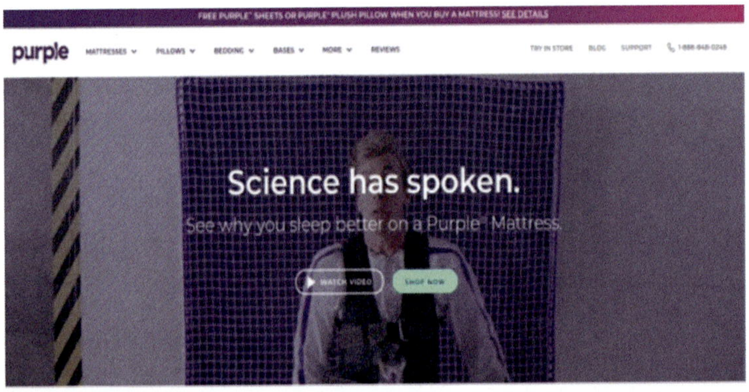

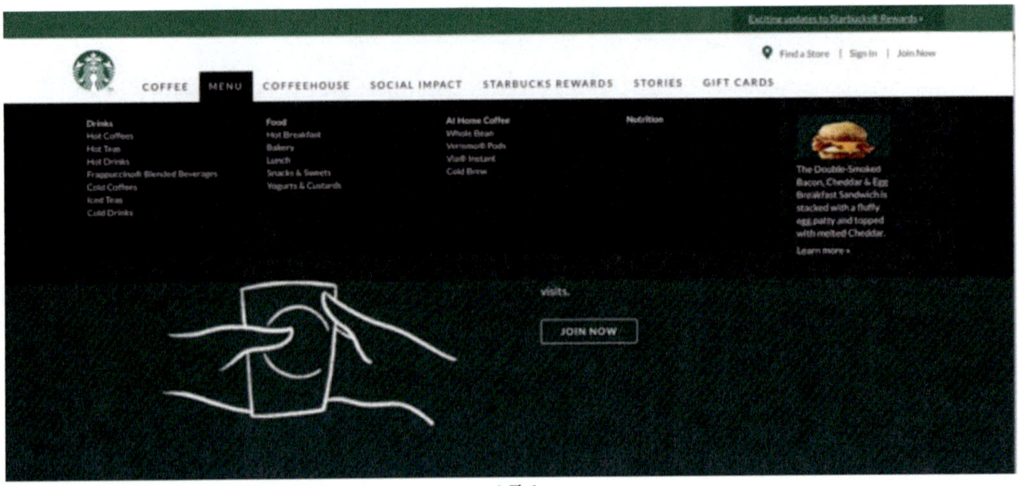

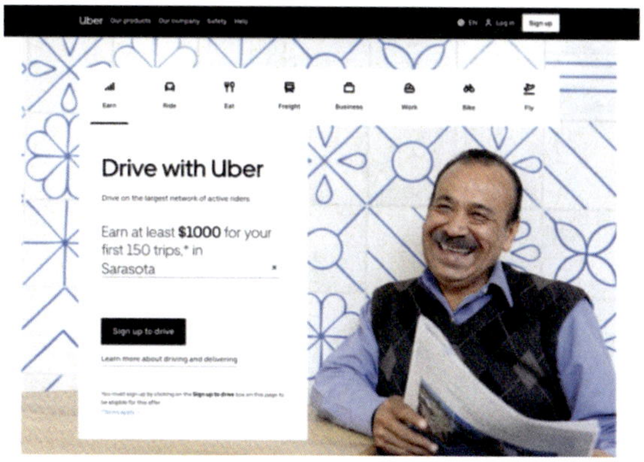

https://www.uber.com

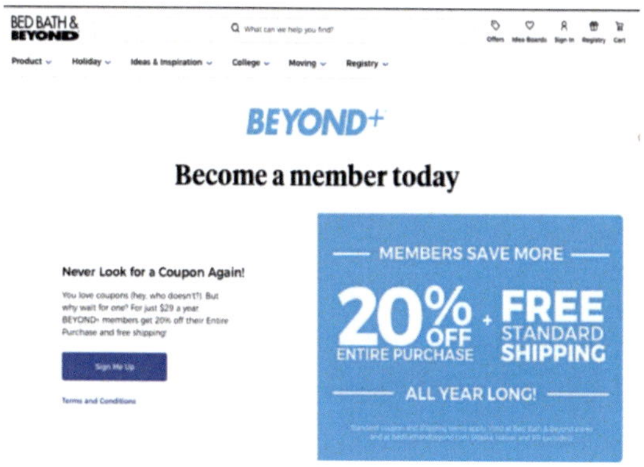

https://www.bedbathandbeyond.com

One way to get someone to click on a CTA is to add a <u>sense of urgency</u>.

- Offer expires May 15th
- Price increase January 1
- Enroll early for discount
- Supplies limited
- Discount Deadline
- BOGO

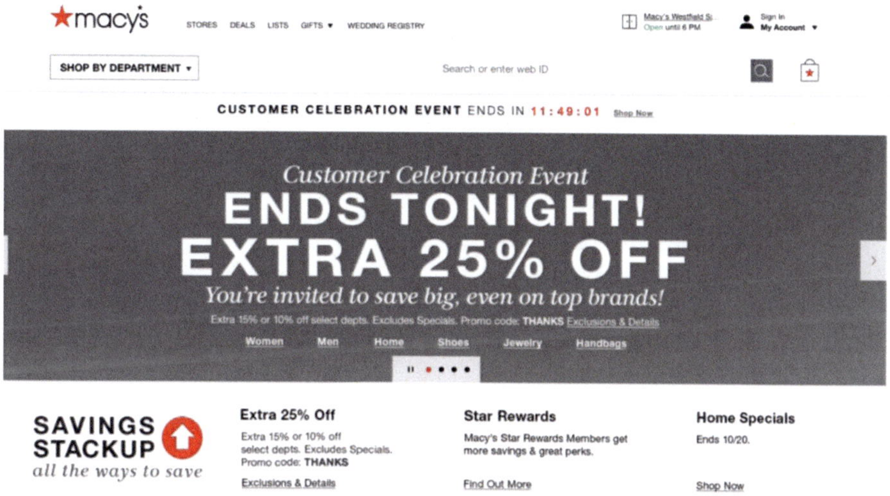

Tips:

- Make the CTA larger and bolder than surrounding elements. Use color. Craigslist highlights its CTA in yellow.

- Place CTA in obvious place on your web page.

https://dorseywealth.com

- Freebies get more traction.

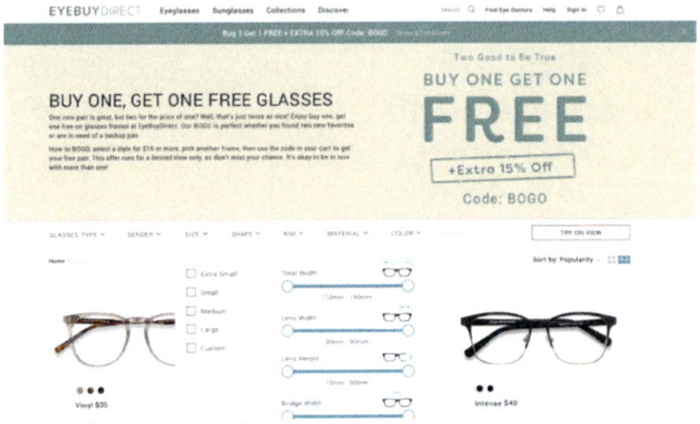

https://www.eyebuydirect.com

- You can use more than one CTA.

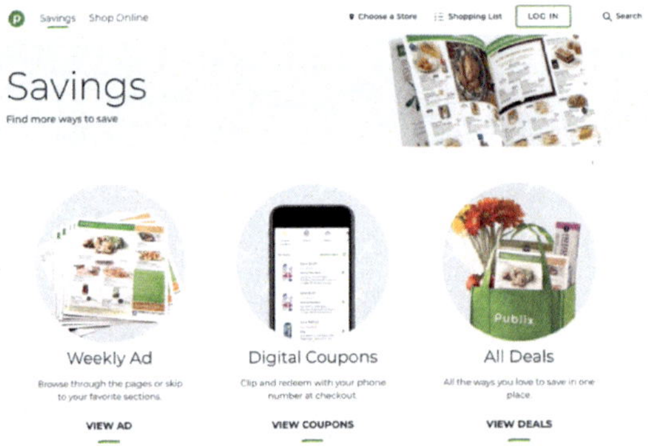

https://www.publix.com

- For fun, try reverse psychology and tell people "not to click".

HOME PAGE

Your home page is the most important page on your website. It is the first thing visitors see when they enter your website. It is the front door to your business. You need to "wow" them.

What makes a home page exceptional?
It gets their attention.

- Identifies who you are/what you do in the heading.
- Tells them why your products/services are needed.
- Speaks directly to your target audience.
- Engages visitors with a call-to-action.
- Makes navigation easy.
- Optimizes for mobile devices.
- Uses quality imagery and impactful headings.
- Is current with weekly updates.

Home Page Layout
Visitors make up their minds in a few seconds whether to stay on your website or leave. Your home page layout will affect that decision.

Your Home page is divided into two parts:

Above-The-Fold
The area seen before scrolling down. 100% of your visitors will see the content in this section. Put your most important (Primary) content above-the-fold.

- Headline -Make it short, clear, and descriptive of who you are and what you do.

- Sub-Headline -A brief description of how your service/product relates to your target audience. Explain how you can help them.

- Call-to-Action – Give them direction-what to do next.

- Imagery-What you see: pictures, a slider, or a video. Make it relevant and try not to use stock images.

- Name/Logo–Locate your name/logo on the top left side of the menu bar.

- Menu Bar-Contains the links to your website pages.

Below-The-Fold

This is the area you see when you scroll down the page. The content in this section supports the Above-The-Fold content.

Two types of content used:

Secondary Information

The second most important information to put on your Home page (the most important is Above-The-Fold). It reinforces your primary content.

- Briefly explain the benefits of your product/services.
- Show you are human, personal, and not a fake.
- List the most important features.

Additional Information

Extras like a location map, list of blogs, newsletters, sign-ups.

Choose a template that includes the About and Contact pages. Drag and drop your content into the template.

Examples of Above/Below-The-Fold: Wix and Squarespace

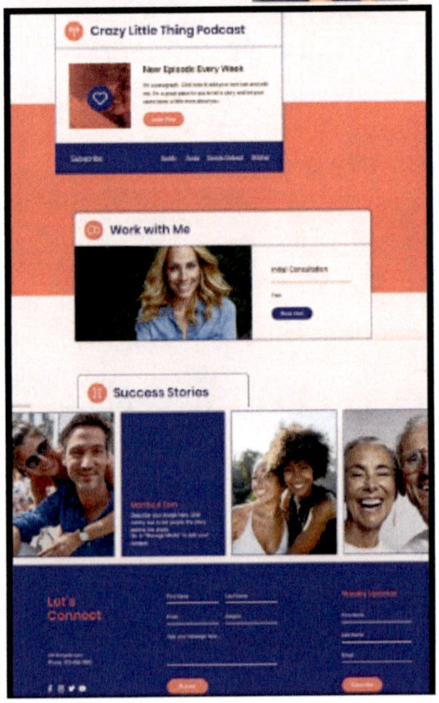

Examples of Above/Below-the-Fold: GoDaddy and Wix

GoDaddy Lulu

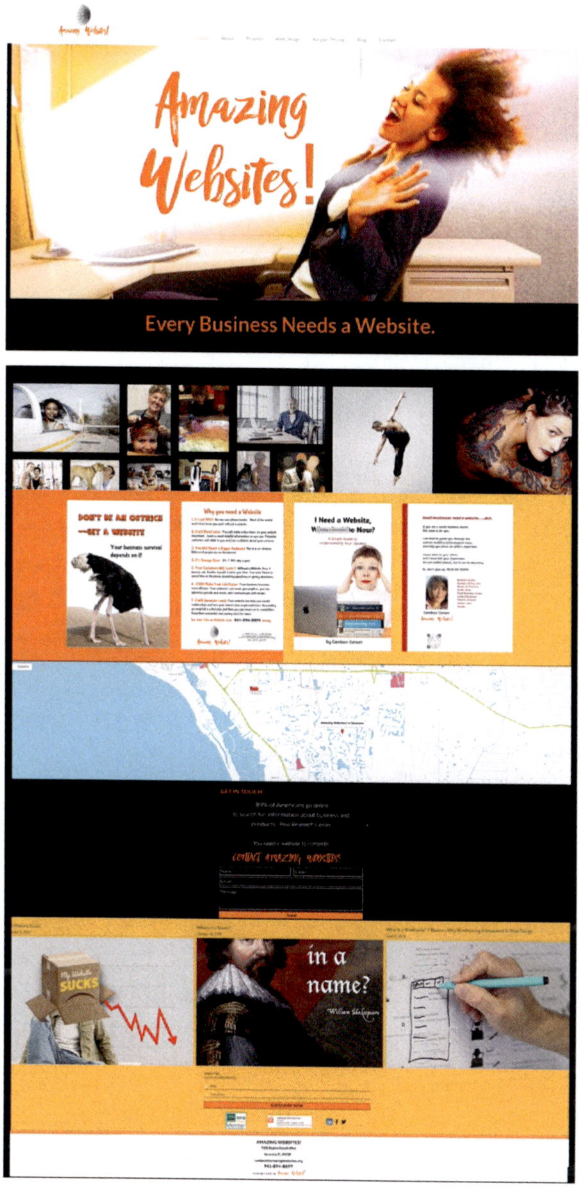

You can make alterations to the template to customize your website. Some templates allow for more changes than others. You can move sections to different areas, eliminate sections, enlarge and shrink areas, change fonts, and alter colors.

ABOUT PAGE

The About page is the second most important website page (after the Home page). Visitors are curious about you and your business. They want to know your story. The page should be interesting, informative, and personal.

You want the viewer to like you and to know that you are credible. Introduce yourself. Review your credentials (education, experience), explain why you like doing what you do, and how you are different.

<u>Tips</u>

- Use the first person ("I").
- Keep it short (under 250 words).
- List accomplishments but don't have an endless list.
- Add an image of yourself and pictures of your staff.
- Be natural. Use your natural voice.
- Be honest and sincere.
- Include a CTA to link to purchase or your email.
- Include a sign-up for subscriptions and/or newsletters.
- Add your favorite quote or try a little humor.
- Smile!

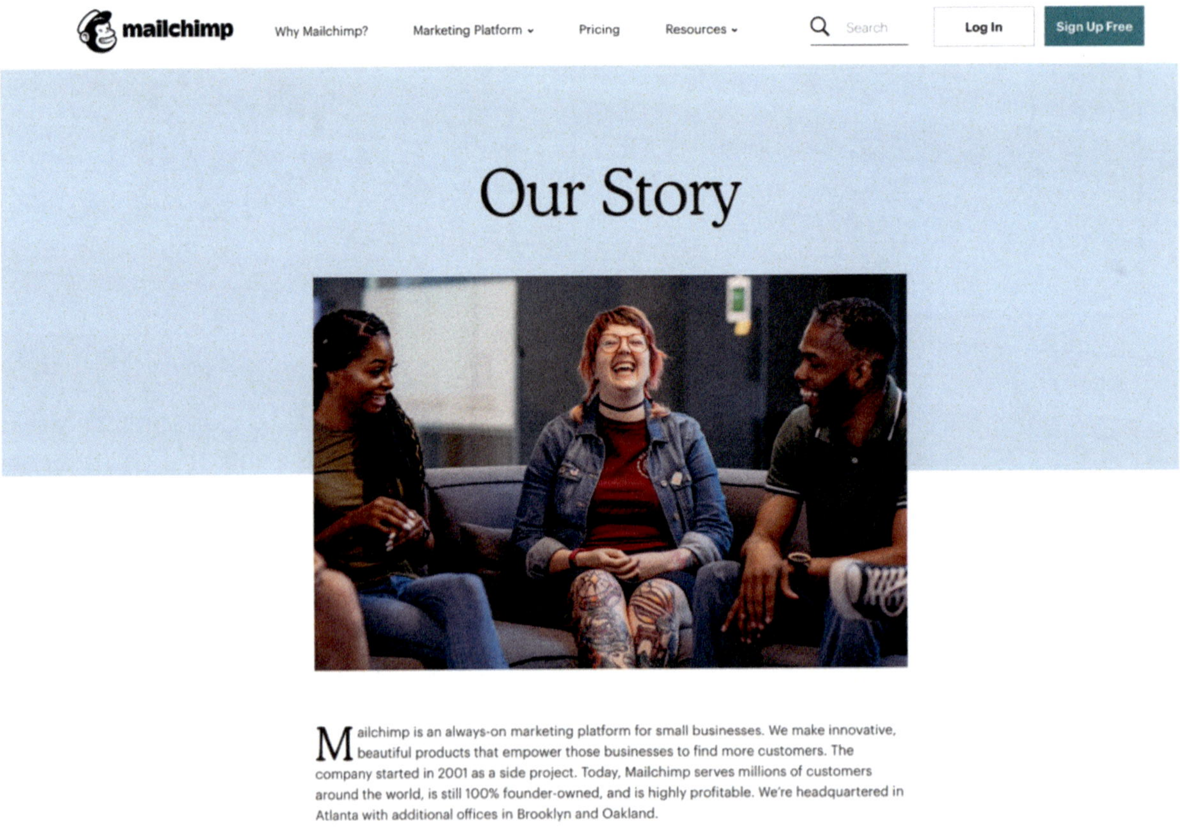

Below are the About pages on the templates depicted on pages 158 and 159. The Wix page is unchanged. The SquareSpace page has added images and text. The GoDaddy page has one added image. The last one is from my website.

GoDaddy Lulu /Apple Pie Woman
Image by Finn Bjurvoll Hansen from Pixabay

SERVICES PAGE

The services page competes with the About Page in viewer interest. It explains what you do and how you are different from the rest of the pack.

<u>Page Layout:</u>

- Title: 1-2 words describing what you do.
- Subtitles: Experience, products, or services.
- Text: Elevator Pitch-What you do and what you offer. List qualifications and services. Keep it brief, 100-150 words.
- Images: Use relevant images; "real" is best.
- CTA: Make your call-to-action obvious and easy to find. No one should have to hunt for it.

To help with your Google ranking, your menu bar should be descriptive. Words like "Services" or "Products" are too generic. "What We Do" is too broad. It is difficult to come up with an original alternative, which is why most websites don't.

Sierra Designs lists the types of products it sells. Notice that it keeps the list to 7 items.

Di Bruno Bros. lists products in general terms. It uses subcategories to further delineate items.

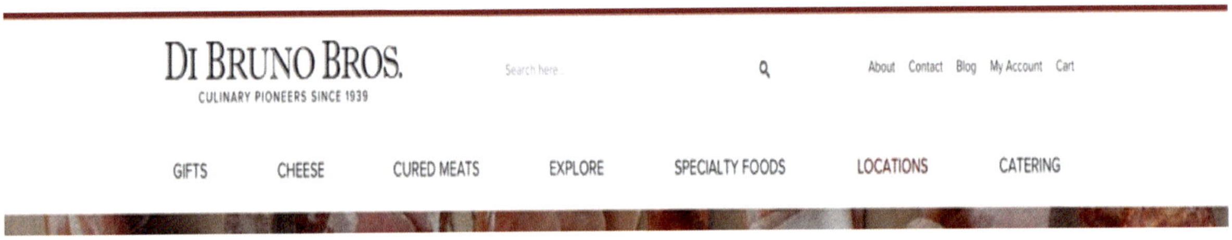

Dogeared lists the types of jewelry it offers.

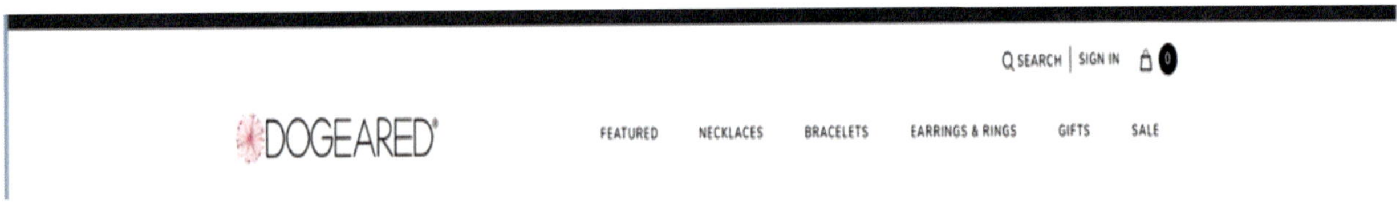

Continuing with the templates that we reviewed on page 158, this is how the Services pages look:

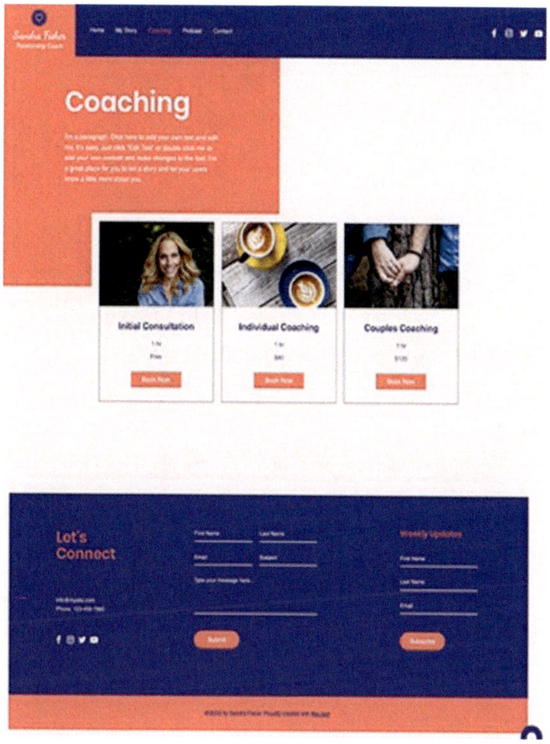

CONTACT PAGE

The Contact Page should be the last item on your menu bar. Everyone knows that. It should be where the viewer expects it to be.

The main purpose of the page is to provide the user with information on how to get in touch with you. It's your last chance to get a potential client.

It's easy to throw a form on the page, add your email address, and phone number–everybody else does. It may be the last page a viewer sees. It should entice the viewer to contact you. Think about how you can make it a little different.

Keep it simple and reflect your personality. Show that you want to be contacted.

All website builders have the contact form on their templates. You can easily add or exchange a form if you prefer something different. Make it brief and don't ask for too much information.

Include:

- Email and Phone number.
- Short Form for user information.
- Call-To-Action
- Add a map.
- Something different–personal.

Always respond ASAP. Once someone fills out the form, make sure you answer promptly.

Examples of Contact Pages

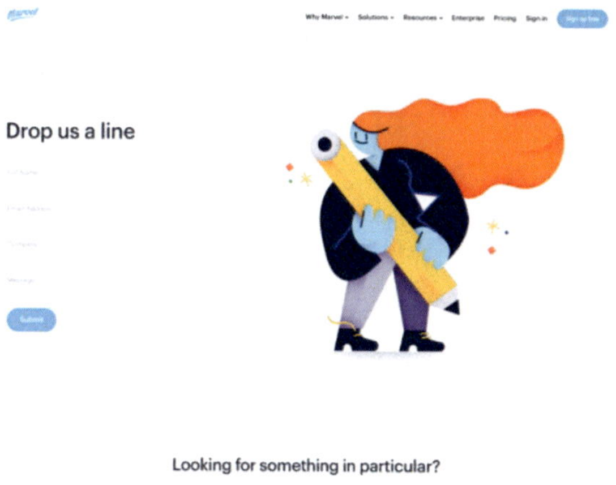

Marvel

Media Proper

G2G Branding and Web Design

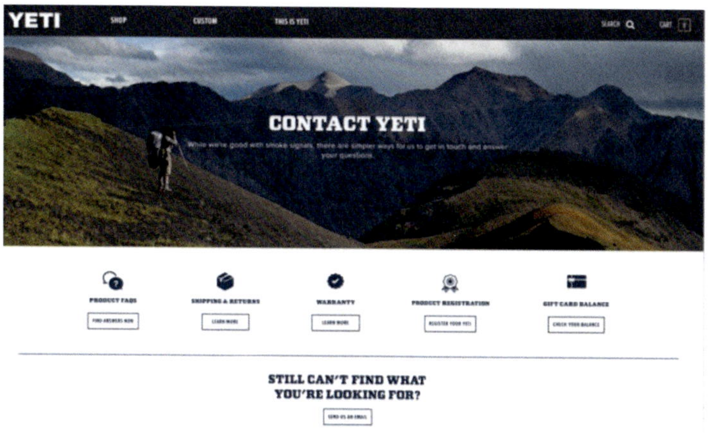

Yeti

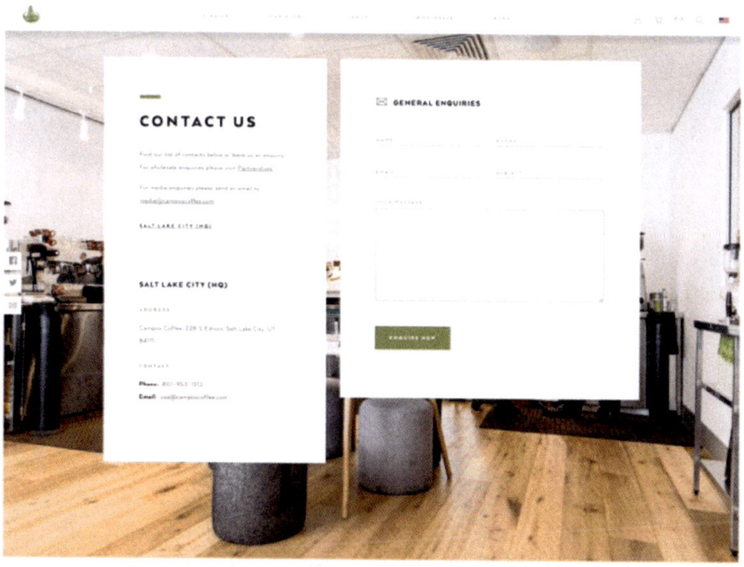

Campo Coffee

Below are pages from the website templates we have been following . You can see how each includes the specific elements we have discussed and each maintains consistency throughout the design.

Home Page

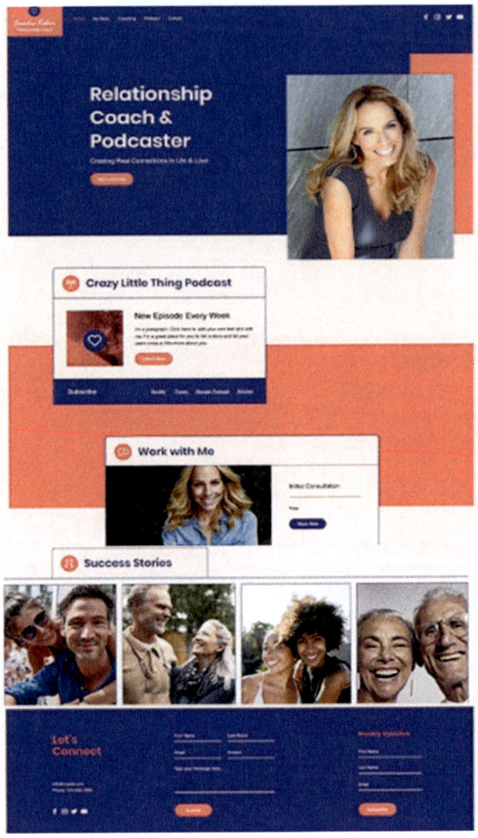

About

Coaching (Services)

Contact

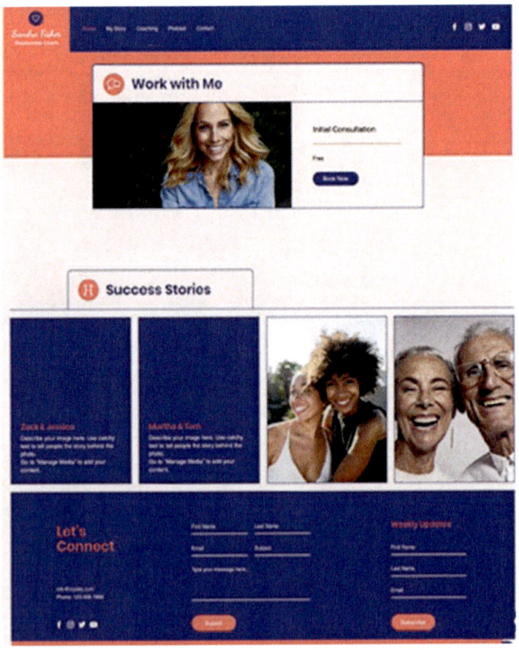

Home Page

About

Our Programs (Services)

Contact

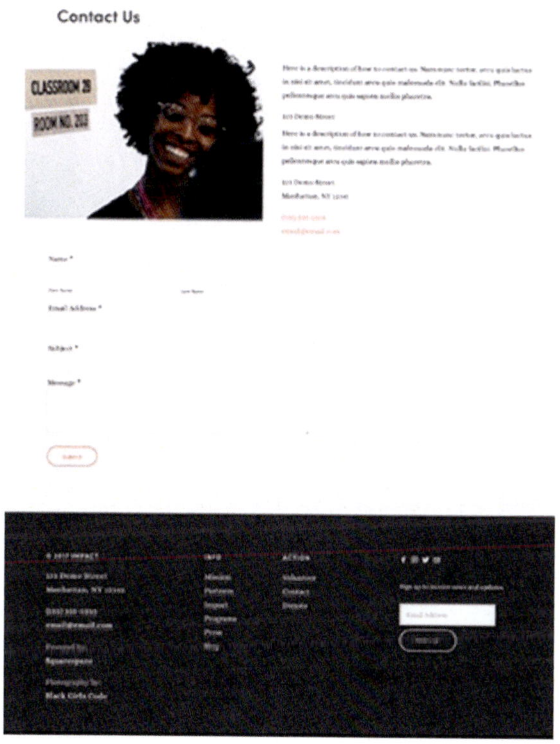

Home

About

Inspirations (Services)

Contact

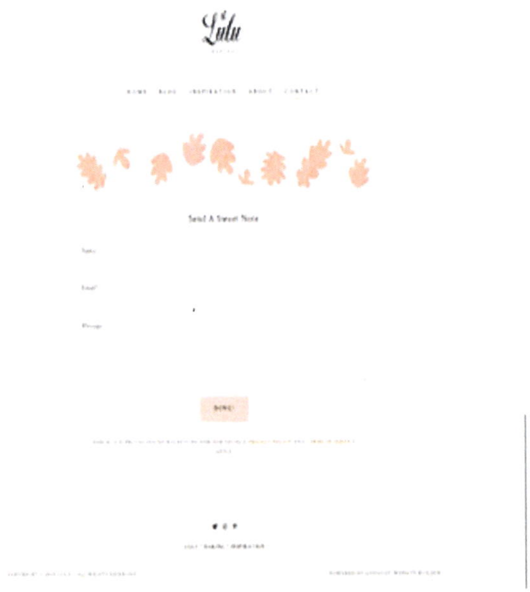

Home

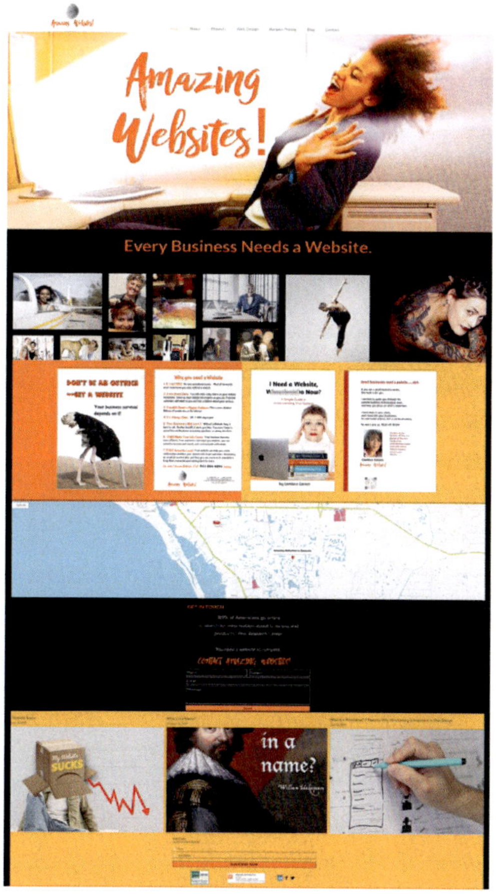

About

Web Design (Services)

Contact

TESTIMONIALS

Testimonials are unbiased reviews that testify to your character, qualifications, business, products, and services. They come from customers who praise your work and encourage others to buy your product or invest in your service. Satisfied customer reviews are a marketing tool that can boost your business. They are persuasive and build credibility.

Testimonials showcase the quality and success of your products and services. They establish trust. They are especially useful for websites because visitors are often skeptical to trust online businesses.

Testimonials should include the person's name, title, company, and picture. A picture makes it real. If they don't want their name used, ask to use their initials. It isn't as good, but better than nothing.

Testimonial Guidelines

1. Use descriptive language that's enthusiastic and detailed to convince the viewer to make a purchase.
2. Highlight specific uses for the product or service.
3. Added visual elements like pictures, videos, audio, and social media prove that the testimonial is from a real person.
4. Always get permission to use the testimonial.

How to Get Testimonials

Some testimonials are user generated. A customer will post a review online. This is a gift. Copy it and add it to your website and social media pages.

The majority of testimonials are solicited. You have to ask. Most clients don't mind telling others that they are happy with your work and they like recommending you to other people. If you find this book helpful, please let me know.

Testimonials build trust. It matters what others think, especially online. They are an important asset that should be included on all websites.

Ways to Get Testimonials

- Send feedback forms after a purchase.
- Send an email request.
    - Make it short, polite, and beneficial by offering to that link the testimonial back to their website if they have one.
    - Make it easy for them to decline so they won't feel pressured.
- Call customers and ask for feedback.

Testimonial Questions

Make it easy for the person giving the testimonial by giving them questions to answer. Example questions:

- How did you hear about us?
- How was your experience with us?
- What product/service did you purchase?
- What did you like about our product/service?
- How did our product/service help you?
- Would you recommend us? Why?
- Is there anything you'd like to add?
- Can we use your comments online?

Where to put Testimonials

Many websites designate a page for testimonials. The testimonial page is the least viewed page on a website. It is a flagrant sales pitch, and everyone knows it.

Sprinkle testimonials throughout your website. A few well-placed testimonials seem more honest than a dull, monotonous list of customer reviews.

Put them:

- Below text advertising your product or service.
- Next to images of the product or service you offer.
- On all pages but especially on your Home, About, and Contact pages because those pages are viewed the most.

Note: If you have a lot of testimonials, add a testimonial page to display the ones not on the other pages. Put the best ones on your Home, About and Contact pages.

Types of Testimonials

- Customer quotes

The most popular form of testimonial. Making a decision is easier when you have the support of satisfied customers. You build credibility when customers advocate on behalf of your brand.

https://hubspot.com

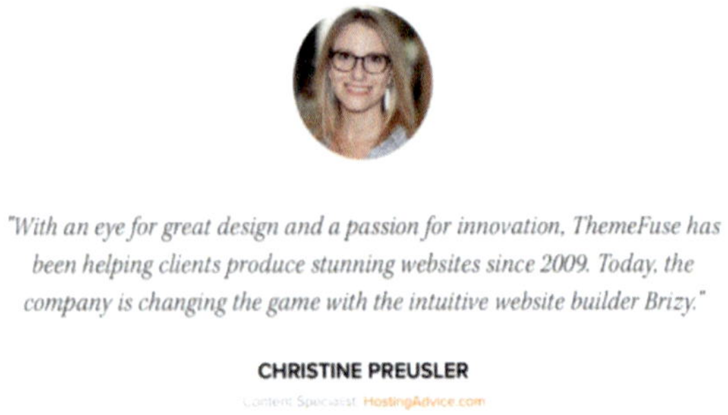

https://themefuse.com

- Customer Interviews

Ask customers to share information about your business and how it played a role in their success. It can be posted as a text, an image, audio, or video.

https://video.search.yahoo.com

https://shopify.com

- <u>Case Studies</u>

  Customers analyze their successful experience with your products or services. Results are backed up with data.

CREW — CASE STUDY

Crew's Website Converts Global Brands Into Loyal Customers

Crew is an app that keeps frontline teams engaged and productive through communication, recognition and scheduling. They're trusted by teams at the largest brands including Taco Bell, KFC and Dunkin' Donuts.

↗ crewapp.com

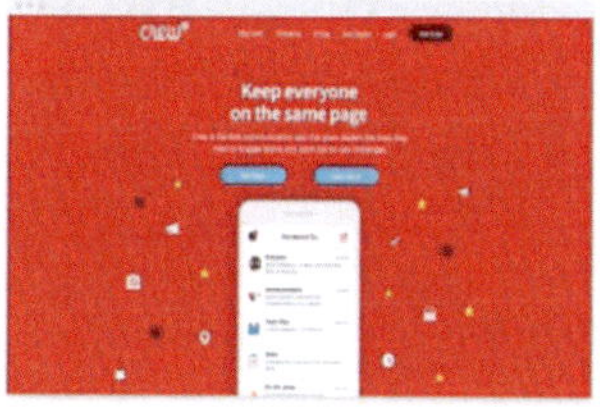

https://www.wix.com/partners/case-study-crew

https://www.bluebeam.com

- <u>Social Media</u>

  Satisfied customers can post a review that can be liked and shared online by others on a number of free online sites. It is popular with everyone.

Examples: **Facebook, Yelp, Instagram.**

Recommendations and Reviews

People talk about "citrus beurre blanc", "filet mignon" and "braised short rib ravioli"

great food, great service 😎😎
October 24

Great food
The foods is really good and the service was excellent..😘
September 20

We had a party of 22 people and the staff was absolutely wonderful t aking care of each an every one ... See More
July 28, 2018

Do you recommend Mattison's Forty-One?

Yes	No

Mattison's Forty One restaurant

- Peer Reviews

  Sites like Yelp and Angie's List offer free online reviews. Many consumers use these sites during the decision-making process. It is beneficial but, dissatisfied customers can also review you. If they do, ALWAYS respond. You want to try to solve their concerns and to make certain others who read the review notice that you are pro-active.

Wimpy's Plumbing & Air

13 reviews

Verified License · Water Heater Installation/Repair, Heating & Air Conditioning/HVAC, Water Purification Services

24/7 Availability

Emergency services

Request a Quote | Responds in about 50 minutes

(941) 212-3566

Serving Sarasota and the Surrounding Area

Wimpy's Dependable Plumbing is a full-service Sarasota plumbing company. We have been providing the area with top-quality services since 1973, and we are proud to have built a strong… read more

https://www.yelp.com

- Write a Blog to tell your story.

Get a Website--YESTERDAY

July 3, 2019 | Candace Carson/AMAZINGE WEBSITES!

Having a website is essential for marketing your small business. A website should be the basis of your advertising and marketing efforts. Without one, you can't hope to compete effectively.

So, why are some small businesses like the Ostrich - keeping their heads in the sand? Here are the main excuses:

MY BUSINESS IS SMALL, I DON'T HAVE A BUDGET.
Your website is your number one marketing asset. It should be part of your budget just like your LLC license. It is essential. 91% of customers have visited a store because of an online experience and 37% use the Internet to find a store at least once per month.

I HAVE ENOUGH BUSINESS. Lucky you, but 97% of people go online to look up your phone number, your location/directions and hours of operation and answer basic questions about your business. They want to know who they are buying from. They want to trust you.

I KNOW SOMEONE WHO WILL MAKE ME A WEBSITE FOR FREE
Having a friend or family member make your website is like trusting a handyman to build your house. A bad website is worse than none at all. "You get what you pay for". Do yourself a favor and save a lot of headaches - - hire a Pro.

https://www.amazingwebsites.org/single-post/2019/07/03/Get-a-Website--YESTERDAY

• <u>Slideshow</u>-Use sliders to show the reviews.

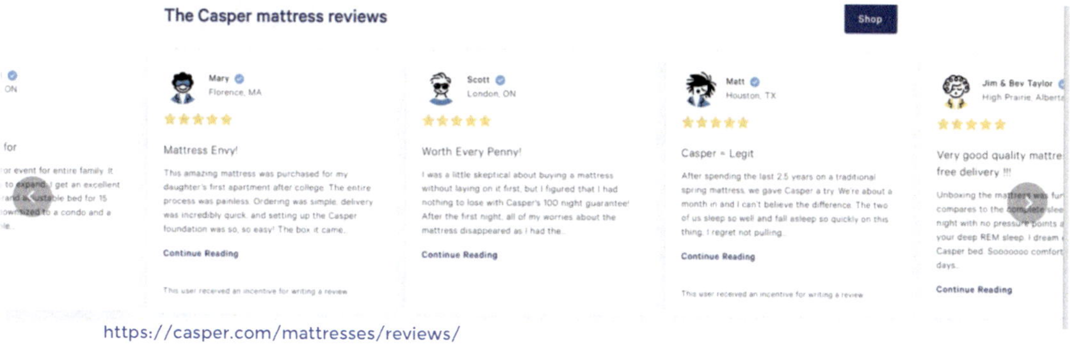

https://casper.com/mattresses/reviews/

• <u>Video</u>

Video is trendy, tells a story visually, and has the potential to go viral. It can be expensive and time consuming but, if good, can reach thousands of potential customers. It is more powerful than any other format.

https://get.chownow.com/testimonials-reviews

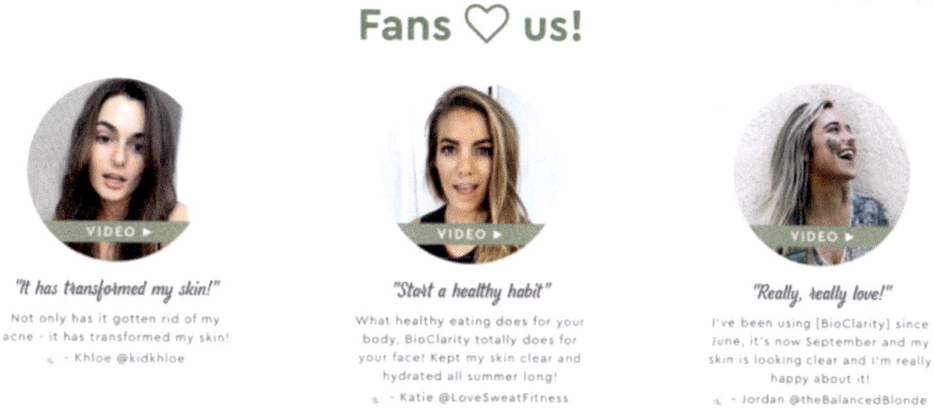

https://www.bioclarity.com/pages/proven-results

• <u>Audio</u>

Audio is easier, cheaper, and uses less data than video. It can be heard anywhere.

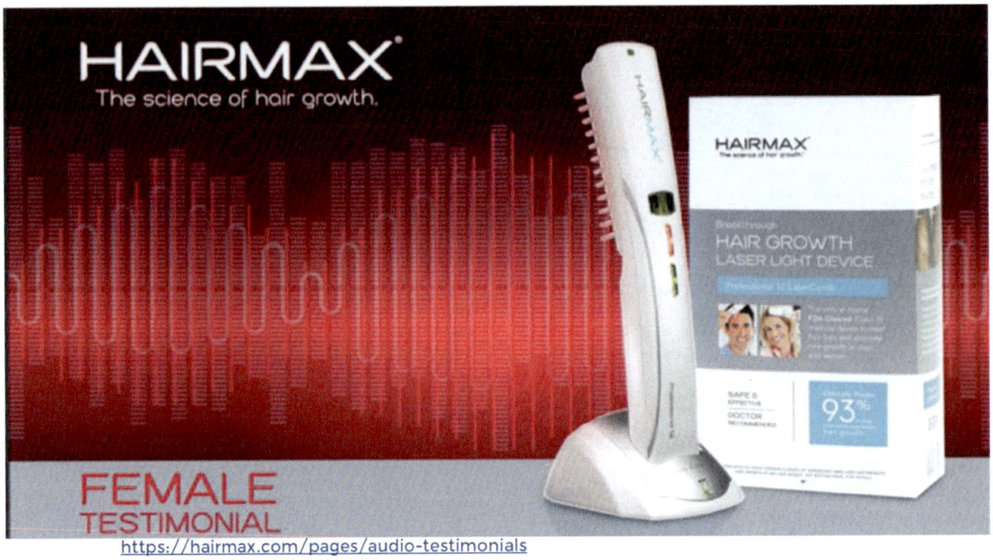

https://hairmax.com/pages/audio-testimonials

• <u>An Endorsement</u> is when a well-known person or company supports your product. It can be expensive but, if successful, is very beneficial.

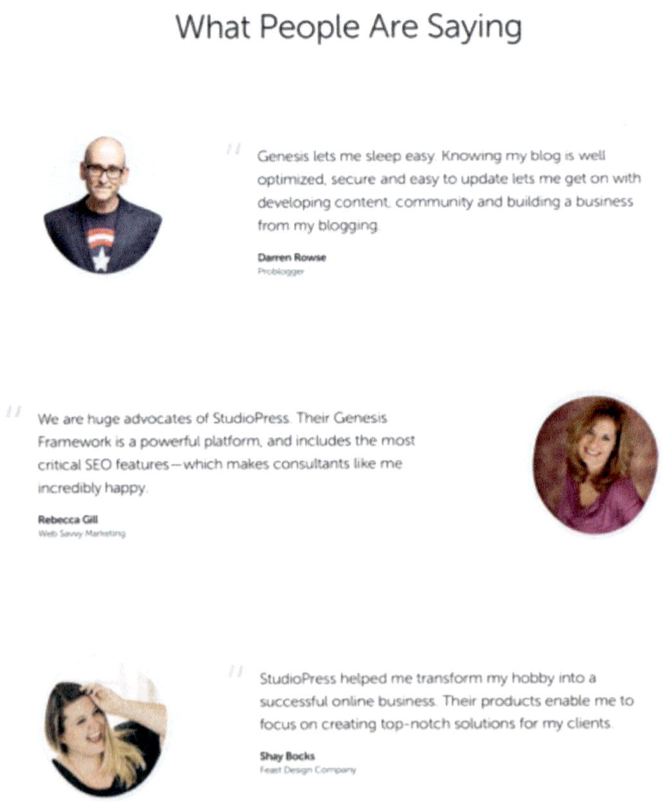

https://www.studiopress.com

- Press

Get your business featured in newspapers, magazines, or on television and then put the content on your website.

IT'S SHOWTIME!

At One of Sarasota's Oldest Restaurants, Great Service Matters

Columbia Restaurant assistant manager Richard Appelgren shares the secrets to the restaurant's success.

10/29/2019 • By Cooper Levey-Baker

https://www.sarasotamagazine.com/eat-and-drink/best-restaurants

"The thing that we are trying to do....is just help people connect and communicate more efficiently."
–**Mark Zuckerberg**

CHAPTER 13

CONNECTIONS

LINKS

A link (or hyperlink) is an icon, text, or graphic that links to another file when clicked. It allows a connection between web pages.

Links give the user more information from another source on the web (ex: URL address, PDF file, web page). They are an integral, interactive part of the internet experience. The internet would be boring without links.

Search engines follow links to discover you online, and point search inquires in your direction. The more incoming links a web page has, the higher it ranks in search results, which helps your SEO.

Links have two parts:

URL address + word(s) to direct the user to the web page

https://www.AmazingWebsites.org/about

Types of Links:

Internal links are between two web pages on the same website. They are usually located in the menu bar and the footer.

External links are between your website and another web page. They provide information to support your website. Always link to high quality, trusted web pages.

Incoming links are when someone else's web page links to your website. They have the highest SEO (Search Engine Optimization) benefit but are the hardest to obtain.

When building your website, focus on internal links. Links make your site stronger by giving supportive information. Website builders make adding links easy.

Guidelines to make your links more usable:

1. Text links should be in the color blue and underlined. Everyone is used to clicking on underlined, blue text.

   Do not use blue or underline text that is not a link. It will confuse the user, who might try to click on it...and it won't work.

   Example from WordPress.org

Our Story

WordPress started in 2003 when Mike Little and Matt Mullenweg created a fork of b2/cafelog. The need for an elegant, well-architected personal publishing system was clear even then. Today, WordPress is built on PHP and MySQL, and licensed under the GPLv2. It is also the platform of choice for over 34% of all sites across the web.

The Technology

Learn about WordPress, where it's been, and where it's going.

- Requirements
- Features
- Security
- Roadmap
- History

The Details

There's so much in the details. Stay abreast with the particulars.

- Domains
- GNU Public License
- Accessibility
- Privacy Policy
- Statistics

The People

Learn about the community and how we get along.

- Philosophy
- Etiquette
- Swag
- Logos and Graphics
- Testimonials

2. Links should become highlighted or change color on mouseover. It makes them seem "alive".
3. Mix letter case to be more scannable. Do not use all upper or lower case. Make it easy to read.
   https://AmazingWebsites.org
4. Links should identify the page title where it leads.
   https://AmazingWebsites.org/about
5. Make your logo an icon link, that when clicked, the user is returned to the home page.
6. Use an image to connect to another web page by embedding the link in the image. The images below act as buttons.

fitbit

airbnb

7. Use descriptive button instructions like "Free Trial". Generic terms ("click here") do not scan well. Users already know they can click; they want to know why they are clicking.

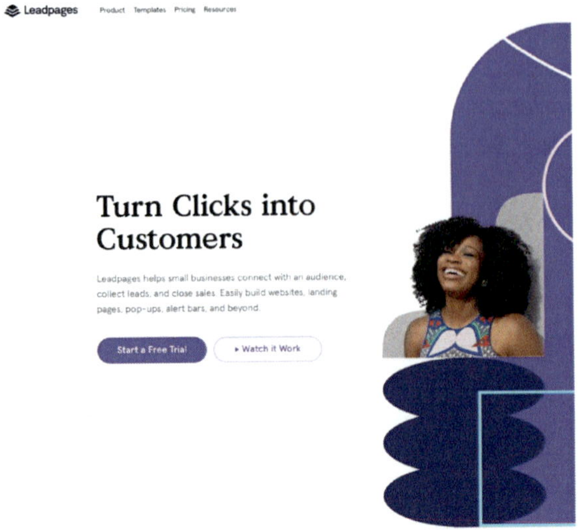

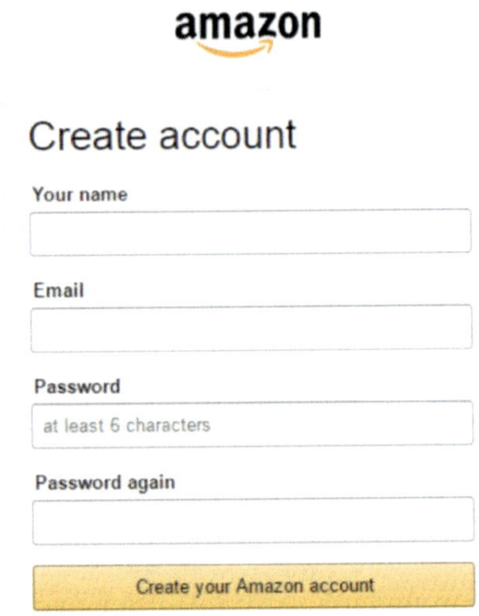

8. Make links obvious and place them prominently on the web page. Users should not have to hunt for them.

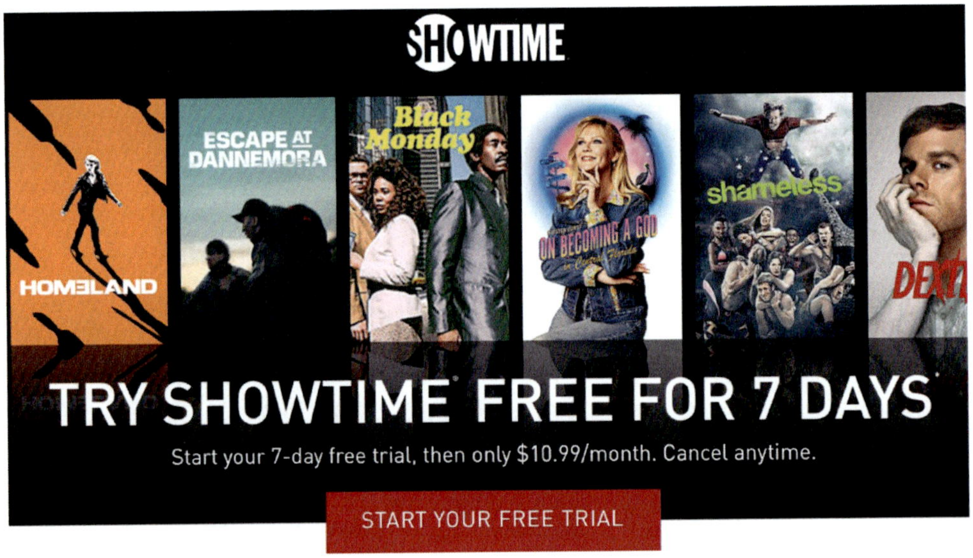

9. If you use buttons, rectangular buttons are more clickable than other shapes. Everyone is used to pushing rectangular buttons. Make it easy.

10. Be consistent with the design you choose. If the button has rounded corners on one page, it should be the same on all pages.

11. Choose the option "open in the same window" if linked to another web page. This keeps your website open, and the user can return to your web page when finished.

12. Open in a different window if the link is to a PDF.

13. Make sure the link works. Web page location can change or be discontinued and will return a 404 error. If a user wants information, but the link doesn't work, it will be frustrating.

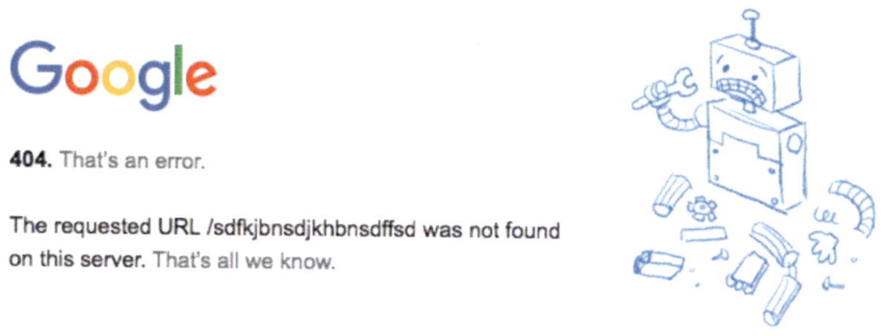

14. Don't clutter your website with too many links.

BUTTONS

Buttons are an essential element of interactive design on the web. They direct users to take action.

Types of buttons

1. Flat, color-filled with squared edges.
   Simple, doesn't distract from content.

2. Color-filled, with rounded edges.
   Draws the eye toward the center.

3. Color-filled with shadows.
   Seems pushable and has an impact.

4. Gradient Button
   Has a dynamic effect and a sense of motion and depth.

5. Ghost Button
   Transparent and usually bordered with a thin line. The page background is seen through it. Trendy, clean, elegant, and supportive of the design.

Button Guidelines

- It should look like a button. Buttons are regarded as "clickable."
- Use rounded or squared-edged rectangular buttons. If you deviate from this basic shape, you risk confusing the user.
- Its color should change when the cursor hovers over it.

- Buttons should be sized according to importance. The larger the button, the more important the action. Adjust the size of the button on mobile devices.

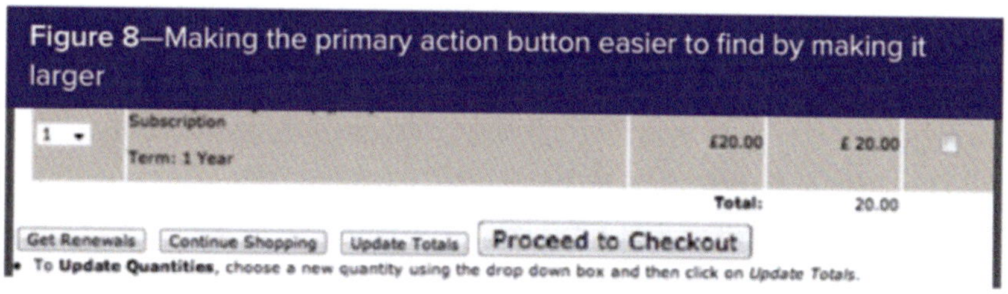

https://uxmatters.com

- Buttons must match. Use the same design, color, fonts, contrast, and hover color on all website buttons.
- Make buttons easy to read and find. Put them where they are expected to be.

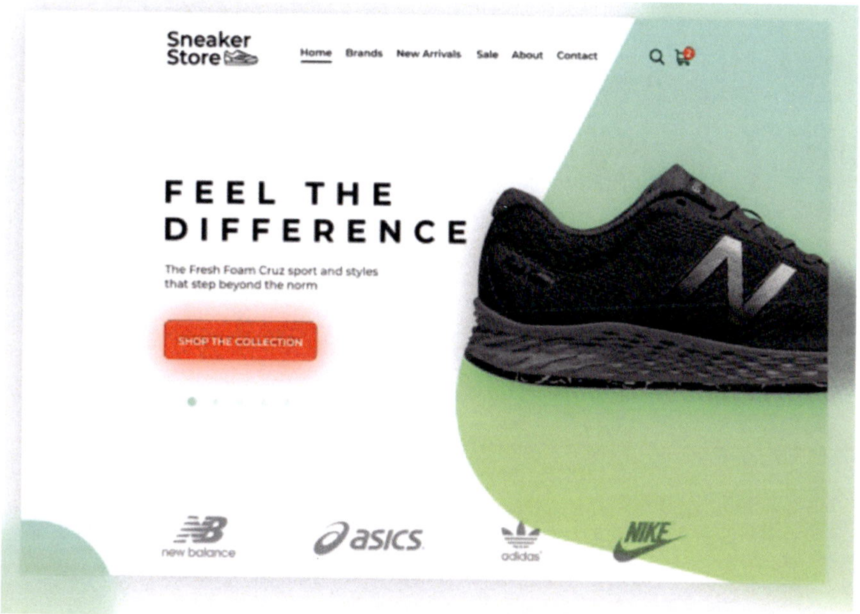

Design by Alexander Bykhovsky.

- Label buttons with what they do. Users expect a particular action followed by clicking on the button. Generic instructions like, CLICK ME, don't get clicked.

- Surround the button with white space. Never put it in the middle of the text.
- Make buttons finger-friendly for mobile users. They should be sized between 10 - 14 mm. Website builders have already figured that out for you.
- Don't clutter with a lot of buttons. Everything does not need to have a button. Too many options are confusing, and users end up doing nothing.

<u>*Button Examples:*</u>

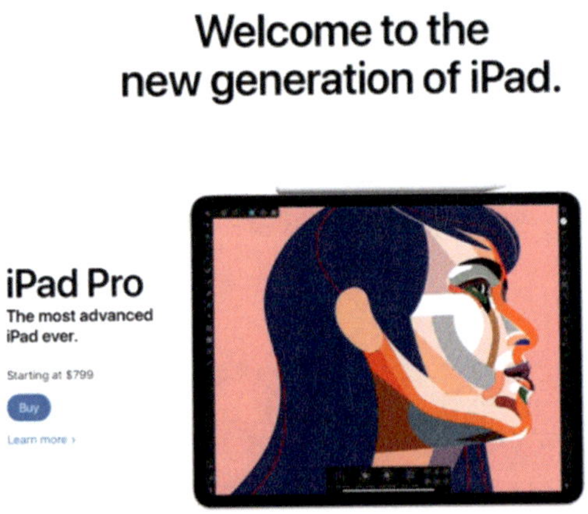

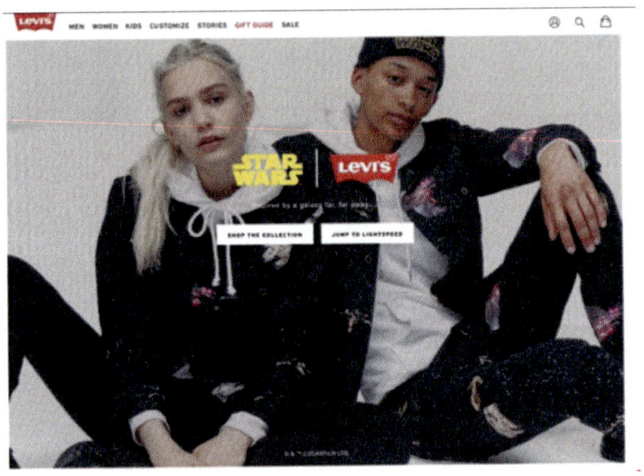

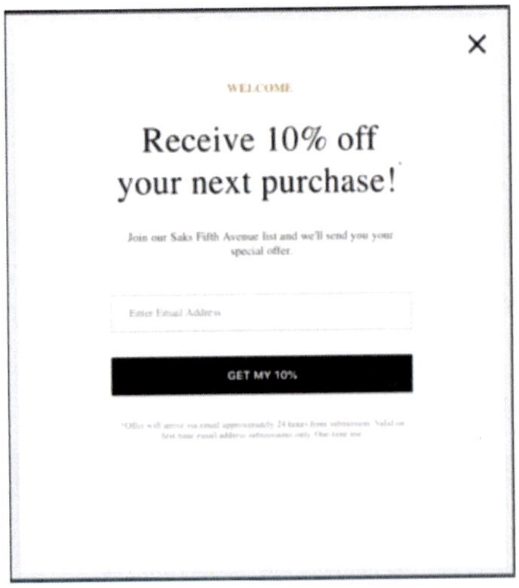

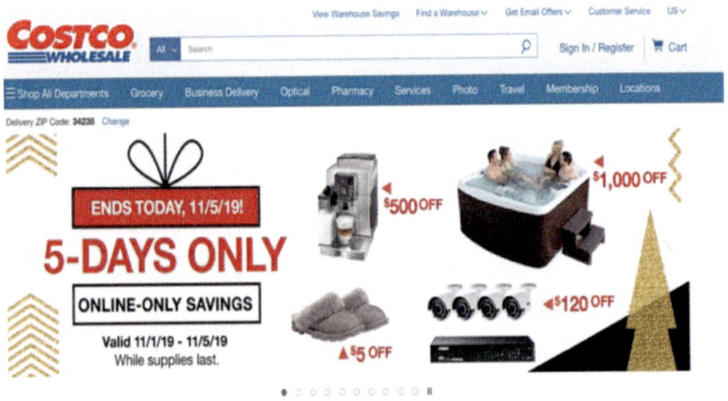

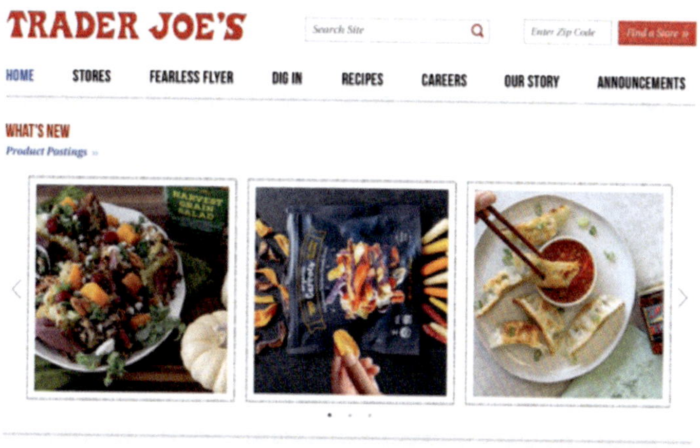
TRADER JOE'S
Search Site
Enter Zip Code
Find a Store »
HOME
STORES
FEARLESS FLYER
DIG IN
RECIPES
CAREERS
OUR STORY
ANNOUNCEMENTS
WHAT'S NEW
Product Postings »
HARVEST GRAIN SALAD

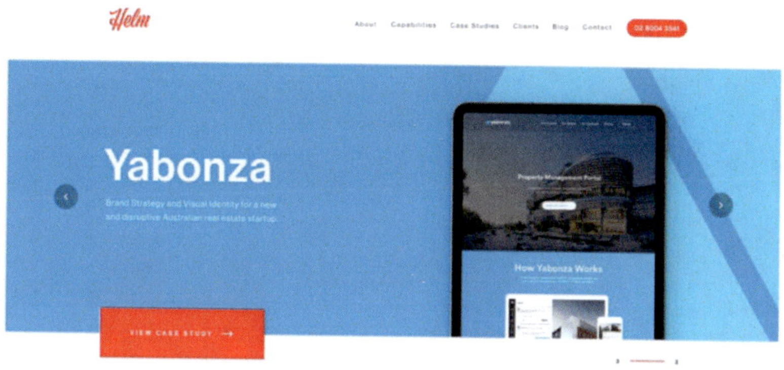
Helm
Yabonza
How Yabonza Works

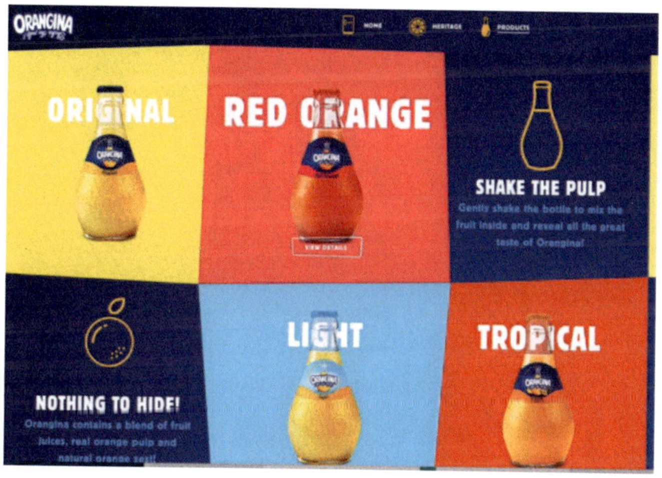
ORANGINA
HOME
HERITAGE
PRODUCTS
ORIGINAL
RED ORANGE
SHAKE THE PULP
Gently shake the bottle to mix the fruit inside and reveal all the great taste of Orangina!
NOTHING TO HIDE!
LIGHT
TROPICAL

INTRODUCING
AIR SHOP

Ivy Lane restaurant in NYC is a good example of how buttons should be used on a website. They are consistent, easy to read, appropriately sized by importance, labeled by action, prominently placed, and have a blue hover col

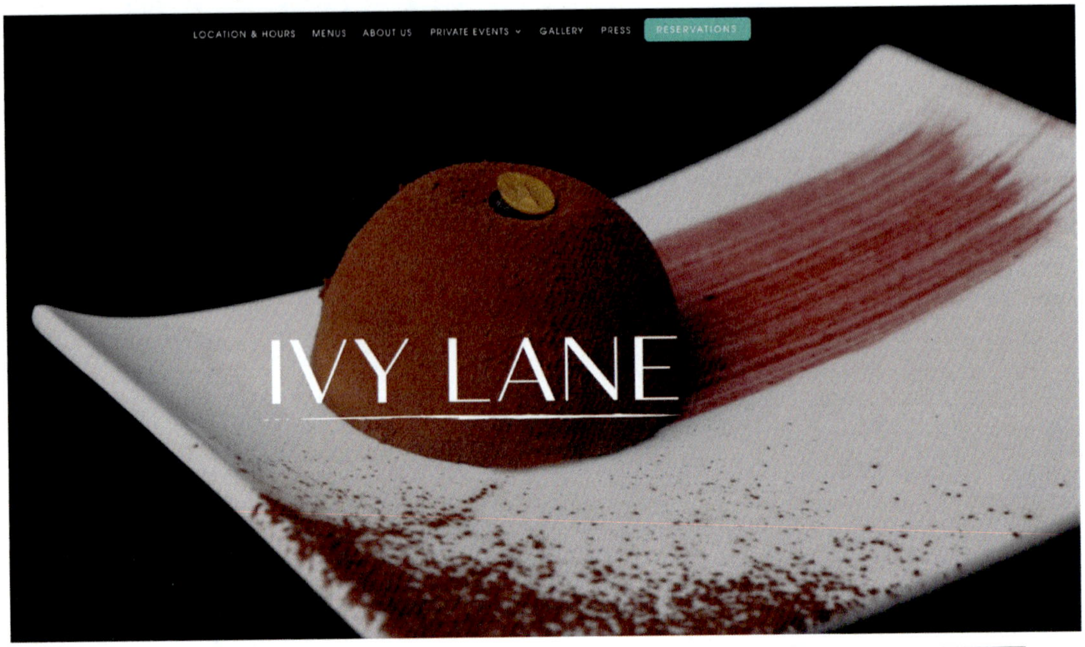

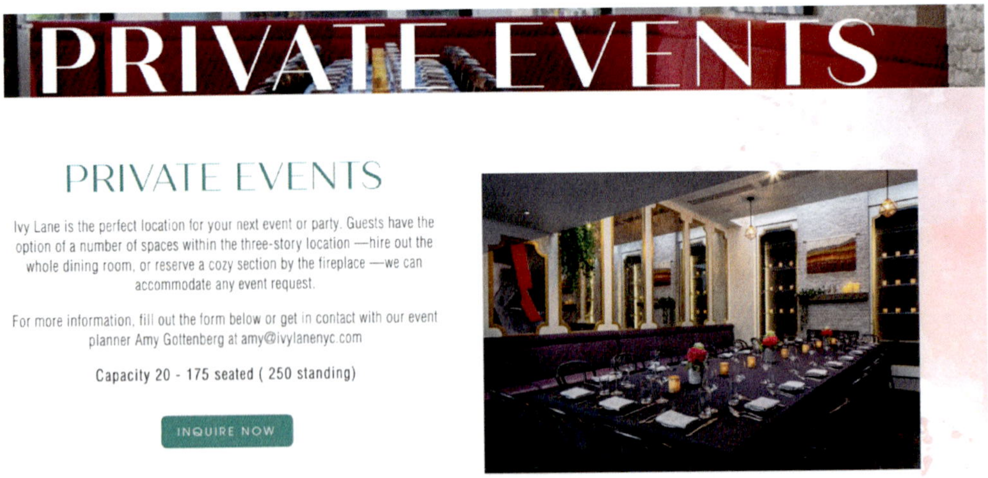

SOCIAL MEDIA

"Eventually everything connects - people, ideas, objects."
–Charles Eames

Social media is an internet platform that links people with other people who share similar interests. More than 3 billion people in the world use social networks. The most popular are:

Facebook is the top social network on the web. Every business should have a Facebook page.

Twitter is a real-time social network where news breaks first. Its unfiltered messages are limited to 280 characters. Content must be interesting.

LinkedIn is a career-oriented social network for professionals. You can join industry-specific groups to share information and advance your brand.

YouTube is the second largest search engine (Google is #1) and is packed with video content on every imaginable topic. You can also upload videos.

Instagram is a social network used for sharing photos and videos. Anyone with a smartphone can share pictures of products and services.

Pinterest uses visual content both in social networking and as a search vehicle. It uses a pinboard platform to showcase images separated into categories. Good for niche businesses.

Tumblr is a content sharing social blogging platform used by teens and young adults. Users can follow, comment, and create blogs on a variety of topics.

Snapchat is a mobile-based social networking app that allows photos or short videos to be sent as a message (a snap). Snaps automatically disappear 24 hours after viewing.

Reddit is a social network that discusses topics and shares photos, videos, and links. Information is displayed and voted upon. The ones that receive the most positive votes get on the first page.

Flickr is Yahoo's most popular photo-sharing network. You can upload over 1,000 GB of free photos, create albums, and share your photos.

Social media is an extension of your website. It can increase your marketing efforts to promote your brand. Use it to push people to your website where you can sell your products and services. It will:

- increase your visibility.
- humanize your business by connecting with followers.
- provide a way to interact directly with customers.
- provide incoming links to your website.
- increase your ranking in search results.

Website builders make it easy to set up social media links. Social media is free, but you will have to commit to making it work.

Tips:

1. Include the social media button links on your header or footer to ensure that the viewer can click on them wherever they are on your website.

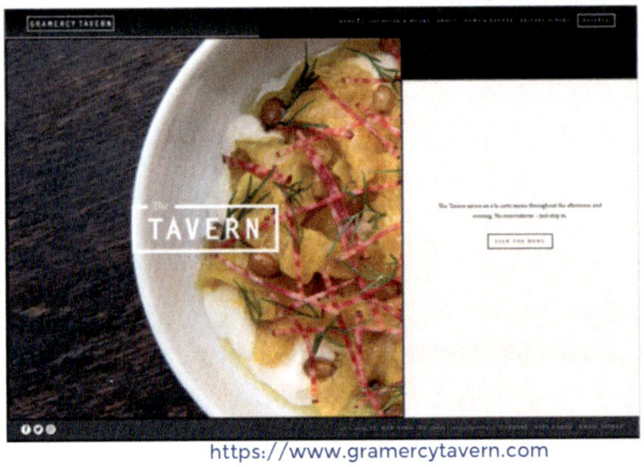

https://www.gramercytavern.com

https://www.onceuponatimein1969.com

2. Keep it simple and choose social media sites that appeal to your target audience. Focus your attention on one platform to start. You can add more later; 2-3 are enough.

3. Set up business pages on social media. Do not link to your personal pages.

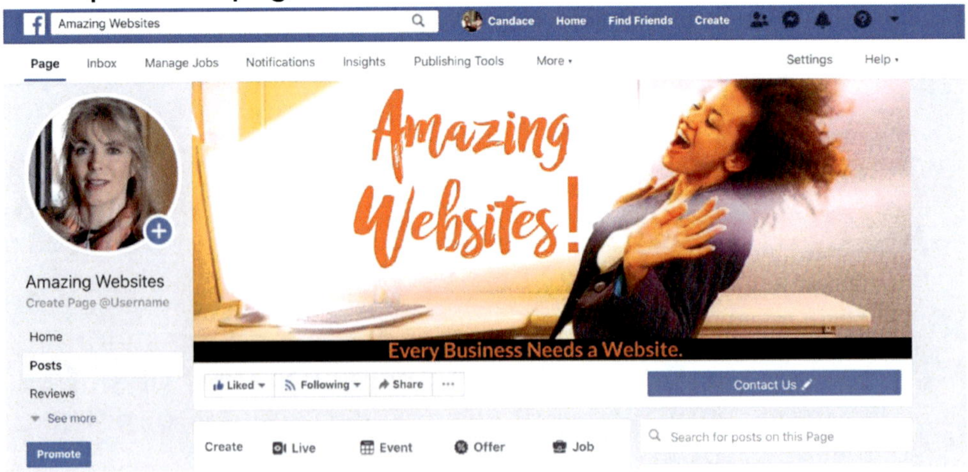

4. Only use the social media networks that you actively manage. Linking to inactive sites makes you look unprofessional.

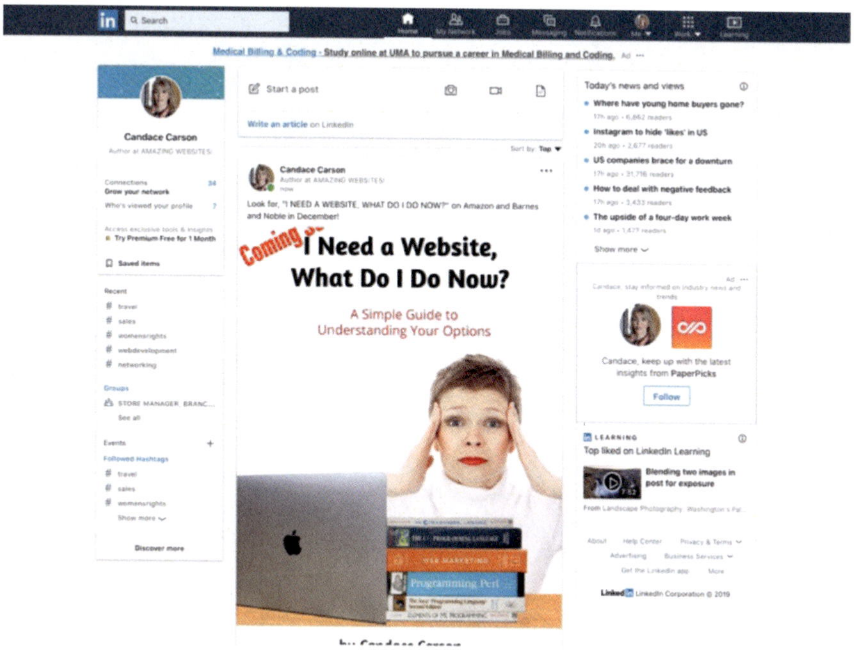

5. Use social media to share information about your business. Make connections by listening and responding to customer comments, even if they are negative. You might not be able to change the mind of the writer of the negative review, but those who read your response will see you as proactive. You care.

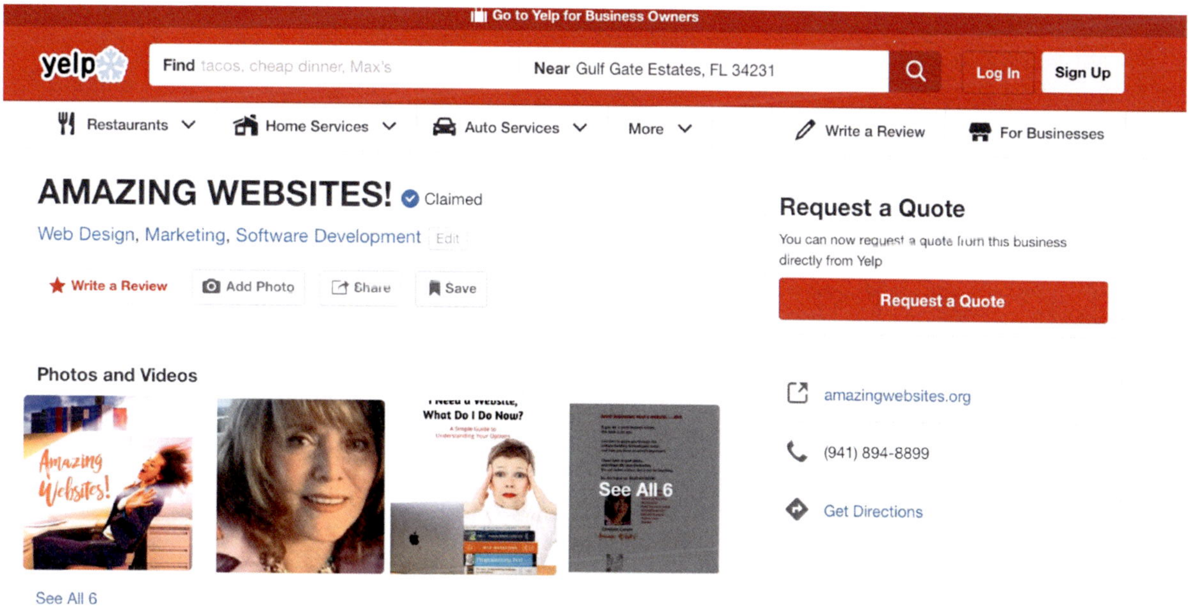

6. Write a blog or a newsletter (or both!). You can use it on your website, post it to your social media site, and then link it back to your website using a CTA button at the bottom. Win, Win.

Your Website Sucks

June 19, 2019 | Candace Carson

You know it does--it has sucked for over a year. You keep telling yourself that it is "good enough". It is not. I sucks....and everyone knows it does.

Perhaps you don't want to spend the money, but you are losing far more in sales than you would ever spend on a good website. Your reputation is at risk, too.

Did you get a discount price on your website? If it's too good to be true—usually it is. You got what you paid for—admit it. It sucks.

Maybe you are one of the thousands that believed a DIY website company who advertised that you could set up a website in one hour. You know how that worked out—you haven't even completed your home page and it's been 6 months.

Maybe you had a reputable website 3 years ago—but technology has changed—and left you behind. Your website is slow and the design is outdated. You have little pictures and lots of verbiage that no one reads. Face it—it is boring. The colors are boring. The pictures are boring. You have done nothing to upgrade it. It has just been sitting there. You have been busy, but don't think no one has noticed. Most people are internet savvy –they know it is old --"behind the times" and out-of-date—that's how they see your business, too.

Is your website interactive? If it isn't, it sucks. It is not a brochure for goodness sakes---it should communicate in real time. Is anyone subscribing to your newsletters or commenting on your blogs---oh, you don't have those?—you should. Does your site have movement? It is mobile optimized? It better be because 90% of consumers use smartphones.

Is is fun?-- it should be fun—like you used to be.

The internet is essential. It has replaced brick and mortar and changed consumer dynamics. You've got to get in the game or die-on-the-vine. If you have a business—any business—you need a good, well designed website. Your success depends on it.

In 2019, a website is EVERYTHING.

https://www.amazingwebsites.org/single-post/2019/06/19/Your-Website-Sucks

7. Keep your social media pages up to date. This is the hardest part. You are busy.

8. It takes time and energy to see the positive results that social media platforms can offer. Schedule 15-30 minutes every day for the first month to develop a foundation. It will take months, but don't give up.

EMAIL

A professional email address gives credibility to your business and is vital in ensuring your target audience can connect with you.

Use your business or domain name in the address to convey professionalism, brand awareness, and consistency. People are more likely to open newsletters if they recognize your business name.

The format is:
your first name + @ your business name and extension

candace@AmazingWebsites.org

Using your first name promotes familiarity. Using use your first initial and last name is more business-like.

ccarson@AmazingWebsites.org

All website builder platforms offer email hosting. It is easy to set up, free of advertising, and cost a few dollars a month. Prices range from $3 to $8 a month.

Keeping your email and website hosting together will work for most small businesses. Growing businesses and large companies should have a separate web hosting site for their emails.

If you prefer to use a separate email hosting solution, the ones listed below are the most popular. They range in price and are billed annually.

bluehost migadu ZOHO Yandex

If security is a priority these companies have built-in security for user protection.

ProtonMail Hushmail Mailfence COUNTERMAIL

For easy access, store all your email accounts on Gmail. You can go to one place to access all your emails, personal and business. It is free and simple to set up.

WEB ACCESSIBILITY

Web Accessibility is the process of designing and developing websites so that people with disabilities can use them. Make sure your CMS (Content Management System or Website Builder) incorporates accessibility in its platform.

Accessibility is not difficult to implement and will ensure everyone can use your website. It will help with your SEO ranking, as well.

Assistive technologies browse the internet to accommodate a variety of special needs. The Web Accessibility Initiative has been working since 1997 to help improve online accessibility. The guidelines outline the steps needed to make sites more user-friendly.

https://www.w3.org/WAI/standards-guidelines/wcag/

WordPress focuses on website accessibility.

https://make.wordpress.org/accessibility/handbook/best-practices/

All good website builders address Accessibility issues.

TEN WAYS TO MAKE YOUR WEBSITE ACCESSIBLE
from Ellice at DreamHost.com

1. Keyboard-Friendly - Webpages that work without the use of a mouse. Common keystrokes for interaction:

Navigate forward	Tab
Navigate backward	Shift + Tab
Link	Enter
Button	Enter or Spacebar
Checkbox	Spacebar
Dropdown menu	Up or Down arrows
Menu Bar	Tab, Enter Scroll
Up or Down arrows.	

See more at: https://webaim.org/techniques/keyboard/

2. Content is Accessible - Usually, this is not a problem. Scanners read text. Do not put text in images because it is not readable.

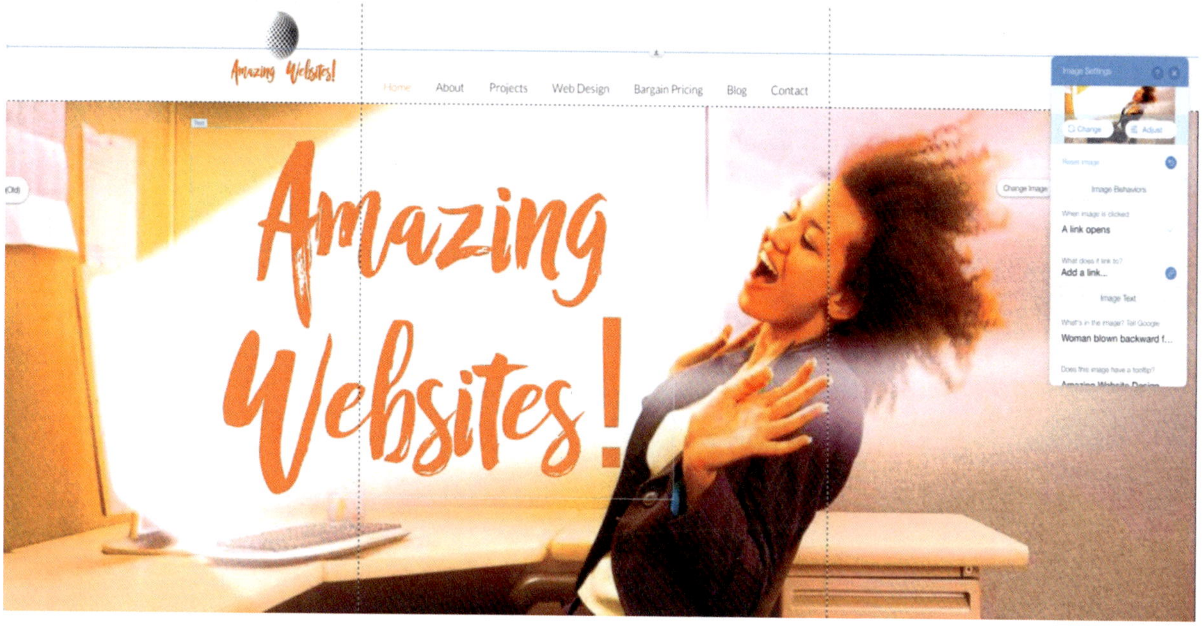

3. Add Alt Text to all Images - Website platforms allow for descriptive text to be added to images.

4. Color Choices - People perceive color differently. Use contrast to make text color legible against the background. (Refer to page 80.)

5. Header Structure - Use appropriate sizes for titles (the largest), subtitles (the second largest), text (the third largest), and image descriptions (the smallest).

6. Form Accessibility -Choose a form design where all areas are clearly labeled and easy to read.

7. Keep Tables Simple

8. Resizable Text - Text should adjust to fit on all devices.

9. Avoid Automatic Media and Navigation because stopping a video or music can be difficult when using a screen reader.

10. Create Accessible Content - Images should have descriptive information and acronyms should be spelled out (ex: SEO-Search Engine Optimization).

You can test your website accessibility at:
https://www.webaccessibility.com/results

"Design is not just what it looks like and feels like. Design is how it works." –**Steve Jobs**

CHAPTER 14

WHAT MAKES A GOOD WEBSITE-PART III

Behind the Curtain.

WEB DESIGN AND WEB DEVELOPMENT

WEB DESIGN
Web Design is concerned with how a website looks and how customers interact with it. This is also called the front-end part of the website. A well-designed website looks great, is user-friendly, and reflects the personality of the owner.

WEB DEVELOPMENT
Web Development is concerned with the coding and programming for all that you see online. This is called the back-end part of the website. Coding and programming make a website function.

All Drag-and-Drop website builders take care of the coding and programming so you can focus your energies on design.

Once the design and the development of your website are complete, you need to focus on getting traffic to your site.

SEO – SEARCH ENGINE OPTIMIZATION

"Google only loves you when everyone else loves you first." —Wendy Piersall

Every second, 40,000 people search for something on Google. Search Engine Optimization is how those searchers can find you. Understanding what type of information people are searching online, the answers they are seeking, and the words they are using allows a connection that increases traffic to your website.

SEO should be an integral part of your website plan, especially if you are in E-commerce.

Developing an SEO strategy requires time and patience. Before you proceed, consider:

- Is your business reliant on online sales?
- What rewards can be gained by increased web traffic?
- How much time and money do you want to invest?

Getting a new website to show up in search results is difficult. It gets easier once you raise your SEO ranking and get more traffic to your website. It's a process.

All website builder platforms have a basic SEO structure. They will get you started but you will need more than what they offer to rank high.

Professional SEO experts offer an invaluable service, but they are costly. If you have an E-commerce site, you should hire an expert to get you started. Once your SEO ranking is high, they will be needed less.

My advice will increase your chances of being found online, but it will only scratch the surface. It will augment the SEO you have with your website builder. I will explain the basics, offer tips, and suggest the best places to look for further information.

CRAWLING, INDEXING, AND RANKING

Search engines, like Google, discover and catalog content on the internet by crawling, indexing, and ranking data by how well it matches search requests.

Crawling - Google sends out a team of robots called Googlebots onto the internet to find new and updated content. They fetch the web page and follow the links to other web pages.

Indexing -New content fetched by the Googlebots is stored in a database called an index.

SEO Ranking - When content from the index is retrieved to match a query, the website ranking increases. The more matches, the higher the ranking.

Note: If you do not update your web content, Googlebots will not crawl your website and your SEO ranking will drop. They are searching for new content.

SERP - Search Engine Results Page - The page of results that Google provides when users type in a search phrase (query).

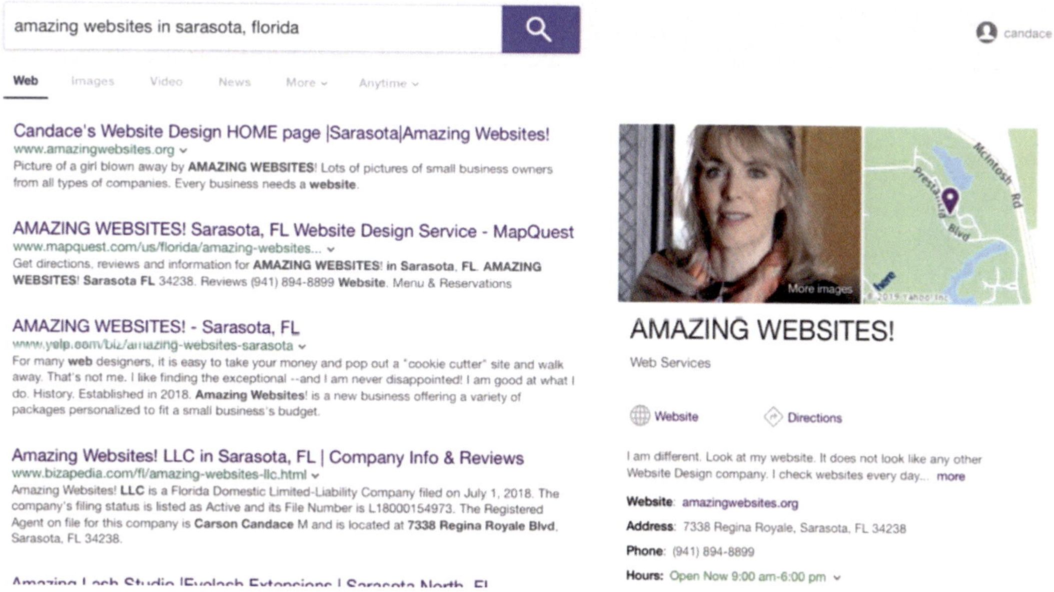

You can increase your SERP ranking by paying for GoogleAds. Your website will be listed higher on the page, but it can be expensive.

KEYWORDS

Keywords are the words that users type into the search box to find information. What kinds of words would users type when looking for your products or services? Use those words on your website. Googlebots will crawl, fetch, index, and match those words to the search.

Appeal to your target audience. They are the ones looking for you.

Who are they?
What information are they looking for?
When are they searching?
Where are they?
Why are they searching?
How do they search?

What words will you use in your content to fulfill their search?

Choosing Keywords

There are several free Keyword Suggestion tools online.

1. Moz Keyword Explorer

https://analytics.moz.com/pro/keyword-explorer/keyword/suggestions?locale=en-US

You must set up a free account. Type in the name of your product or service and click on the search icon. I used "website design".

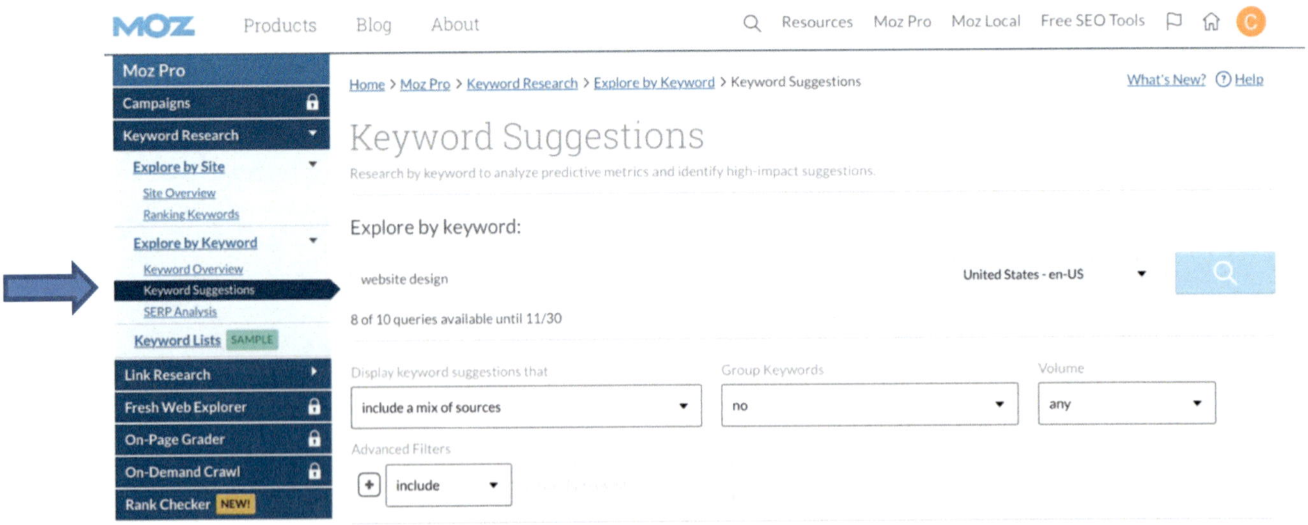

Website design had 1000 keywords ranked by relevancy. 5 (best) - 1 (worst).

All Keyword Suggestions

☐	Keyword	Relevancy
☐	website design	●●●●●
☐	website design software	●●●●●
☐	website design company	●●●●●
☐	website design templates	●●●●●
☐	website design ideas	●●●●●
☐	website design services	●●●●●
☐	website design cost	●●●●●
☐	website designers	●●●●●

2. Answer the Public

https://answerthepublic.com

You don't need an account unless you opt to "Go Pro." I typed in "website design" and clicked GET QUESTIONS.

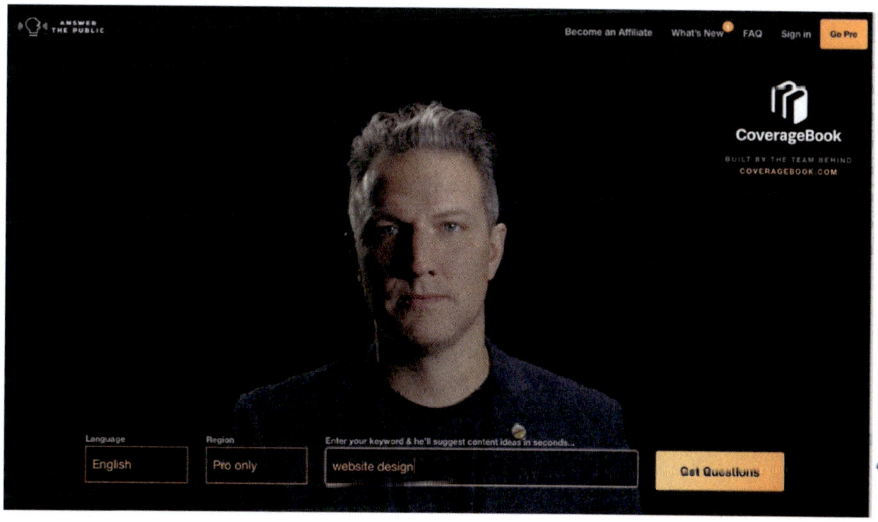

Results can be viewed in two formats: Visualization

and Data:

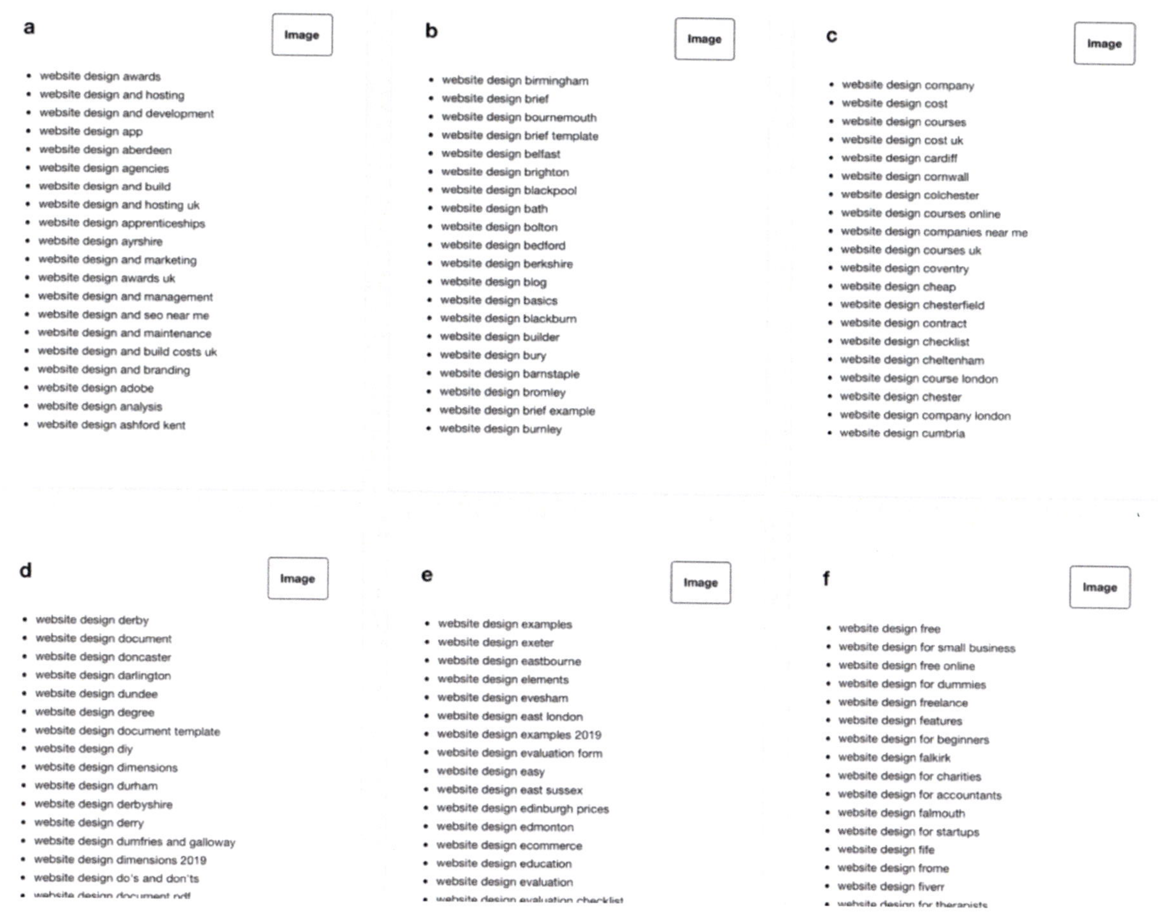

3. SpyFu

https://www.spyfu.com/?alt=1

SpyFu provides your competitor's keyword choices. Type into the website and click the search icon. Basic information is free.

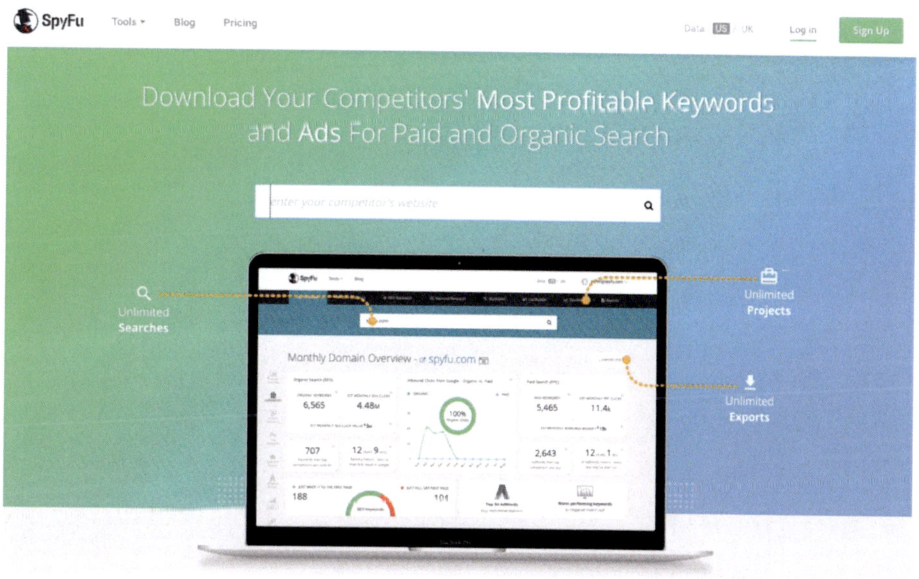

4. Keyword Tool

https://keywordtool.io

Free alternative to Google's Keyword Tool (which is not free).

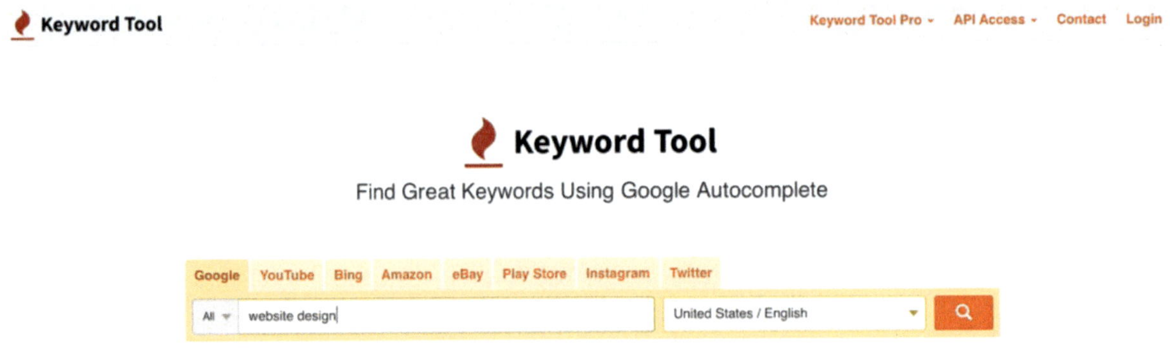

Once you have keywords, you want to use them on each page of your website. Create content that features your keywords naturally. Avoid needless repetition. Google calls that "keyword stuffing" and will penalize you for it.

IMAGE OPTIMIZATION

Image Optimization is important in SEO performance by improving website speed. Images occupy a significant amount of space and are the biggest culprits of slow web pages. The best way to solve the problem is to compress your images. We covered image optimization on page 121.

META TAGS

Meta Tags are snippets of text in a web page source code that describe a page's content. They are only visible to search engines and tell them what the page is about. Use keywords in your meta tags.

Website builders create meta tags for each page. You can easily add meta tags to your web page. Below is an example using Wix.com.

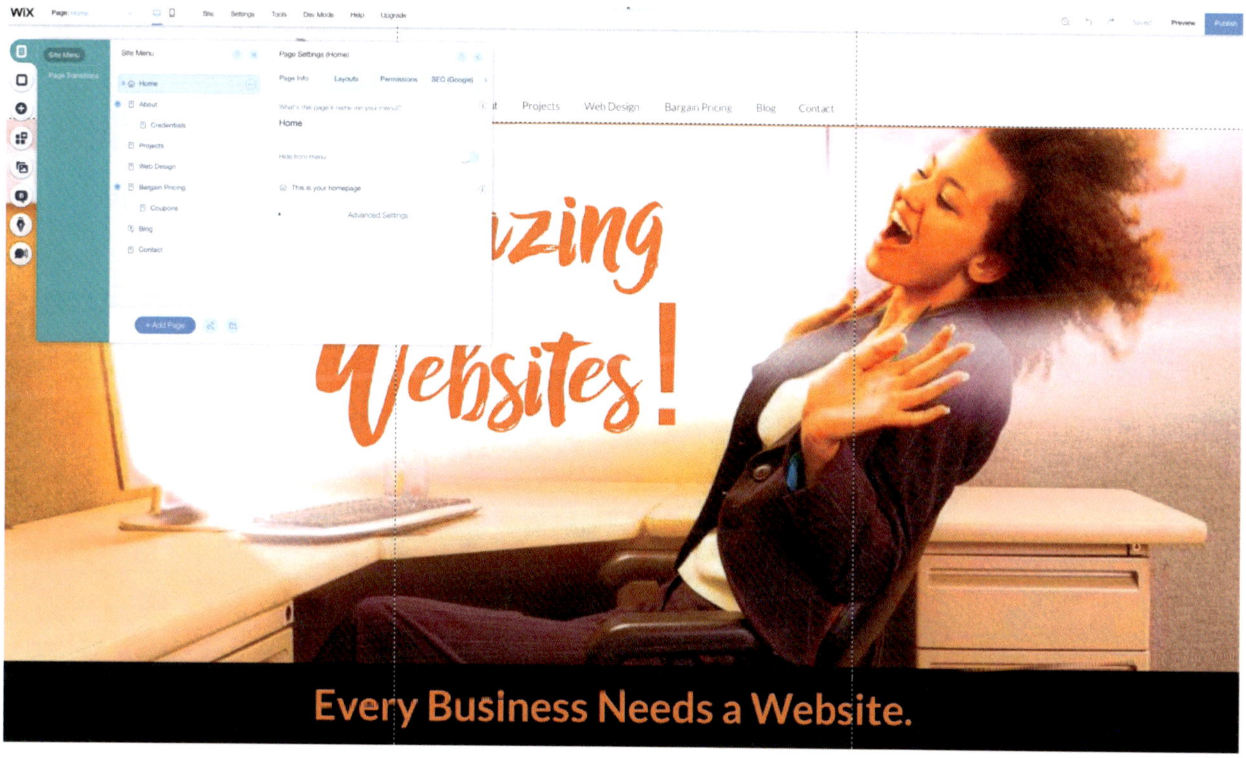

ALT TEXT

Alt text is a brief, written description embedded in an image. Search engines can't see images, but they can read the description. Describe your image to boost your SEO.

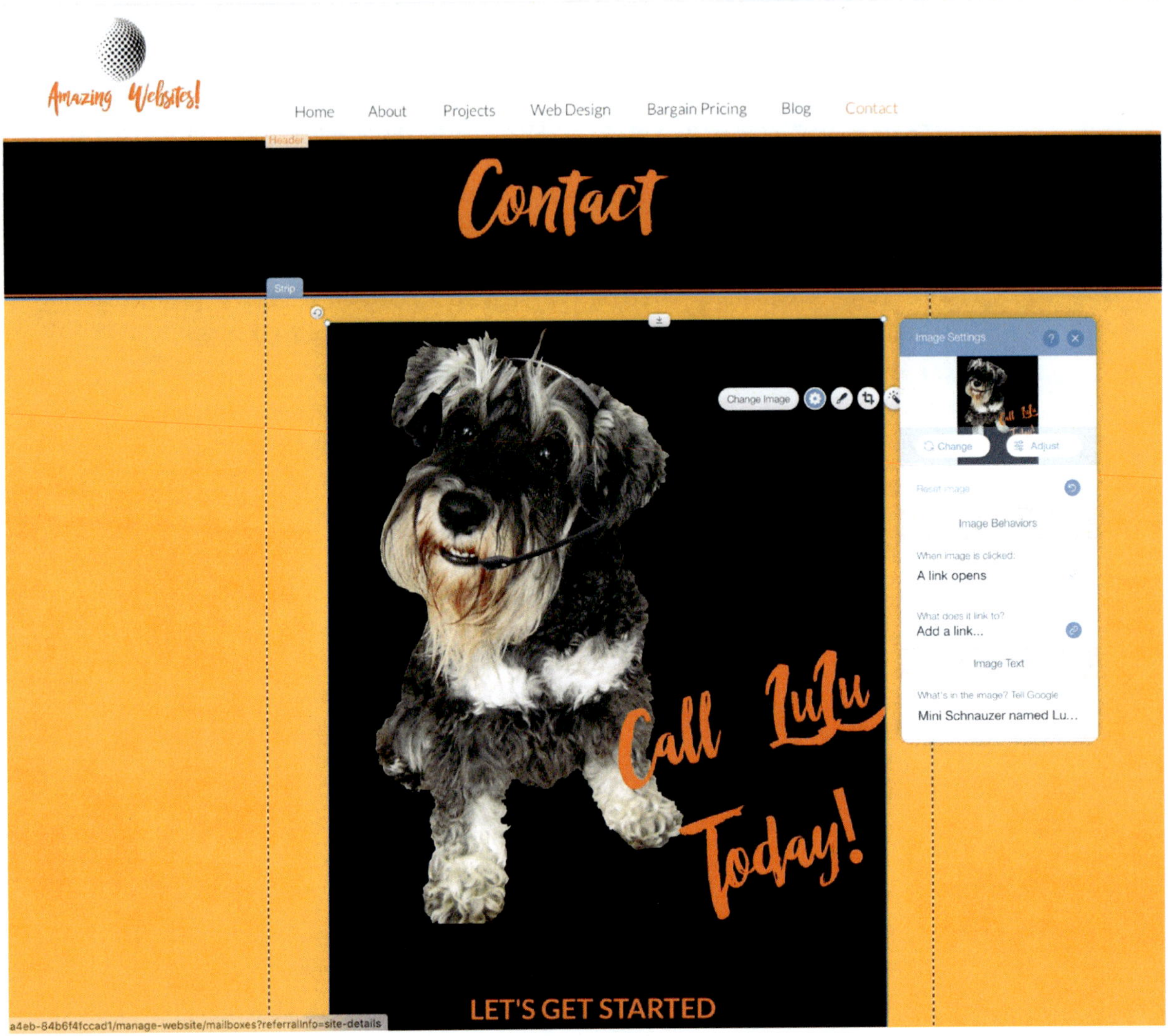

SEO is addressed by all website builder platforms. You can add to the basic framework. If you are in E-commerce and rely on internet sales, hire an SEO specialist to improve your online presence. Once you have a solid framework set up and have been online for a few months, you will see your ranking increase. It takes time.

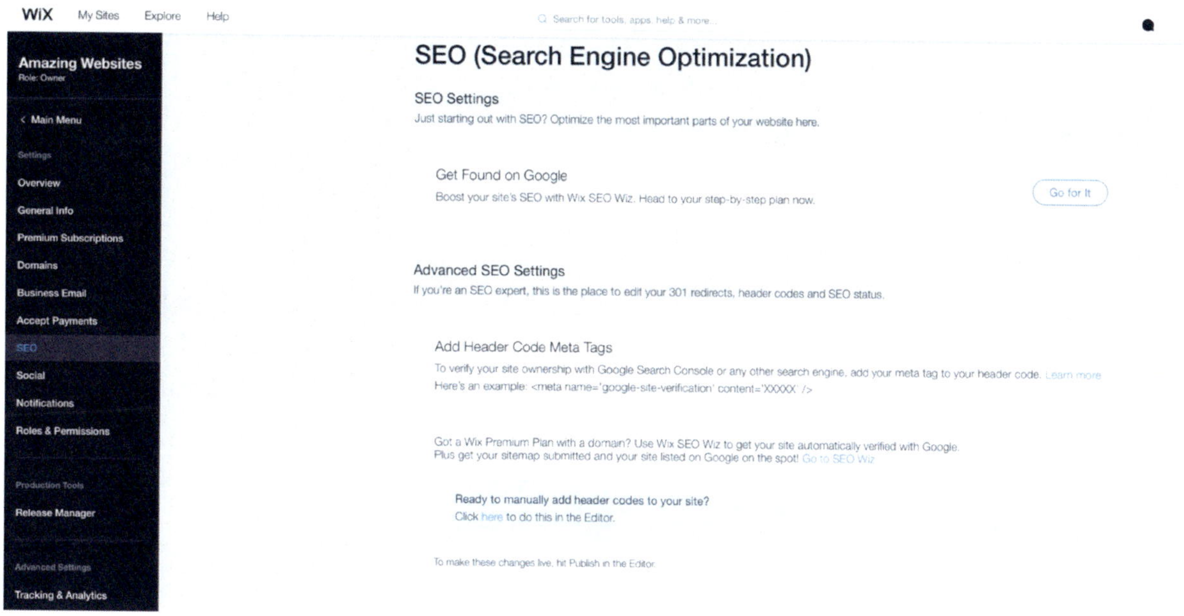

GOOGLE ANALYTICS

Google Analytics measures the success of your website. It is the most widely used website analytics service on the web. You can track performance and adjust problem areas.

Set up a free account using your gmail account.

https://analytics.google.com

"I'm a perfectionist, so I always feel there's room for improvement."
–Ludacris

CHAPTER 15

ENHANCEMENTS TO WEBSITE DESIGN

APPS

Website Applications (Apps) are computer software programs that add a variety of functions to websites. They can be contact forms, sliders, blogs, site search, events, bookings, videos, etc.

All website builders custom build apps or offer apps that are built by third-party developers. Some are free and some are paid.

Examples:

WIX has hundreds of easy to install apps.

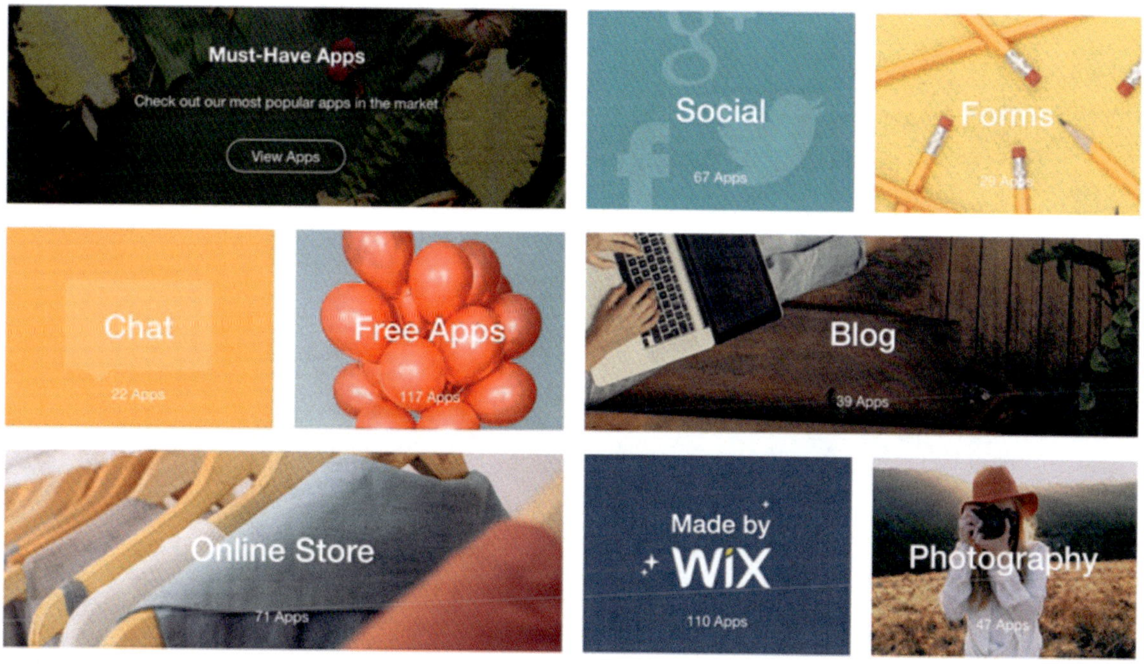

Weebly offers several hundred apps.

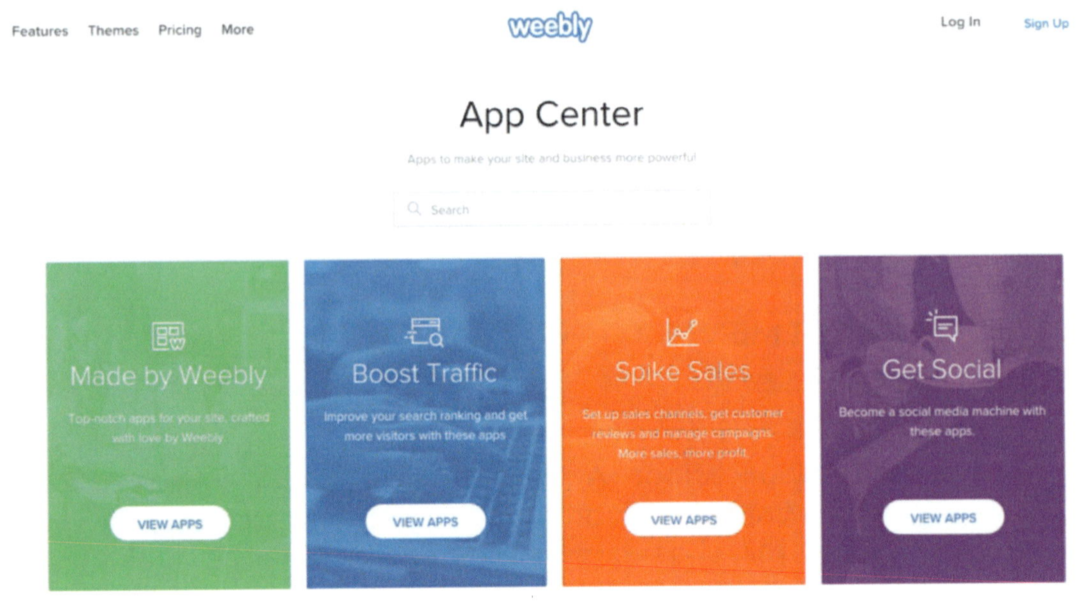

WordPress apps are called "plug-ins." There are over 50,000 from which to choose.

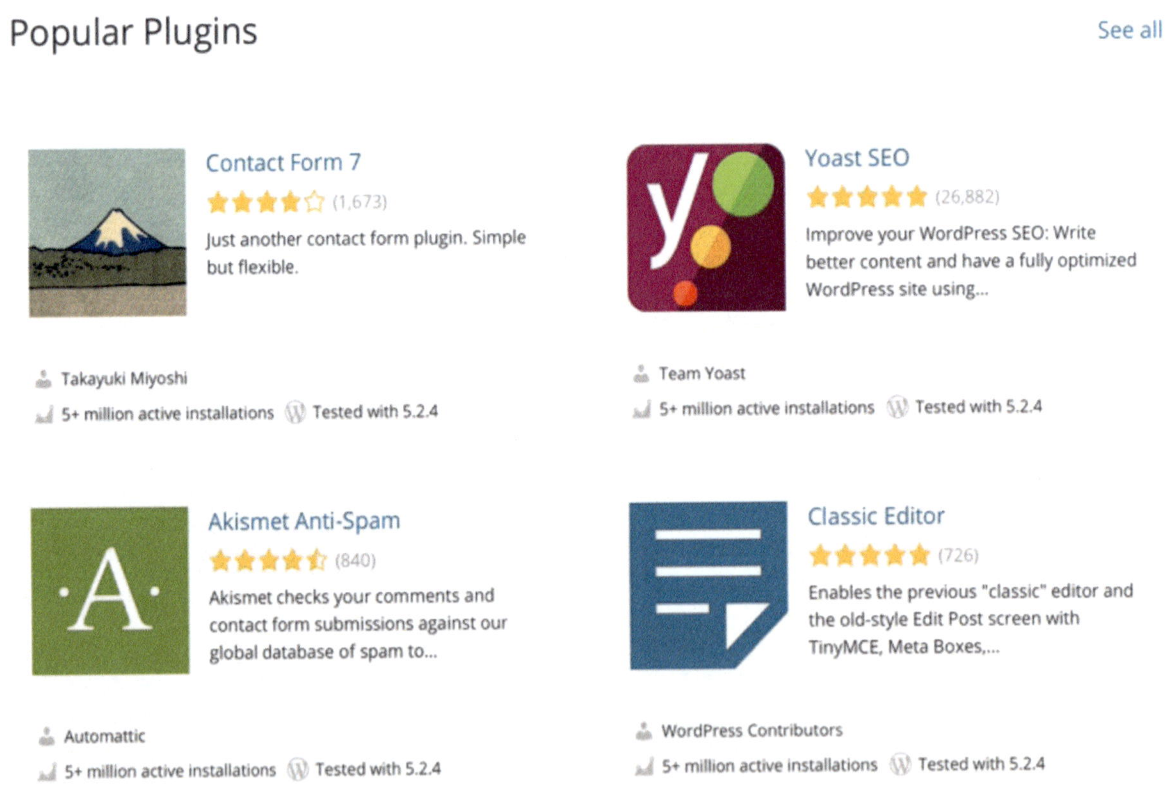

FAVICON

A favicon ("favorites icon") is a 16 x 16 pixel icon displayed before the URL in a web browser.

Favicons are free and easy to design. All website builders offer favicon creation.

Examples:

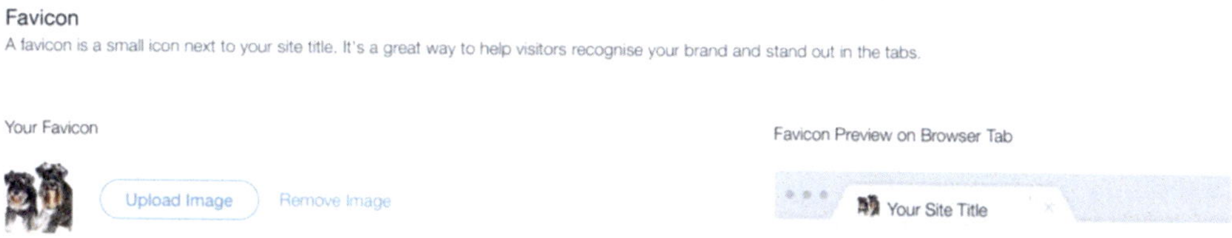

- Wix explains favicons in their general information section.

- WordPress allows creation of favicons:

  Administrative Screen>Appearance> Customize>Site Identity>Site Icon

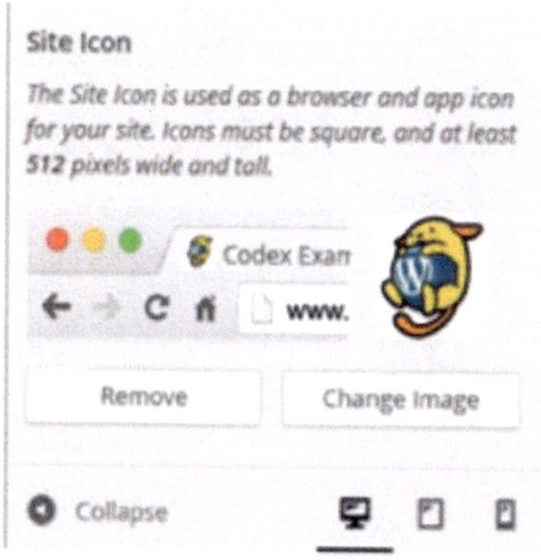

- SquareSpace has a video explaining how to add a favicon.

- Weebly gives step-by-step instructions.

You can also create a favicon through free sites like Favicon Generator.

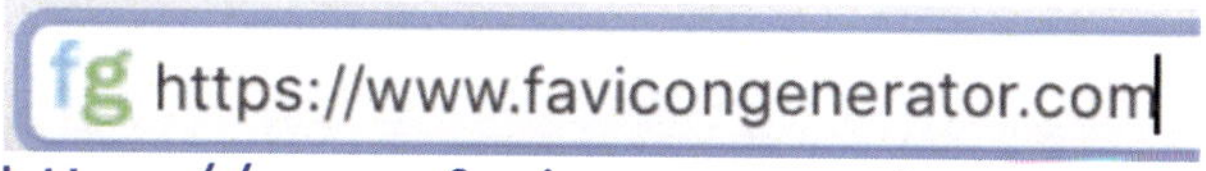

https://www.favicongenerator.com

BLOGS

A blog is an online news column. It keeps your website current and gives potential customers a reason to return. Blogs help build brand values and improve traffic to your website. A blog is today's newsletter.

You do not need to be a great writer to write a successful blog. People read website blogs to get information about what you do and what you offer. Content should be interesting and relevant to your target audience. The best blogs are informal and written in a conversational style. Write about what you know.

<u>How to Start a Blog:</u>

1. Know your target audience and speak to them.
2. Make a list of topics useful to your target audience.
3. Write in your natural voice, as if you were talking with your customers.
4. Post a blog twice a week.

<u>Why You Should Have a Blog:</u>

- Search engines love content and blogs are informative content.
- Writing a blog will help your SEO ranking.
- It's a way to promote your products and services.
- It connects with your target audience.
- Linking blogs to your social media platforms will link back to your website. Creating backlinks is good for your SEO ranking.
- Sharing your blog is another opportunity for potential customers to find your website.
- Writing a blog establishes you as an authority.

All website builders make it easy to add a blog. Designate a page in your menu for blogs and provide internal links on your home page directed to the most current blogs. Google will love it!

EMAIL SUBSCRIPTION

Email Subscription is a Call-To-Action (CTA) that allows visitors to receive updates via email. It is a great way to grow your mailing list and keep your customers informed about sales, coupons, events, etc.

All website builders have Email Subscription forms that make it easy for users to use. Put it on the bottom of the Home page.

"Another flaw in the human character is that everybody wants to build and nobody wants to do maintenance."
—**Kurt Vonnegut**

CHAPTER 16

WEBSITE MAINTENANCE

"Digital design is like painting, except the paint never dries."
–**Neville Brody**

The hard part is over, but you are never finished. You cannot put your website online and then forget about it. It will "die on the vine" without care.

Regular maintenance is critical to the function of your website. It will help attract, educate, and expand your customer base.

WHY WEBSITE MAINTENANCE IS IMPORTANT

Keeping your website current and relevant ensures traffic growth and strengthens your SEO and Google rankings. Google ignores websites that are not updated.

SEO (Search Engine Optimization)

You need customers and SEO drives them to your website. Updates, blogs, new content, and new keywords keep Google interested.

Customer Interaction

Interact with customers and potential customers with updated information and Call-to-Actions. Keep them engaged. If your website is stale, no one will revisit. Why bother?

Security
Many website builder platforms include built-in maintenance functions that make maintenance easier. Make sure you are installing software updates.

Professionalism
Customers relate to businesses that are current. If you don't update, you look lazy.

WHAT NEEDS UPDATING

You can update anything, anywhere on your website. Some areas require more maintenance than others.

Blogs
Your latest blogs should be within the last month.

Home Page
Refresh sliders with new images. Add new pictures, information, links.

About Page
People are curious about you and your staff. Add new pictures, update information.

Product/Services
New products and services. Add pictures and new text, FAQ, pricing updates, promotions, coupons, etc.

Links
Make sure all links work.

Social Media links
Make sure social media has current information about your products, services, and company updates.

Testimonials
When you make a customer happy, get a testimonial and post it.

ONLINE TESTING FOR YOUR WEBSITE

SEO, Performance, URL on Google Search Console
https://www.google.com/webmasters/#?modal_active=none

Make sure your website is mobile friendly:
https://search.google.com/test/mobile-friendly

Performance and Speed:
https://www.thinkwithgoogle.com/feature/testmysite/
https://developers.google.com/speed/pagespeed/insights/

Check for safe browsing: malware and phishing status:
https://transparencyreport.google.com/safe-browsing/search

Check the security of your website:
https://accounts.google.com

Google Analytics Test:
https://marketingplatform.google.com/about/analytics/

Check Readability:
https://app.readable.com/text/

Website Accessibility:
https://www.webaccessibility.com/results

Remember to optimize all images.
https://shortpixel.com
https://imagecompressor.com
https://compressjpeg.com
https://compressor.io/compress
https://www.iloveimg.com
https://imagecompressor.com

WEBSITE MAINTENANCE SCHEDULE

If you don't set up a schedule, you won't do it.

Weekly

1. Check your web pages to make sure they are loading.
2. Check your load speed. If slow, optimize your images.
   https://www.thinkwithgoogle.com/feature/testmysite/
   https://developers.google.com/speed/pagespeed/insights/
3. Add updates. (New Products, Sales, New Hires, Blogs)
4. Make sure your forms are operating.
5. Make sure your links are linking to the right places.
6. Check animated features like sliders, and videos.
7. Review emails.
8. Write one or more blog posts. Blogs keep your visitors interested and drive SEO traffic to your website with backlinks.
9. Check Google Analytics to see how you can improve.
   https://marketingplatform.google.com/about/analytics/
10. Check your website on a mobile device.
    https://search.google.com/test/mobile-friendly
11. Back-up your website. Website Hosting companies backup on their servers.

Monthly

1. Check the SEO guide on your website builder site to ensure you are doing all you can to improve your Google ranking.
2. Check Google Analytics to see your progress from the previous month.
   https://marketingplatform.google.com/about/analytics/
3. Review local search visibility with Google.
   Are you being found online?
4. Update blogs and social media connections.
5. Check for security updates.
   https://accounts.google.com
6. Check your competition.

Quarterly

1. Review your website design and structure. Do you need to add new features or pages? Check for new trends in design and technology.
2. Update content. Add text and new images.
3. Update Meta tags and descriptions.
4. Make sure all features work (popups, forms, buttons, and calls-to-action).
5. Test your website on all devices and browsers to see if it displays correctly–this is especially important for mobile devices.
6. Dump out-of-date information. (Expired sales coupons, etc.)
7. Review meta data and meta description tags.

Annually

1. Update names and email addresses on subscription lists.
2. Renew your domain name, website subscriptions, SSL, and email box.
3. Update your website design. New tools and apps are available every day. Be aware of the current trends. Looking outdated makes you seem inconsequential.
4. Make sure your copyright date on your footer is the current year.

Website maintenance is not rocket science, but it does require time. It is a good business practice to check your website every day, to monitor its success, do updates, and make changes that will generate interest.

Some business owners do not want to invest in the time to do website maintenance. Many companies will maintain your website. Costs vary widely. Small business costs range from $40-$1000 a month.

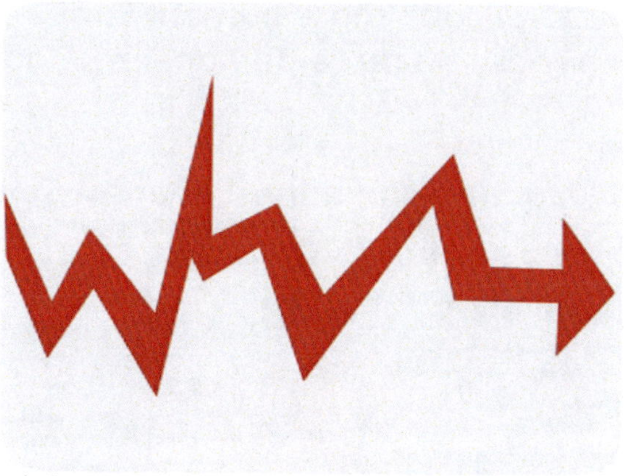

pixabay.com

"Trend currents are big-picture, unstoppable, inexorable forces that are shaping the world we live in." —**Steve Woodruff**

CHAPTER 17

TRENDS

Website technology is developing at a rapid pace. The 2020s will see many new trends and the exit of others.

<u>2020s TRENDS</u>

- PWA - Progress Web Apps
  Applications enhanced with modern web technologies. They will load quickly and continue to work when offline.

- VUI - Voice User Interface Optimization
  Siri, Alexa, and Google Assistant have lead the way. Voice search enablement will make up 50% of all web searches in 2020. Soon, voice assistants will be able to answer questions.

- Security
  Unsecure websites that start with *http://* are unsafe. Make sure your URL starts with *https://* which means that your website has an SSL Certificate and is secure.

- Mobile First
  60% of web traffic is mobile-based. Make sure your website is mobile-ready.

- Speed will be faster.
  Load time will be less than two seconds.

- Websites will look more human. Simple line drawings give a website a more personalized look.

- Design
  - Bold Structure and honest shapes. Simplicity rules.

https://soundboard.heihei.resn.co

  - Oversized Typography and Fullscreen Images.

https://studiovoila.com

  - Minimal Design - Fewer elements, fewer colors, fewer fonts. Web users scan. Make it easy for them by eliminating fluff.

https://vspicer.com

- Gradient color gives depth to flat design.

https://www.awwwards.com/sites/julien-renvoyes-portfolio

- Solid color blocks break up content.

wix

- White Space makes a website more spacial, clearer, less complicated.

https://store.google.com/us/product/pixelbook_go?hl=en-US

- Split screen content is uncluttered, with equal emphasis on each side.

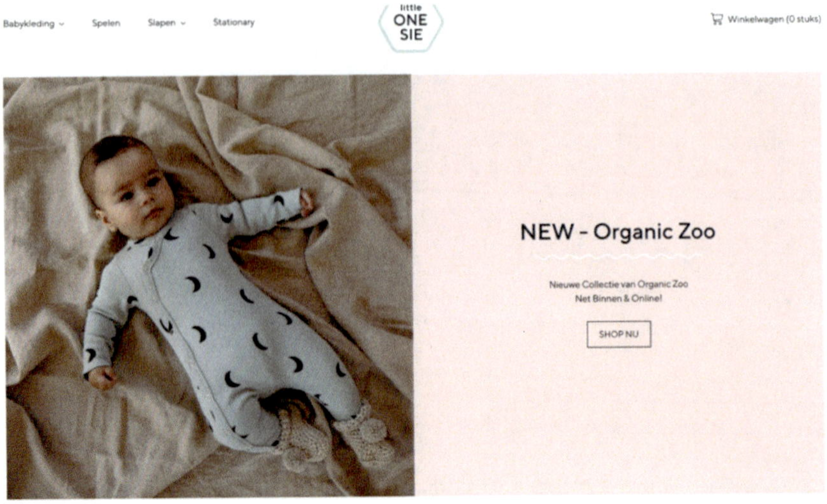

https://www.littleonesie.shop

- Overlapping layers can add depth to flat a screen.

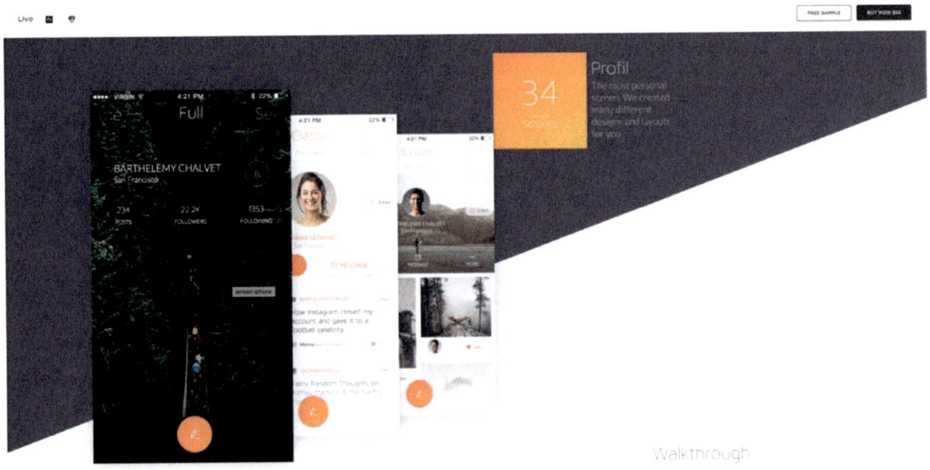

https://www.market-me.fr/Livo/

- Kinetic design uses videos, sliders, and animation.

https://dopper.com

- Asymmetric Layouts will be popular with personal websites. No longer is the grid format necessary.

Tread carefully. This type of structure can become cluttered.

https://bullyentertainment.com

<u>TRENDS THAT WILL BE OBSOLETE in 2020</u>

- Parallax Scrolling

  Parallax scrolling looks great but is not good in terms of user experience. It slows loading speeds. What was once "different" has become overused and bothersome.

- Flat/One Page Design

  One Page Design is too long. Too much information slows download speed. Users dislike scrolling down endlessly. It is easier to access pertinent information on separate pages.

- Complicated Typography

  The use of multiple fonts makes a website look cluttered. A clean, concise, uncomplicated type is the new norm.

- Overly Complicated Design

  Less is more. Make it easy. Don't clutter.

"Never trust a computer you can't throw out the window."
—**Steve Wozniak**

AFTERWORD

WHEN TO HIRE A FREELANCER

Small businesses need a website—duh.
You know it's true. You bought my book. It is important today and will be even more important in the future. An online presence is crucial for your business. Do you remember Blockbuster? How about Borders bookstore? Both ignored the internet.

You read my book and learned the basics, bought your domain name, selected a website builder, and paid the annual subscription fee.

You were assembling your website and then stopped. It's been weeks since you have done any work on your site. There are many reasons why you stopped.

- You just need help in one area.
- You aren't enjoying designing a website.
- You don't have the time.
- A friend or a relative offered to help and didn't.

Some of my readers will find website design easier than others. Some won't like it at all, but ***all*** of my readers will learn about website design and have a handy reference tool for future use.

Find a professional to finish your website. The information in my book will help you explain to a freelancer what kind of website you want for your business.

Get online. Now is the time.

ABOUT THE AUTHOR

I wanted to build a website and searched for information to guide me through the process. The books on website design and development were either too detailed or specific to one area or one platform.

The information I needed was spread all over the web. There are thousands of blogs and websites with information about website design and development. I feel like I have read them all!

Website builder platforms have eliminated the necessity of learning code and programming, thus making website creation accessible to everyone. They also offer generalized design concepts that can be applied to a variety of business types.

I did not want a website that looked like everyone else's. I wanted a custom look that reflected who I am and why my business is different.

"I Need a Website, What Do I Do Now?" is a simple guide to assist in producing innovative, well-designed websites for small businesses.

GLOSSARY

ABOVE-THE-FOLD
The screen area first seen by website visitors. It is under the menu bar and contains information to interest your viewer. All other information is obtained when scrolling downward.

ALGORITHMS
The process of retrieving and ordering stored information.

ALIGNMENT
How content is placed on a web page.

ALT TEXT
A brief description of an image.

APPLICATION
An "APP" is software that is installed on a computer.

ACCESSIBILITY
Making content accessible to people with disabilities.

BACKLINK
A link on another website that refers back to your website.

BACK-END TECH
A person who designs and develops programs that process data and perform tasks that the user doesn't see.

BANDWIDTH
The rate of speed that data is transferred.

BELOW-THE-FOLD
The area you see when you scroll down the web page. It supports Above-The-Fold content.

BLOG
An online column.

BOTS
Crawlers (Spiders) that search the internet for new content. Google's bots are called Googlebots.

BOUNCE RATE
The number of users that enter a website and leave after visiting one page. A bounce rate of 75% means that 75% of the visitors left without reading any other pages.

BRAND
A brand is the face of your company.

BROWSER
A software package or mobile app that displays web pages, graphics, and online content. Examples: Internet Explorer, Safari, Chrome.

CLOUD
Information stored online and borrowed and installed on a computer. Files can be saved in the cloud and accessed by different devices.

CMS
Content Management System is a platform that helps users generate, manage, and store content on websites.

CONTENT
Text, pictures, video, or anything you see on a web page.

CONVERSION RATE
The ratio of visits to conversions. Tallies how many website visitors are answering call-to-actions on a website.

COOKIE
Tokens that store small amounts of data on your computer when you visit a website. Example: shopping carts, personal preferences.

COPYRIGHT
Protection for published work that helps to prevent it from being used without prior authorization. A Copyright may be indicated by the word "Copyright" or a C surrounded by a circle (©). The Copyright might also be followed by the date of when the work was published.

CRAWL
The process of looking for new or updated web information.
Google crawls the web looking for new pages, retrieves the information, and then indexes it.

CRAWLER
Automated software that crawls (fetches) pages from the web and indexes them.

CREATIVE COMMONS
A nonprofit organization that specifies which rights of creative work are reserved and which are waived.

CTA
A Call-to-Action prompts the user to take a specific action.

CURSOR
An object that is used to point, click, drag, and drop an item.

DOMAIN NAME
A website address. How people find you on the web and remember you. A link between the real and virtual world.

DOMAIN REGISTRAR
Where your domain name is stored.

DOWNLOAD
Transferring information on the internet to your computer. *Examples*: music, files, photos.

DPI
Dot-per-inch is a measurement of resolution indicating how many ink dots the printer can place in one square inch. The higher the DPI, the sharper the image. 72 DPI is sufficient for websites.

DRAG AND DROP
The action of selecting content and moving it to another space.

DRIVER
Software that controls the input and output of a device.

DROP-DOWN MENU
A style of website navigation used when the user places the mouse over a menu item, and another menu is exposed. Search engines have difficulty reading the links in the menu, but if constructed properly, these issues can be resolved.

E-COMMERCE
Electronic Commerce is the transaction of selling and buying online. *Examples:* Amazon, eBay, Paypal.

E-MAIL
Electronic Mail is the sending/receiving of messages on computers.

EMBEDDED COMMAND
Invisible commands that enable additional functions.

EXTERNAL LINKS
Links between a website and another web page outside the website. They provide supportive information.

FAVICON
A 16px by 16px icon in the URL address on the web browser created by using an icon generator such as favicon.cc

FILE EXTENSION
The ending of a file that identifies the type of file. *Example*: .jpg

FIREWALL
A barrier to protect computers from hackers and viruses.

FLASH DRIVE
A device that is used to store data transferred from a computer. Known as a pen drive or thumb drive.

FONT
A graphical representation of text that may include a different typeface, size, weight, color, or design.

FOOTER
The area at the bottom of a web page that contains information.

FRESHNESS
Update, update and update some more. Add new pages, new information. Keep your website current.

GFX
Abbreviation for graphics.

GOOGLE ANALYTICS
A tool that gives insight into how people are engaging with a website.

GOOGLE SEARCH CONSOLE
A free program provided by Google that allows website owners to access website performance.

GOOGLEBOT
The name of Google's crawler. Googlebots crawl the web constantly.

GUI
Graphical User Interface pronounced "Gooey". The interactive visual pieces for computer software. The pieces change color, size, or visibility when the user interacts with them. (icons, buttons, etc.)

HARD DRIVE
Where data is stored.

HARDWARE
Computer equipment: the computer, monitor, keyboards, and mouse.

HEADER
The area at the top of a web page that contains the logo or company name and the navigation menu.

HERO
The main focal point in a website.

HOME PAGE
The hub of your website which links to the other pages.

HTML
Hypertext Markup Language is the programming language of web pages.

HTTP
Hypertext Transfer Protocol is the data communication standard of web pages. It's how you find web documents.

HTTPS
Hypertext Transfer Protocol Secure indicates that the web page has a layer of encryption to make it more secure.

IMAGE OPTIMIZATION
When the code of an image is altered so it uses less memory.

INDEX
Google fetches a web page, reads the content, and stores it the index. Once indexed, a web page can be displayed as a result of an inquiry.

INTERNAL LINK
Links between pages on the same website.

INTERNET
Inter + networks. A network infrastructure linked by technology.

ISP
Internet Service Provider is a company that provides services to access the internet. *Examples*: Comcast, Verizon.

KEYBOARD
A device used to type on to input data into a computer.

KEYWORD
Search words and phrases used in website content to help users find information. Good keywords help SEO.

KEYWORD STUFFING
Overuse of keywords in the content.

LANDING PAGE
The first web page a visitor visits when entering a website.

LAYOUT
The appearance of a webpage designed to make it more appealing.

LINK
A hyperlink is what connects web pages to other web pages.

MALWARE
Malicious software designed to damage your computer.

MEGA DROP DOWN MENU
Menus containing all the categories on one plane. Good for sites with large category lists or businesses with a lot of services.

MENU
Sections of the website (Categories) that are links to other pages on the website. (ex: About/Pricing/Blog/Contact)

META TAG
Snippets of text in a web page source code describing the page's content.

MODEM
A Modulator-Demodulator connects you to the internet.

MONITOR
A device that displays images from a computer.

MOUSE
A device used to move a cursor on the computer screen.

NAVIGATION
Links that help users go to web pages.

OS
Operating System manages the hardware and system resources. Examples: Windows, Mac OSX, Android, iOS.

PHISHING
Emails that try to lure you into releasing secure information.

PIXEL
The smallest portion of an image that a computer can display.

PUBLIC DOMAIN
The free use of work without any restrictions. It is not copyrighted, the copyright has expired, or the license allows its use by the public.

QUERY
Words typed into the search bar.

RAM
Random Access Memory describes the amount of data a computer can hold at any one time. The more memory a computer has, the more tasks it can perform, and the faster it can work. Once the computer is turned off, the data is lost.

RANK
Parts of content that best answer a query. Results are ordered by most relevant to least relevant.

RESPONSIVE DESIGN
Makes your website look good on different devices.

ROM
Read-Only Memory is memory retained by a computer even after it is switched off.

ROUTER
The wired or wireless hardware device that routes internet traffic to your computer.

SEARCH ENGINE
An information retrieval program that searches for items in a database that match queries. *Examples:* Google, Bing, Yahoo.

SEO
Search Engine Optimization arranges keywords on a web page to boost the page's placement on search engine results.

SERP
Search Engine Report Page-the results of a query.

SLIDER
Slideshow to showcase work, products, or services.

SOCIAL MEDIA
Any free online site that enables computer users to interact with other computer users. *Examples*: Facebook, Twitter, LinkedIn, YouTube, Instagram, Pinterest, Snapchat, Tumbler, Reddit.

SOFTWARE
Programs on computers that tell them what to do.

SPAM
Unwanted and unsolicited email.

SSL
Secure Sockets Layer is used for transmitting encrypted data to protect information.

STOCK PHOTO
Professional high-quality images online for free or a fee.

STORAGE
Where data is saved. Computers save data on an internal and external hard drive.

TEMPLATE
A predesigned framework to help make web design easier. Templates are professionally designed layouts with carefully selected fonts, color schemes, graphics, and built-in functionality.

TESTIMONIALS
Unbiased reviews that testify to character, qualifications, business, products, and services.

TM
Trademark is a registered word, logo, or symbol that distinguishes one company from another. They are registered with the government, preventing others from using them without consent. They are often denoted with a symbol of the letter "R" in a circle.

TRAFFIC
Visits to a website.

TYPEFACE
A design that defines the look of type.

URL
Uniform Resource Locators are the web addresses of pages and files. Example: https://www.amazingwebsites.org

USABILITY
Usability defines how easy or difficult it is to use a website. It may be determined by the design, content, or speed.

USB
Universal Serial Bus is a system for connecting devices to computers.

VPS
A Virtual Private Server is a hybrid between shared hosting and dedicated hosting. Fewer sites are housed on the same server than shared hosting. Each website has its resources when spikes in usage occur.

WEB HOST
A company that stores your website's content online. When someone types in your domain name, the web retrieves it from your website host. They deliver content, keep your site open to the public 24/7, and offer support.

WEB PAGE
What you see in your browser when you are on the internet.

WEBSITE STRUCTURE
How you organize your content.

WHITE SPACE
The portion of the webpage that is blank. It can be white or any other color but is free of text or images.

WIFI
Wireless Fidelity is a wireless mobile network for homes and offices.

WIDGET
An APP that links to another page: Calendar, Posts, etc.

WIREFRAME
A wireframe shows the underlying structural composition of a website.

WP
A Word Processor is a software program capable of creating, storing, and printing typed documents. Microsoft Word is the most popular.

WWW
World Wide Web is the space online where web resources are accessible.

APPENDIX

https://amazingwebsites.org
https://analytics.google.com
https://analytics.moz.com
https://answerthepublic.com
https://app.readable.com
https://apps.apple.com
https://audiomicro.com
https://awwwards.com
https://bigcommerce.com
https://bigstock.com
https://bluehost.com
https://business.tutsplus.com
https://canva.com
https://commons.wikimedia.org
https://compressjpeg.com
https://compressor.io/compress
https://computerhope.com
https://constantcontact.com
https://coverr.co
https://creativeblog.com
https://css-snippets.com
https://csswinner.com
https://designshack.net
https://designshard.com
https://developers.google.com
https://digitalsynopsis.com
https://diker.com/
https://dreamhost.com
https://entrepreneur.com
https://envato.com
https://etsy.com
https://facebook.com
https://favicon.cc
https://favicongenerator.com
https://fingerprintmarketing.com
https://fiverr.com
https://flickr.com
https://fonts.google.com
https://fontsquirrel
https://forbes.com
https://freeimages.com
https://freesound.org
https://gettyimages.com
https://godaddy.com
https://google.com
https://search.google.com
https://hostgator.com
https://hubspot.com
https://iloveimg.com
https://imagecompressor.com
https://istockphoto.com
https://jimdo.com
https://keywordtool.io
https://kylesteed.com
https://lifewire.com
https://linkedin.com
https://mailchimp.com
https://mashable.com
https://mazwai.com

https://moz.com
https://online-tech-tips.com
https://orbitmedia.com
https://pcmag.com
https://pexels.com
https://picjumbo.com
https://pinterest.com
https://pixabay.com
https://publicdomainarchive.com
https://publicdomainpictures.net
https://red-dot-geek.com
https://renegade-empire.com
https://sarasotamagazine.com
https://shopify.com
https://shortpixel.com
https://shutterstock.com
https://smashingmagazine.com
https://soundsnap.com
https://spyfu.com
https://squarespace.com
https://stockfootageforfree.com
https://support.microsoft.com
https://techwalla.com
https://thebalancesmb.com
https://tinkerwatches.com
https://tweeter.com
https://tympanus.net
https://udemy.com
https://unsplash.com
https://upwork.com
https://usabilitygeek.com
https://uspto.gov/trademark
https://utterweb.com
https://uxmatters.com
https://uxplanet.org
https://venngage.com
https://videezy.com
https://videohive.net
https://videvo.net
https://vimeo.com
https://w3.org
https://web.com
https://webaccessibility.com
https://webaim.org
https://webascender.com
https://webdesign.tutsplus.com
https://webfx.com/web-design/color-picker/
https://webs.com
https://website.com
https://websitebuilderexpert.com
https://websitecriteria.com
https://weebly.com
https://wikipedia.org
https://wix.com
https://wordpress.com
https://wordpress.org
https://yahoo.com
https://yelp.com
https://yoast.com
https://youtube.com
https://whois.com

Made in United States
Orlando, FL
04 November 2026

90201288R00150